CW01084347

The Diaries of Cornelius Ashworth 1782-1816

The Diaries of
Cornelius Ashworth
1782-1816

Edited by
Richard Davies, Alan Petford and Janet Senior

Indexed by
Nigel Smith

Hebden Bridge
Hebden Bridge Local History Society, 2011

© 2011, Richard Davies, Alan Petford and Janet Senior

Published by
Hebden Bridge Local History Society
The Birchcliffe Centre
Birchcliffe Road
Hebden Bridge
HX7 8DG
www.hebdenbridgehistory.org.uk

Typeset in Palatino Linotype by
Hebden Bridge Local History Society

The publication of this volume has been assisted by a generous grant
from the Marc Fitch Fund

ISBN: 978-0-9537217-2-6

Printed and bound in Great Britain by
The Amadeus Press, Cleckheaton, BD19 4TQ

CONTENTS

Preface

This book has its origins in a three-year research class organised by the Hebden Bridge Local History Society that commenced in September 2008. The three editors co-operated closely in the transcription and editing of the text as well as in the research and writing of the introductory material. They would like to place on record the support they have received from the Society in preparing this publication. They would also like to thank Nigel Smith for his work in preparing the very thorough indexes and Ian Bailey for his assistance in preparing the book for the press. David Cant and Neville Ingrey have been kind enough to read the proofs and their vigilance has saved us from many errors.

The editors gratefully acknowledge the Halifax Antiquarian Society, the depositor and legal owner of the Cornelius Ashworth Diaries, for permission to publish this transcription of the original text, which is on permanent loan by the Halifax Antiquarian Society to the West Yorkshire Archive Service (Calderdale) whose conditions prohibit any unauthorised reproduction of the document for commercial purposes.

We are grateful to the West Yorkshire Archive Service (Calderdale), Calderdale MBC Museums and Galleries, Kirklees Cultural Services and the Yale Center for British Art for permission to reproduce illustrations from documents and works of art in their collections. The references for these illustrations and the appropriate acknowledgements are given in the relevant captions.

The Hebden Bridge Local History Society would like to place on record its gratitude to The Marc Fitch Fund, to a benefactor who wishes to remain anonymous and to John Leach, a Vice-President of The Halifax Antiquarian Society, all of whom have given generous support towards the cost of publication. David and Sybil Lee of Walt Royd have kindly allowed access to their farm on many occasions, which has been much appreciated.

List of Illustrations

Introduction

The Hebble Brook runs down from the moors north of Halifax. On the gentle west facing slope of the Wheatley valley, at a height of just over 625 feet above sea level, lies Walt Royd. From 1775 to 1819 Cornelius Ashworth farmed at Walt Royd and his four surviving Diaries give a fleeting glimpse of the life of a small farmer who, like so many of his kind, supplemented his income by a number of other occupations. At various times Ashworth was also a handloom weaver, quarryman, builder and hop dealer.

Ashworth's Diaries have been known and used by historians since the early twentieth century and he features in the margins of social and economic history as a typical farmer and handloom weaver. However, he is anything but typical. He wrote a diary, which immediately sets him apart from the majority of his contemporaries. Nor was Cornelius Ashworth a poor weaver struggling to make ends meet. At the age of twenty-three he married Margaret Marsden, a modestly prosperous widow, who owned Walt Royd.[1] Thus he became, through his wife, one of the relatively few farmers in this part of the parish of Halifax who owned their own farm. The farmhouse at Walt Royd is a pleasant late seventeenth century two storey building with an extension at the east end added in the eighteenth century. Early twentieth century photographs show that the building was rendered and whitewashed but this has now been removed to reveal the original masonry (see *Figures 1* and *2*).

Walt Royd is situated in the district of Wheatley in the township of Ovenden, part of the parish of Halifax. Eighteenth century commentators were fond of pointing out that the parish of Halifax was larger than the whole county of Rutland and indeed, until it was divided in the later nineteenth century, it was amongst the largest parishes in England. This huge parish was divided into twenty-three townships (see *Figure 3*). These townships provided the basic structure for local administration, much of which revolved around provision for the poor.

---

[1] See below p.12.

Figure 1   *The front of Walt Royd from the south. An early twentieth century photograph. (Halifax Antiquarian Society)*

Figure 2   *The rear of Walt Royd. An early twentieth century photograph. (Halifax Antiquarian Society)*

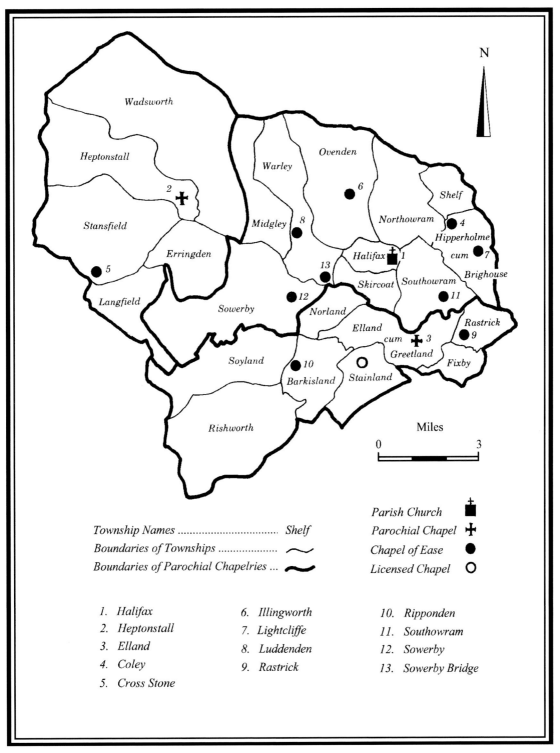

N

Wadsworth

Heptonstall

Stansfield

2

Ovenden

Warley

6

Shelf

Northowram

4

Midgley 8

Hipperholme

Erringden

Halifax 1

cum 7

13

Brighouse

Langfield

5

Skircoat Southowram

Sowerby

Norland 12

11

Elland

Rastrick

Soyland

cum 3

9

Greetland

Fixby

10

Barkisland Stainland

Rishworth

Miles

0   3

Township Names .... *Shelf*   Parish Church ■

Boundaries of Townships .... ∿   Parochial Chapel ✝

Boundaries of Parochial Chapelries ... ∿   Chapel of Ease ●

Licensed Chapel ○

1. Halifax	6. Illingworth	10. Ripponden
2. Heptonstall	7. Lightcliffe	11. Southowram
3. Elland	8. Luddenden	12. Sowerby
4. Coley	9. Rastrick	13. Sowerby Bridge
5. Cross Stone		

Figure 3   Map of the Parish and Townships of Halifax. (P.M. Buckley and A.J. Petford)

Cornelius Ashworth played his part in the administration of the township and we find him serving his turn as Overseer of the Poor from November 1780 to April 1781.[2] For ecclesiastical purposes ten chapels of ease and two parochial chapels augmented the parish church. The chapel of ease which served the people of Ovenden was at Illingworth and Cornelius Ashworth often referred to local people being buried there.

The Halifax of Cornelius Ashworth

Walt Royd is still surrounded by the fields that Ashworth tilled and he would still recognise the immediate environs of his farm. Lower down the Hebble Brook, however, the landscape that Ashworth knew has been transformed beyond recognition by successive waves of industrialisation. When Ashworth was a young man, Halifax ended at the north end of Northgate and the division between town and country was abrupt (see *Figure 43*). To walk from Walt Royd to Halifax was to walk from country to town (see *Figures 4* and *37*).

The Halifax that Ashworth knew was always distinctly urban. The narrow streets in the centre boasted an impressive range of shops and here and there were town houses to rival those of the Leeds merchants. There were three market squares, Bull Green, Cow Green, and Market Place, and round each was the usual cluster of inns.

During his lifetime Ashworth saw Halifax more than double in size. In 1764 some 6,360 people lived in the Township of Halifax,[3] predominantly in the built-up area depicted on the map of the town made for John Watson in 1759 (see *Figure 5*). By the time of Ashworth's death in 1821 the census recorded 12,628 people living in the Township.

---

[2] E. Webster, 'Cornelius Ashworth of Walt Royd, Wheatley', *Transactions of the Halifax Antiquarian Society*, 1985, 30-48 at p.42.
[3] J. Watson, *The History and Antiquities of The Parish of Halifax in Yorkshire*, London, Lowndes, 1775, p.146.

Figure 4   *Halifax from the south east. (J.Watson, The History and Antiquities of The Parish of Halifax, 1775)*

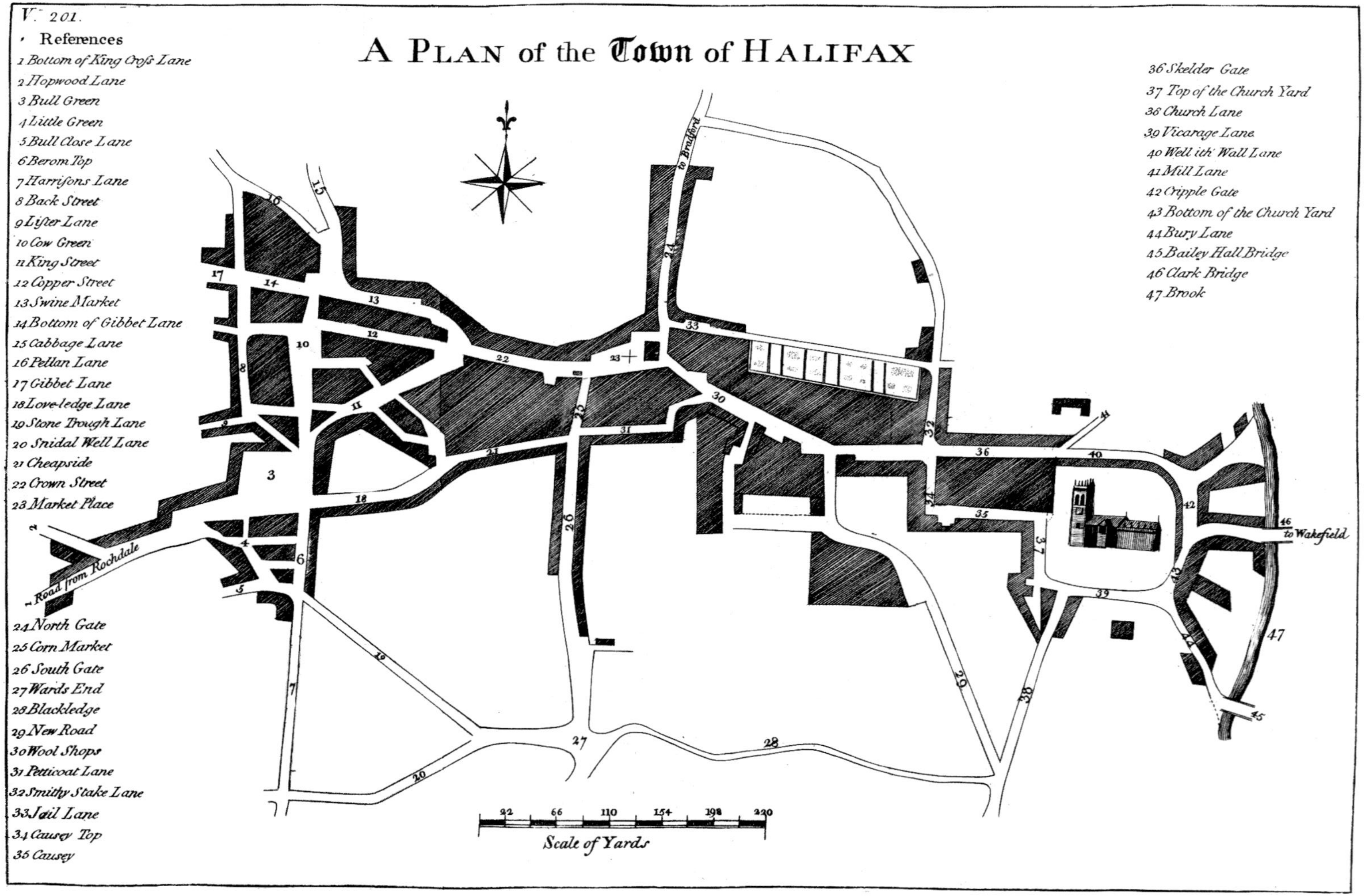
V. 201.
References
1 Bottom of King Cross Lane
2 Hopwood Lane
3 Bull Green
4 Little Green
5 Bull Close Lane
6 Berom Top
7 Harrisons Lane
8 Back Street
9 Lister Lane
10 Cow Green
11 King Street
12 Copper Street
13 Swine Market
14 Bottom of Gibbet Lane
15 Cabbage Lane
16 Pellan Lane
17 Gibbet Lane
18 Love-ledge Lane
19 Stone Trough Lane
20 Snidal Well Lane
21 Cheapside
22 Crown Street
23 Market Place
24 North Gate
25 Corn Market
26 South Gate
27 Wards End
28 Blackledge
29 New Road
30 Wool Shops
31 Petticoat Lane
32 Smithy Stake Lane
33 Jail Lane
34 Causey Top
35 Causey
A PLAN of the Town of HALIFAX
36 Skelder Gate
37 Top of the Church Yard
38 Church Lane
39 Vicarage Lane
40 Well ith' Wall Lane
41 Mill Lane
42 Cripple Gate
43 Bottom of the Church Yard
44 Bury Lane
45 Bailey Hall Bridge
46 Clark Bridge
47 Brook
to Bradford
to Wakefield
Road from Rochdale
22 66 110 154 198 220
Scale of Yards

Figure 5 *Plan of Halifax in 1759. (J.Watson, The History and Antiquities of The Parish of Halifax, 1775)*

This dramatic growth in population was sustained by a buoyant economy that was founded principally on textiles for which Halifax had long been famous. Writing in 1795, John Aiken remarked that:

> For some time past, the staple manufactory of the place and neighbourhood has been tammies, shallons, drawboys, known best under the title of figured lastings and amens, superfine quilled everlastings, double russels, serges de Nisme & du Rome. These are all made from combing wool.[4]

These were all worsted fabrics, predominantly the type of cloth sold in the Piece Hall, which opened in 1779. According to Aiken:

> the value of goods at one time in it is reckoned never less than £50,000.[5]

Only a few years before Aiken was writing the majority of cloth sold in the Piece Hall had been in an unfinished state and had been bought by London merchants who had made much of their profit by finishing the cloth and then selling it at a much enhanced price, often to the European market. However from the 1780s the Halifax merchants had begun to finish their cloth before sale so that an increasing amount was being bought by factors who were shipping it directly to Europe.

Aiken was writing when worsted manufacture was at its peak in Halifax. Soon after the turn of the century Bradford was to become the pre-eminent centre of the West Riding worsted trade. However the prosperity of Halifax did not depend solely on the worsted trade for, as Aiken noticed, there was also a flourishing woollen industry based on kerseys, bockings, baizes and half-thicks. Significantly Aiken pointed out that it was the woollen industry that was being developed most enthusiastically at the time he was writing so that, he asserted:

> the most promising branch of manufactory is that of cloth and coatings, which has been introduced within these few years by a few persons of enterprise, who have, at vast expense, erected mills on the Calder, and other small streams…..[6]

The complex and rapidly changing textile trades intimately concerned Cornelius Ashworth and he recorded a number of occasions when he or a neighbour began to weave a new type of cloth. All the types of cloth with which Ashworth was concerned were worsteds. This might be expected because the main area of woollen cloth production lay to the south-west of

---

[4] J. Aiken, *A Description of the Country from Thirty to Forty Miles Round Manchester*, London, Stockdale, 1795, p.564.
[5] Aiken, *Description of the Country*, p.563.
[6] Aiken, *Description of the Country*, p.564.

Halifax, especially in the area of Sowerby and the Ryburn Valley, whereas Ashworth lived in the worsted area to the north-west of the town.

In the 1760s the prosperity of the town had been expressed by a number of opulent merchants' houses. David Stansfield had built Hope Hall, a distinguished classical composition, which nevertheless housed his warehouse as well as domestic accommodation. Most impressive of all was Somerset House, designed as a warehouse and residence for the merchant John Royds. With a frontage over sixty yards long, Somerset House impressed not only by its size but also by the quality of its decoration, notably the exquisite plasterwork by the Italian stuccatore, Giuseppe Cortese.[7] In the last thirty years of the eighteenth century a number of public buildings, all built in classical style, helped to change the face of Halifax. They included Square Chapel, Holy Trinity Church and the long-vanished Baths in Lily Lane. Furthermore, Halifax had a vigorous urban culture. By the end of the eighteenth century it could boast a subscription library and a theatre, and the town was populous and prosperous enough to support the weekly *Halifax Journal*.[8] It was into this developing town that Ashworth walked several times a week.

[7] C. Giles, *The Buildings of Halifax*, Halifax, Calderdale Council in association with English Heritage, 2010, pp.14-15.

[8] J.A. Hargreaves, *Halifax*, Edinburgh, Edinburgh University Press, 1999, p.86.

Cornelius Ashworth and his Family

Cornelius Ashworth was baptised on 20 October 1751.[1] On his gravestone in the yard of Pellon Baptist Church it was recorded that he died on 1 June 1821 and that he was sixty-nine years of age.[2] He had three brothers, Abraham, John and William and one sister, Hannah.[3] William is mentioned only once in the Diaries, when his son was born on 29 December 1785. Abraham and John were both employed at various times at Walt Royd and probably lived locally. In the spring of 1809 both brothers helped Cornelius to sow his oats and set the potatoes.[4] Brother John worked at Walt Royd later in the year weeding and manure spreading and the Diary for 1815 records that he was employed for slightly more days on the farm in that year.

Cornelius Ashworth was described as being of Ovenden when he married and it is clear from the Diaries that his parents lived close by, although it is not known precisely where. On 5 August 1783 he recorded in his Diary:

Our Mother Ashworth came to see us and went home that night

Three months later Ashworth wrote:

I went to Halifax by Wheatley and to John Greenwoods & Benj Rigleys at Haley Hill and Came back by my Fathers[5]

After Cornelius Ashworth had been ill in 1785 his father came and helped out with the threshing at Walt Royd.[6] Ashworth's father was called Abraham but, at present, his mother's name is not known (see *Figure 6*).

---

[1] West Yorkshire Archive Service (Calderdale), MAC: 1/1-27, *Mixenden Congregational Church Records.*

[2] T.W. Hanson, 'The Diary of a Grandfather', *Transactions of the Halifax Antiquarian Society*, 1916, p.247. The gravestone has since been removed.

[3] West Yorkshire Archive Service (Calderdale), MAC: 1/1-27, records Hannah's baptism on 7 October 1750. At present no other references to her have been found.

[4] Sowing oats: Diary, 23 March 1809. Setting potatoes: Diary, 26 and 28 April 1809.

[5] Diary, 11 November 1783.

[6] Diary, 17 and 18 March 1785.

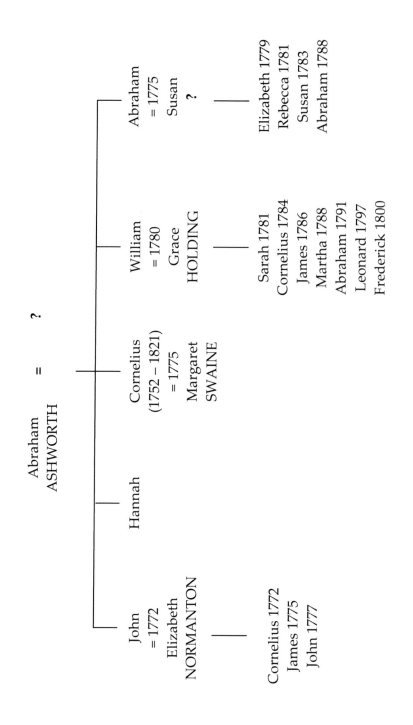

Abraham
ASHWORTH
= ?

John
= 1772
Elizabeth
NORMANTON

Cornelius 1772
James 1775
John 1777

Hannah

Cornelius
(1752 – 1821)
= 1775
Margaret
SWAINE

William
= 1780
Grace
HOLDING

Sarah 1781
Cornelius 1784
James 1786
Martha 1788
Abraham 1791
Leonard 1797
Frederick 1800

Abraham
= 1775
Susan
?

Elizabeth 1779
Rebecca 1781
Susan 1783
Abraham 1788

Figure 6   The Ashworth Family.

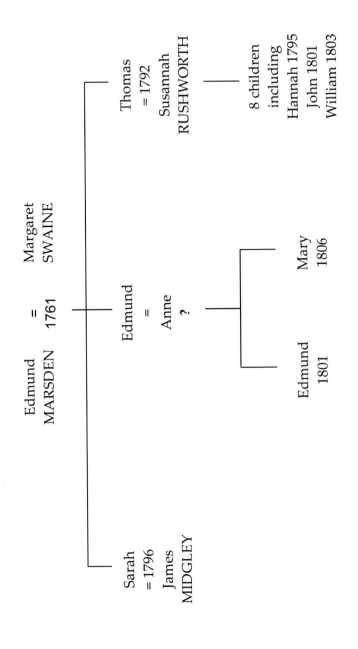

Figure 7   The Marsden Family.

11

On 15 October 1775 Cornelius Ashworth married Margaret Marsden at Halifax Parish Church.[7] She was the widow of Edmund Marsden, who came from an old-established Ovenden family, which had owned Walt Royd since at least the beginning of the eighteenth century. Edmund Marsden had married Margaret Swaine in Batley parish church on 3 April 1761 (see *Figure 7*).[8] Previous to the marriage, a settlement had been made which transferred Walt Royd to the hands of two trustees. They were Thomas Swaine, father of Margaret, and Eli Cordingley her uncle. After Edmund Marsden's death Walt Royd was to pass to his wife and then to his eldest son.[9] It is worth noticing that by 1791 the property comprised not just the farmland and associated buildings but also seven cottages. These were occupied by Ashworth's tenants, one of whom, George Town, frequently worked on the farm.[10]

The date of Edmund Marsden's death is not known but Margaret was first described as a widow in 1768.[11] It is not known how Cornelius Ashworth and the widow Margaret Marsden met but when they married Cornelius Ashworth must have been aware that, because of the settlement deed of 1761, the farm at Walt Royd would always remain his wife's property. Edmund and Margaret Marsden had three children, Sarah, Edmund and Thomas. Sarah was christened in 1762, and the two boys in April and October 1765.[12] Sarah married James Midgley in 1796 and Ashworth referred to him as 'son James' in the Diary.[13] He worked on the farm at Walt Royd quite extensively in 1809 and 1815. The very first entry in Ashworth's first Diary reads:

Cornelius Ashworth Book Sep[tm] 25th 1782

Edmund Marsden Set off for London the above mention,d Day

This is a reference to Margaret Marsden's eldest son, not quite seventeen years old, travelling to London where he worked in his grandfather

---

[7] West Yorkshire Archive Service (Wakefield), WDP 53, *Registers of the Church of St John the Baptist, Halifax.*

[8] West Yorkshire Archive Service (Wakefield), WDP 37, *Registers of the Church of All Saints, Batley.*

[9] West Yorkshire Archive Service (Wakefield), *West Riding Registry of Deeds,* Vol. AU, p.83, Deed 113, 1761.

[10] West Yorkshire Archive Service (Wakefield), *West Riding Registry of Deeds,* Vol. DK, p.63, Deed 94, 1791.

[11] West Yorkshire Archive Service (Calderdale), HAS: 89/1, *Ovenden Assessment for Poor Rate,* 1768.

[12] West Yorkshire Archive Service (Wakefield), WDP 73, *Registers of the Church of St Mary, Illingworth.* Sarah was christened on 28 July 1762, Edmund on 8 April 1765 and Thomas on 12 October 1765.

[13] West Yorkshire Archive Service (Wakefield), WDP 53, *Registers of the Church of St John the Baptist, Halifax,* Marriage of James Midgley and Sarah Marsden, 2 July 1796.

Swaine's family business as a hop merchant. He is recorded as coming from London to Walt Royd twice in June 1785 and for one extended visit in 1809. It is significant that on one occasion Cornelius Ashworth referred to him as Mr Edmund Marsden, an indication of his prosperity and status as a merchant.[14] Edmund Marsden had one daughter, Mary, and one boy who was called Edmund after his father.[15] Cornelius Ashworth knew his step-grandson Edmund well for he was sent north to be educated at Ewood Hall School and Edmund spent at least one of his holidays at Walt Royd (see *Figure 9*).[16]

After his mother's death, Edmund Marsden inherited Walt Royd and leased it at a rent of £25 per annum for twenty-one years to his stepfather Cornelius Ashworth, who was still living there..[17] Margaret Marsden's second son Thomas was apprenticed as a carpenter and went to London.[18] In 1782 he came back to Walt Royd to spend his Christmas holidays there.[19] Thomas married Susannah Rushworth at Halifax Parish Church in 1792 and set up house in London. All their eight children were baptised at St George's Church, Southwark.[20]

Cornelius Ashworth himself had no children. Ashworth recorded that his stepson Thomas paid extended visits to Walt Royd in both 1809 and 1815, on the latter occasion accompanied him to one of the meetings about the enclosure of Ovenden Moor.[21] Like his brother Edmund, Thomas sent his children north for their education, placing his sons John and William with John Fawcett at Ewood Hall and his daughter, Hannah, at the Moravian school at Gomersal, where she was to die from scarlet fever in February 1809 (see *Figures 8* and *10*).[22]

---

[14] Diary, 27 July 1809.

[15] London Metropolitan Archives, P92/GEO, *Registers of St George, Southwark*. Edmund was christened on 30 November 1801 and Mary on 4 June 1806.

[16] Diary, 30 March 1809.

[17] West Yorkshire Archive Service (Calderdale), FW: 102/13, Lease of Walt Royd from Edmund Marsden to Cornelius Ashworth, 15 June 1815.

[18] West Yorkshire Archive Service (Wakefield), WDP 53, *Registers of the Church of St John the Baptist, Halifax*. Marriage of Thomas Marsden and Susannah Rushworth, 23 January 1792. Thomas is described as a carpenter of Southwark.

[19] His holiday lasted from 24 December 1782 to 7 January 1783. See Diary for those dates.

[20] London Metropolitan Archives, P92/GEO, *Registers of St George, Southwark*.

[21] See below p.55.

[22] West Yorkshire Archive Service (Bradford), *Yearly Report of Gomersal Moravian School, 1809*.

Cornelius Ashworth's wife Margaret was a member of the Swaine family of Shelf. However, Margaret's father, Thomas, had been an innkeeper in Southwark. (see *Figure 11*).[23] Thomas Swaine was one of nine children and at least four of his siblings lived in London at some time.

Two of Thomas Swaine's brothers, Edmund and Joseph, were described respectively as hostler of Southwark and tapster of London and his sister Susannah married Eli Cordingley, cordwainer of Gildersome.[24] It is clear that for at least some of her early life Margaret Swaine lived in London. Although Margaret Swaine returned to Yorkshire to marry, her two brothers William and John remained in London and both became hop factors in Southwark. Both are recorded in the Diaries visiting Walt Royd and Cornelius Ashworth almost invariably referred to Thomas as Mr Thomas, perhaps a clue to his prosperity and social standing. William was usually 'Brother Swaine'.

Margaret Swaine's sister Susannah married Shechaniah Rhodes at St Saviour's Southwark on 12 August 1775.[25] The visits of Shechaniah, Susannah and most of their children to Walt Royd are recorded in the Diaries (see *Figure 12*).

Cornelius Ashworth seems to have made a conscious effort to think of Margaret's children as his own. Very often when he mentioned them in the Diaries he called Edmund and Thomas his sons and sometimes he made a correction to this effect. For instance on 17 June 1785 he wrote:

> a hot day I work'd in the Garden all day ᵐʸ Brother Willᵐ Swaine & [Ed] my Son Edmund Marsden [from] Came from London & Sister Rhodes & her Daughter Sally & and Charlotte Came to our house in the Evenⁱⁿᵍ
> (see *Figure 13*).

---

[23] The National Archives, PROB 11/978, Will of Thomas Swaine, proved 22 May 1772.
[24] The occupations of Edmund Marsden and Joseph Swaine are given in West Yorkshire Archive Service (Wakefield), *West Riding Registry of Deeds*, UU/399/536, 16 July 1746. West Yorkshire Archive Service (Wakefield), WDP 53, *Registers of the Church of St Mary the Virgin, Elland*, Marriage of Eli Cordingley and Susannah Swaine, 28 August 1744.
[25] London Metropolitan Archives, P92/SAV, *Registers of St Saviour, Southwark*. Marriage of Susannah Swaine and Shechaniah Rhodes, 12 August 1775.

It must have been his wife's family connections that enabled Ashworth to become a dealer in hops, an occupation he first mentioned in 1785.[26] Certainly his wife's family and wider kinship connected Ashworth to the world beyond Halifax. Perhaps inevitably because of their ownership of Walt Royd, his wife's family had a great effect on Cornelius Ashworth and it is probably significant that he mentions them rather more often than he does his own relatives.

Figure 8   *Gomersal Moravian School. A nineteenth century illustration. (Kirklees Cultural Services)*

---

[26] Diary, 13 December 1785.

Figure 9   *J. Holland: 'Ewood Hall From Greenfields', 1869. Ewood Hall can be seen above the centre of the picture (Calderdale MBC Museums and Galleries)*

John Fawcett D.D.

Ætat 75.

Figure 10   *John Fawcett. (Frontispiece to 'An Account of the Life, Ministry,*
and Writings of the Late Rev. John Fawcett, D.D., London and
Halifax, 1818)

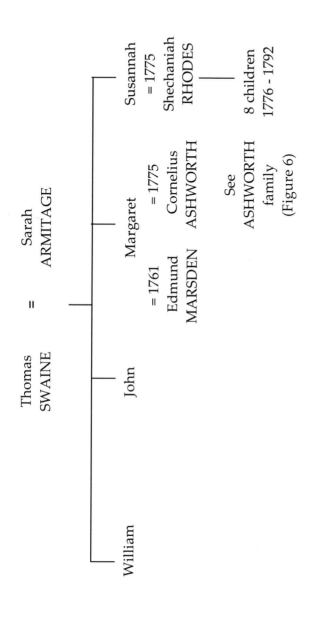

Thomas   =   Sarah
SWAINE   ARMITAGE

William

John

Margaret
= 1761
Edmund
MARSDEN

= 1775
Cornelius
ASHWORTH

See
ASHWORTH
family
(Figure 6)

Susannah
= 1775
Shechaniah
RHODES

8 children
1776 - 1792

Figure 11   *The Swaine Family.*

18

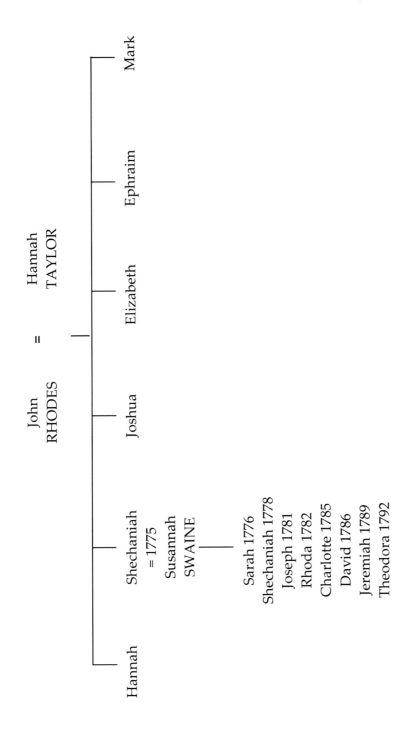

John
RHODES

=

Hannah
TAYLOR

Hannah

Shechaniah
= 1775
Susannah
SWAINE

Sarah 1776
Shechaniah 1778
Joseph 1781
Rhoda 1782
Charlotte 1785
David 1786
Jeremiah 1789
Theodora 1792

Joshua

Elizabeth

Ephraim

Mark

Figure 12   The Rhodes Family.

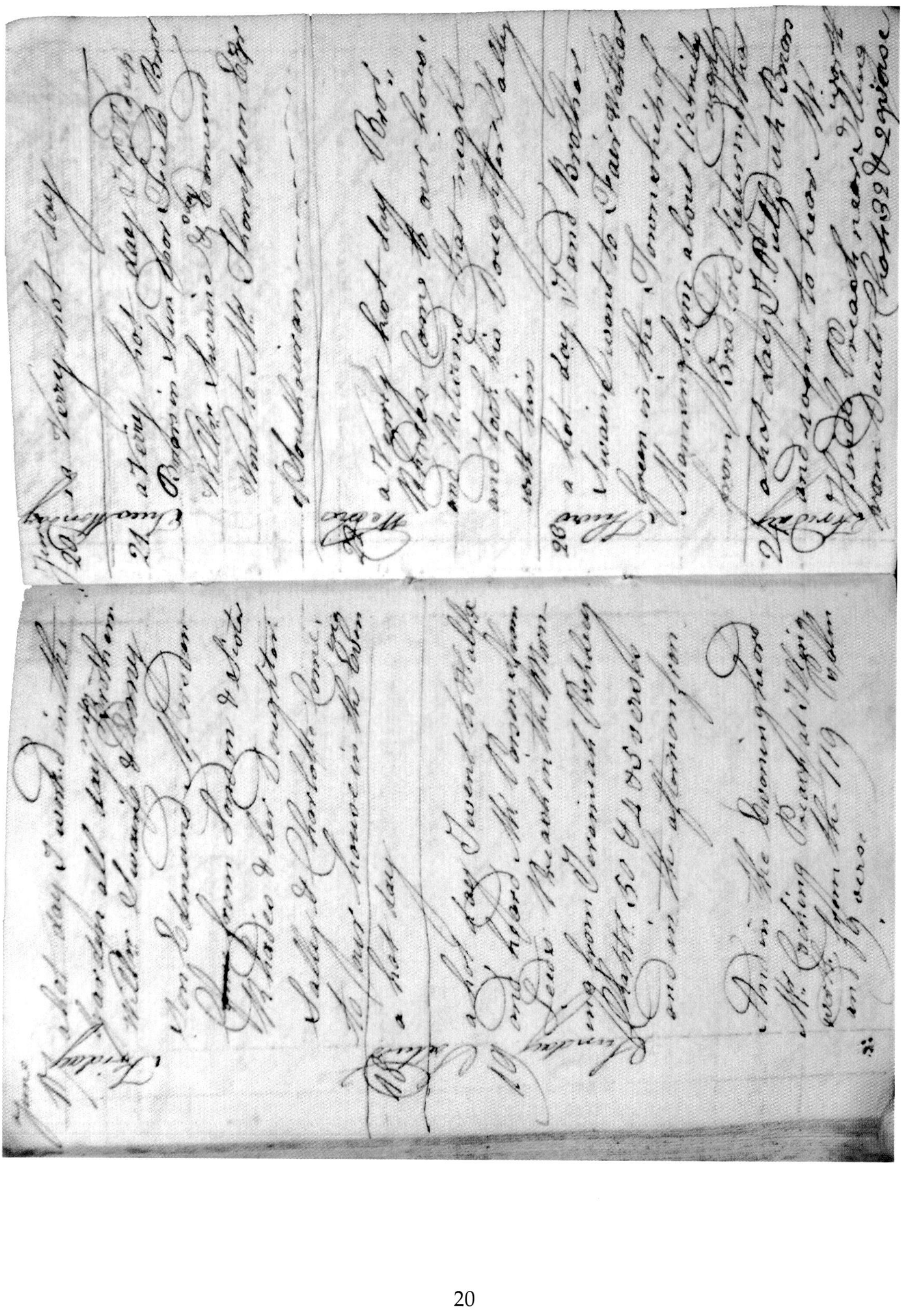

Figure 13   The Diary, 17 – 24 June 1785.

Ashworth's Religious Beliefs and Practice

The Evangelical Movement in the West Riding

Cornelius Ashworth was a child of the Evangelical revival and he grew up in a world of religious ferment. Nowhere in England had been more affected by the Evangelical movement than the West Riding. During the early 1740s the vicinity of Halifax experienced the evangelistic ministries of Benjamin Ingham, John Nelson, William Darney and William Grimshaw. Towards the end of the decade, the work of John Wesley consolidated and extended the first fruits of the revival with the emerging structures of Methodism.

As early as 1737 Benjamin Ingham, a member of Wesley's Holy Club at Oxford, had begun to preach with great effect in the vicinity of Ossett, his birthplace. By 1740 he was itinerating throughout the Dewsbury, Spen Valley and Halifax districts and was reported to have 'two thousand constant hearers in sixty places'.[1] By the following year Ingham's preaching had resulted in the formation of some forty societies. Only two years later he had handed the administration of these societies over to the Moravians. Ingham had been impressed by the Moravians ever since he and John Wesley had first encountered them on their voyage to Georgia in 1735. Indeed, Ingham had been Wesley's companion in 1738 when he visited the Moravian communities in Bohemia and had himself applied for admission to the Moravian church.[2] Ingham's enthusiasm for Moravianism ensured that this essentially quietest church played a larger part in the Evangelical awakening in the West Riding than might have been expected. Moravians welcomed members of all denominations at their schools at Fulneck and Gomersal and these institutions were well patronised by Evangelical parents of many persuasions for the rest of the century. Cornelius Ashworth's niece Hannah Marsden was, briefly, a pupil at the Gomersal school.[3]

---

[1] John Rylands University of Manchester Library, MAM P11B, *Church History Collected from the Memoirs and Journals of Mr Ingham and the Labourers in Connection with Him by William Batty.* Quoted in H.M. Pickles, *Benjamin Ingham*, Coventry, published by the author, 1995, p.19.

[2] C. J. Podmore, 'Ingham, Benjamin (1712 – 1772)', *Oxford Dictionary of National Biography*, Oxford, Oxford University Press, 2004.

[3] See above p.13.

In 1741 John Nelson, the Yorkshire stone mason converted by hearing Wesley preach in London, founded the first Methodist society in Yorkshire in his native town of Birstall. In the following year John Wesley visited the West Riding for the first time, meeting John Nelson and preaching at Birstall. Looking back in 1781 Wesley recalled this visit and the effect of Nelson's preaching:

> I went to Birstall, and found his labour had not been in vain. Many of the greatest profligates in all the country were now changed. Their blasphemies were turned to praise. Many of the most abandoned drunkards were now sober; many Sabbath-breakers remembered the Sabbath to keep it holy. The whole town wore a new face. Such a change did God work by the artless testimony of one plain man! And from thence his words went forth to Leeds, Wakefield, Halifax, and all the West Riding of Yorkshire.[4]

Later in 1741, John Nelson's preaching at the house of Abraham Kershaw at Skircoat Green led to the formation of the first Methodist society in the immediate vicinity of Halifax. Wesley visited this society in 1746 and preached for the first time in Halifax itself in 1747. The historian of Halifax Methodism, J.U. Walker, dated the formation of the first society in Halifax to the period around Wesley's second visit to the town in August 1748.[5] Certainly the cause prospered rapidly enough for the first meeting room to be rented in 1749 in Mount Street and the first chapel was built in 1752 in Church Lane. At the head of the list of trustees of this chapel stands the name of Titus Knight (see *Figure 14*).[6] He was a collier of humble birth, who had already made considerable progress in educating himself when he was converted as a result of hearing Wesley preach in Halifax. At Wesley's instigation he had received further education and became a schoolmaster and one of the most effective Methodist local preachers.[7]

An important factor in the rise of Evangelicalism in the West Riding was the presence of a number of Anglican clergy who promoted the movement in their own parishes and gave encouragement to the Wesleys and their itinerant preachers. First among these was William Grimshaw who had begun his journey towards Evangelicalism when in 1734, as curate of Todmorden, he had begun the serious practice of religion. The death of his

---

[4] J. Wesley, *A Short History of the People Called Methodists*, 1781, in R.E. Davies (ed.), *The Works of John Wesley* Vol. 9, *The Methodist Societies*, Nashville, Abingdon, 1989, p. 434.
[5] J.U. Walker, *A History of Wesleyan Methodism in Halifax and Its Vicinity*, Halifax, Hartley and Walker, 1836, p.71.
[6] Walker, *History of Wesleyan Methodism*, pp.86-87.
[7] See Appendix, p.302.

wife deepened Grimshaw's concern for religion and his conversion seems to have taken place early in 1742, just before he moved to the curacy of Haworth. Almost as soon as he arrived at Haworth in 1742 Grimshaw's preaching began to attract large congregations. Not long after his arrival, Grimshaw began an itinerant ministry in the Haworth area, gathering his adherents into classes. His ministrations soon extended to the societies founded by William Darney, a Scottish peddler who had evangelised the upper Calder valley and Lancashire border area in 1744. After Charles Wesley visited Haworth in 1746, followed by his brother the next year, Grimshaw worked closely with the Wesleys and took charge of the Methodist preaching circuit known as the Great Haworth Round. Grimshaw's evangelism extended further afield and he was instrumental in raising money to build the first Methodist chapel in Halifax where Titus Knight was the leading light.[8] However Grimshaw did not entirely agree with the Wesleys' theological position; he questioned their belief in free will and has been accurately described as 'an eirenic, undogmatic Calvinist'.[9] As such he co-operated readily with George Whitefield, on one occasion administering communion with him at Haworth to a congregation so numerous that thirty-five bottles of wine were required. Like Whitefield, Grimshaw became a close friend of Selina, Countess of Huntingdon, who did much to advance the cause of Calvinistic Methodism.

John Wesley's remarks about the people of Huddersfield when he encountered them in 1757 are well known. 'A wilder people I never saw in England' he wrote in his Journal, an opinion that appears to have been fully justified.[10] Two years later however Henry Venn was appointed to the living of Huddersfield and commenced a remarkable ministry, preaching some twelve sermons a week in the town and surrounding villages. As a result of Venn's labours, Huddersfield was the first provincial town gained for the Evangelical cause. Venn was a moderate Calvinist but, as was the case with Grimshaw, he maintained cordial relations with the Wesleys.

---

[8] J.U. Walker, *A History of Wesleyan Methodism in Halifax and Its Vicinity*, Halifax, Hartley and Walker, 1836, p.86.

[9] J. Walsh, 'Grimshaw, William (1708–1763)', *Oxford Dictionary of National Biography*, Oxford, Oxford University Press, 2004.

[10] J. Wesley, *Journal*, 9 May 1757, in W.R. Ward and R.P. Heitzenrater, *The Works of John Wesley* Vol. 21, *Journal and Diaries IV (1755-65)*, Nashville, Abingdon, 1992, p.101.

Figure 14   *Titus Knight. (The Evangelical Magazine, London, Chapman, 1793)*

By the time Henry Venn left Huddersfield in 1771 the West Riding was one of the great centres of the Evangelical movement.

Perhaps it is a sign of their vigour that divisions soon appeared amongst the Evangelicals. In 1777 Wesley and Whitefield split over the issue of free will. Wesley unswervingly maintained the doctrine of free will and the majority of Methodists supported that position. A minority followed George Whitefield who took the Calvinist position on predestination. Amongst his supporters was Selina, Countess of Huntingdon, whose wealth and influence were considerable. These divisions were felt in Halifax where, under the influence of William Grimshaw and Lady Huntingdon, Titus Knight adopted Calvinist views. In 1762 he reluctantly ceded from the Church Lane Methodist Society, taking almost half the congregation with him. He continued to command a considerable following and with the help of William Grimshaw financial assistance was obtained from Lady Huntingdon, which enabled his supporters to build a chapel in Gaol Lane, Halifax.[11] The chapel was registered as:

> a place of religious worship for a society or congregation of Protestant Dissenters from the Church of England commonly called Independent or Congregational.[12]

Knight was ordained as pastor of this congregation in 1763 and Cornelius Ashworth became a member eight years later.

The case of Titus Knight makes the point that the Evangelical awakening in the West Riding should not be seen simply in terms of Methodism and the ministries of a few charismatic clergy of the established church. The old dissenting denominations experienced a considerable increase in numbers, often due to the establishment of completely new churches. This was especially true in the Huddersfield area where many people evangelised by Henry Venn formed dissenting churches after his departure because his successor's views were unacceptable to them. Both the Independent chapels at Holmfirth and Highfield in Huddersfield owed their origin to this process. Significantly several of the preachers whom Cornelius Ashworth heard were men who had been converted by Henry Venn but eventually became Independent ministers. Joseph Cockin, minister

---

[11] *The Life and Times of Selina, Countess of Huntingdon*, London, Painter, 1840, Vol. I, pp.283-284.
[12] G.P. Wadsworth, *The History of Square Road Congregational Church, Halifax*, Reprinted from the Halifax Courier, Halifax, Stott, 1889, pp.8-9.

successively at Kipping and Square Chapel, Halifax is the best example. In addition to preaching in his own pulpit Cockin exercised an itinerant ministry, preaching in other chapels and to small, scattered congregations at cottage meetings. It was in this way that Joseph Cockin became a frequent visitor to Walt Royd (see *Figure 15*).

When Ashworth joined Knight's congregation in 1771 it was still worshipping in modest premises in Chapel Fold, Gaol Lane, Halifax. Originally the congregation seems to have consisted of poor people; indeed a near contemporary described Knight's auditors as: 'a number of poor people in Jail-Lane'.[13]

Titus Knight's ministry at Chapel Fold was strenuous:
> He laboured with much assiduity and zeal, preaching twice on the Lord's Day in the winter-season, and three times in the summer, and giving a lecture on every Thursday throughout the year. He administered the Lord's Supper regularly every month; and on the Friday evening preceding the celebration of it, he met the members of his church, and delivered an address suited to the approaching solemnity.[14]

The result was that Knight's congregation not only increased in numbers but saw the accession of several wealthy and influential individuals.

When Ashworth formally became a member of the Chapel Fold church, Titus Knight's congregation was already contemplating building larger premises. These were provided at the instigation and largely through the liberality of James Kershaw, a wealthy merchant and former member of the Unitarian congregation at Northgate End Chapel. He had been converted to Evangelical doctrines by Titus Knight and Henry Venn of Huddersfield. Kershaw joined the congregation in Chapel Fold in April 1770.[15] He was the prime mover behind the building of Square Chapel, which, when it was opened in May 1772, ranked as one of the largest and most elegant Independent chapels in the country (see *Figure 16*).

---

[13] J. Cockin, *Memoirs of The Rev. Joseph Cockin*, Idle, printed for the author, 1829, p.128.
[14] *The Evangelical Magazine*, London, Chapman, September 1793, p.94.
[15] West Yorkshire Archive Service (Calderdale), SC 3, *Square Chapel, Church Membership Books*, 1772-1935.

Figure 15   *Joseph Cockin. (Frontispiece to J.Cockin, 'Memoirs of the Rev.*
Joseph Cockin', Idle, 1829)

Figure 16   *Square Chapel. (E. Jacob, The History of The Town and Parish of*
Halifax, Halifax, 1789)

Knight's congregation had suddenly moved from back-street obscurity to the most fashionable building in Halifax. As John Cockin remarked:

> The transition from the Conventicle in Jail-Lane to the new Square Chapel, was perhaps as great as any minister and congregation ever made.[16]

It is intriguing to realise that for twenty-three years Ashworth worshipped amidst new-wrought classical elegance in a building in which he had a considerable stake. For Ashworth was a member of the church and not just a 'hearer' or 'attender' and the difference is significant. Members had a say in the affairs of the church and a duty to make a financial contribution towards the running of it. Those who simply attended the services had no voice in church affairs and equally no financial commitment to the chapel. Although Knight's congregation was large, the actual members of the church numbered only about twenty-five when it moved from Gaol Lane to Square Chapel; member number twenty-four was Cornelius Ashworth.[17]

Ashworth's Religious Beliefs

There is plenty of evidence to reconstruct the doctrines that prevailed amongst the congregation at Square Chapel. Titus Knight published a number of sermons, several tracts and perhaps most revealingly *Amyntas and Philetus; or Christian Conversation Illustrated in a friendly Visit into the Country in Seven Dialogues*.[18] Loosely modelled on classical precedent, and no doubt influenced by Knight's extensive reading, it is a fascinating work that serves as a perfect vehicle for an exposition of his core beliefs of Calvinism and evangelical mission (see *Figure 17*).

The attraction of the Calvinist system was that it celebrated, and indeed institutionalised, the majesty of God. Salvation was to be seen entirely as His gift, a gift not to be merited by any efforts of sinful man but emanating entirely and wholly from the grace of God bought by the sacrifice of Christ on the cross.

---

[16] Cockin, *Memoirs*, p.130.

[17] West Yorkshire Archive Service (Calderdale), SC 3, *Square Chapel, Church Membership Books*, 1772–1935.

[18] T. Knight, *Amyntas and Philetus or Christian Conversation. Illustrated in a friendly Visit into the Country in Seven Dialogues*, Leeds, printed for the author, 1770. There is also a reprint: T. Knight, *Christian Conversation*, Halifax, Martin, 1845.

Amyntas *and* Philetus ;

OR,

CHRISTIAN CONVERSATION.

Illuſtrated in a friendly

VISIT into the COUNTRY.

I N

SEVEN DIALOGUES.

Talk ye of all his wonderous works. Pſ. cv. 2. *And thou ſhalt talk of them when thou ſitteſt in thine houſe, and when thou walkeſt by the way, and when thou lieſt down, and when thou riſeſt up.* Deut. vi. 7.

For all people will walk every one in the name of his God, and we will walk in the name of Jehovah our God for ever and ever. Mic. iv. 5.

By TITUS KNIGHT,

Miniſter of the Goſpel, at HALIFAX, in YORKSHIRE.

L E E D S :

Printed for the AUTHOR,

And ſold by many of the Bookſellers in Town and Country.

Figure 17   Title page of T. Knight, 'Amyntas and Philetus', 1770.

This appealed to the Evangelicals, who had a lively sense of their own unworthiness, and often related their conversion from an immoral course of life in dramatic terms. Indeed, for some, the conversion experience became a test of the sincerity of their faith. Impressed with the omnipotence of God they argued that He had foreknowledge of their conversion and that they were therefore predestined to salvation. The concept of predestination gave due weight to the majesty of God and the unworthiness of man. Taken to its logical conclusion however it might militate against the purpose of all evangelical activity and especially preaching. After all, what purpose was to be served by exhorting all to come to Christ when the doctrine of predestination made it perfectly clear that the elect were predestined to salvation and the reprobate to damnation? Some ministers did indeed reach the conclusion that God's grace should only be offered to the elect, most famously the High Calvinist John Gill, Baptist minister of Horselydown, Southwark. To those like Titus Knight, whose religious development had been nurtured in the evangelistic fervour of the Wesleyan revival, this was a contradiction of their ministry and quite unacceptable. Within Independency, High Calvinism had been debated pretty thoroughly in the so-called 'modern question'; and the result had been a defeat for the High Calvinists. Thus, like many of his fellow Independents, Titus Knight managed to combine a belief in the Calvinist scheme of predestination with an evangelistic fervour that never dimmed in twenty-seven years of active ministry.

For Titus Knight and for many of his persuasion the great enemy to religion was the rationalism of the Unitarians (or Socinians as they were often known to contemporaries). They took a generally benign view of human nature, which struck at the very heart of the Evangelical system. Unitarians argued that with diligent attention to Christian morality the vast majority of people were likely to find a place in heaven. According to the Unitarian view Christ was 'a teacher sent from God',[19] not to save mankind by his sacrifice on the cross but to lead an educated and amenable generation to heaven by good example. In short they argued that Christ was merely human and not the divine son of God. Within a quarter of a mile of Square Chapel lay Northgate End Chapel, the home of an old established congregation that had been regarded as Unitarian since 1744.

---

[19] T. Knight, *Amyntas and Philetus or Christian Conversation*, Leeds, printed for the author, 1770, p.216.

Many in the Halifax area had been influenced by the preaching of the Rev. William Graham, former minister at Warley Independent Chapel who had adopted Unitarian opinions and left Warley in 1763. Graham moved to Halifax and preached frequently at Northgate End Chapel until his death in 1796.[20] William Graham was a good friend of Joseph Priestley whose Unitarian ministry at Mill Hill Chapel, Leeds from 1767 to 1772 greatly alarmed the orthodox because of the steady stream of persuasive publications that flowed from his pen.

Titus Knight wrote slightingly of the Unitarians in his sixth Dialogue in *Amyntas and Philetus*. A Unitarian minister appears in the person of Theologos, a thinly disguised Joseph Priestley:

> A man of much erudition; but very heterodox in his principles. He is said to be an affable and good-natured gentleman; but a strenuous asserter of what is called "new light scheme."[21]

The worldly wisdom of Theologos is suspect to Knight who, speaking in the person of Amyntas, has already pointed out that it is precisely such people who, throughout the ages, have been the real enemies to religion. Amyntas instances the opposition to Paul in Athens:

> When preaching at Athens, a city populous and polite, and where worldly wisdom seemed to have erected its throne, how was his doctrine derided! Was it by the rabble and ignorant mob? No. "Certain philosophers," &c., - men who have always been the pest of true religion.[22]

Amyntas warns Theologos directly:

> You must know, Sir, men of sense and understanding are not ordinarily the subject of gospel grace; nor are sense and understanding at all a qualification for glory. Not wisdom but holiness fit us for heaven.[23]

It is quite likely that Knight's anti-Unitarian message, which he enforced in the pulpit as well as in his publications, resonated with Cornelius Ashworth because both he and his father had been baptised at Mixenden Chapel. Under the influence of its ministers, beginning with John Smith, pastor from 1736 to 1753, the congregation there had moved from Presbyterianism to Unitarianism.[24] Perhaps Ashworth joined Titus Knight's congregation to escape the increasingly heterodox doctrines at

---

[20] J.G. Miall, *Congregationalism in Yorkshire*, London, Snow, 1868, p.377.

[21] T. Knight, *Amyntas and Philetus or Christian Conversation*, Leeds, printed for the author, 1770, pp.197-198.

[22] Knight, *Amyntas and Philetus*, pp.23-24.

[23] Knight, *Amyntas and Philetus*, p.213.

[24] Miall, *Congregationalism*, p.318.

Mixenden. Certainly as a member of Square Chapel he must have followed his pastor in deploring such views. It may be significant that despite its proximity to Walt Royd, Ashworth only once recorded visiting Mixenden Chapel. That was after the death of the minister John Bates in April 1815, when Ashworth went to hear Joseph Harrison who was temporarily supplying the pulpit and whose doctrines seem to have been perfectly orthodox.

In Titus Knight's dialogue Amyntas attempts to convince his Unitarian opponent that he was wrong to speculate on the nature of Christ. Amyntas challenges Theologos directly:

> Whether Jesus Christ be Creator, or creature: and consequently worshipped, or not; - whether we are to depend upon the merits of Christ, for salvation; or are to be saved by the works of our own righteousness; &c. &c. : I presume you do not number these amongst points of mere speculation.

The easy-going and tolerant Theologos replies:

> I may conceive of them as such, Sir; and leave you to esteem them something more if you please. [25]

For Titus Knight this was anathema. For him:

> the Son of God must assume the human nature; conflict with the powers of darkness; suffer the insults of men; and, as the surety of his people, discharge their debt of sin; finish a sorrowful life by a painful and ignominious death, in order to purchase, at the inestimable price of his blood, that mercy and forgiveness which, according to the Rational Scheme, can be dispensed without any such apparatus.[26]

Predictably when Theologos states his view of Holy Communion he sees it as simply another service of the church:

> I do not affirm, Sir, it is a declaration of any extraordinary degree of sanctity that we make, when we attend the Lord's Supper. It is professing no more than we do whenever we say we are Christians.[27]

For Titus Knight this was to deny the real significance of his monthly celebration of the Lord's Supper, which was reserved strictly to members of the church, of whom Cornelius Ashworth was one. Knight argued that Communion was a remembrance of the saving merits of Christ and an important reminder that none could hope for admission to heaven by their

---

[25] T. Knight, *Amyntas and Philetus or Christian Conversation*, Leeds, printed for the author, 1770, p.227.

[26] Knight, *Amyntas and Philetus*, p.242.

[27] Knight, *Amyntas and Philetus*, p.211.

own merit but that all required the sacrifice of Christ. For this reason Knight restricted Communion to those who had declared their belief by becoming members of the church:

> all the world knows the difference is wide between a nominal professing Christian and a true believer. I grant, the children of God, in coming to their Father's table, do not trumpet forth their superior sanctity, in the contemptuous language of the boasting Pharisee, - "Stand off! I am holier than thou;" yet an extraordinary degree of sanctity is implied in their professed faith in the Lord Jesus Christ; - without which, I say again, they have no right to that holy Ordinance.[28]

Here, of course, Knight was touching on one of the attractions of Dissenting congregations, which at the same time was their Achilles heel. They rejoiced in being the chosen of God, a position that gave their members a certainty and an often unconscious superiority which their detractors found infuriating and in flat contradiction to their rhetoric about being the worst of sinners. As Theologos says:

> Your system has a tendency to elate the heart with pride and self-conceit; and is the very bane of humility.[29]

Knight did not always occupy the pulpit at Square Chapel for he spent two months every year preaching in the chapels of Whitefield's Connexion in London. Nevertheless the other voices in the pulpit all proclaimed the same doctrine as Knight and Cornelius Ashworth heard no discordant note. In 1783 Knight left for London on 9 June and returned on 8 August. Nine ministers supplied Knight's pulpit during the eight Sundays of his absence; all were of impeccable orthodoxy and Ashworth heard them all. In 1785 Knight left for London on 2 May and returned in time to take Sunday service on 10 July. During Knight's absence on this occasion Ashworth went twice to hear Samuel Medley preach in Bradford. It is not known why Ashworth did not attend Square Chapel on these two Sundays but in choosing to attend the ministrations of Samuel Medley he was deliberately seeking out a minister of known orthodoxy. Medley had experienced a conversion that had led to his becoming an Independent minister. He had written popular hymns, preached in the pulpits of

---

[28] T. Knight, *Amyntas and Philetus or Christian Conversation*, Leeds, printed for the author, 1770, pp.211-212.

[29] Knight, *Amyntas and Philetus*, p.240.

Whitefield's Connexion and done battle against the errors of High Calvinism.[30]

On several occasions students from the Northowram Academy preached at Square Chapel. Again one can be quite sure that their doctrine was orthodox for this Academy was the successor to the one founded at Heckmondwike in 1756.[31] The Academy at Heckmondwike had been founded specifically to train ministers in orthodox doctrine to equip them to combat the heresy of Unitarianism. Under the guidance of its tutor, James Scott, it had produced a steady stream of effective preachers, such as Joseph Cockin, John and Jonathan Toothill, Robert Galland of Holmfirth and William Tapp.[32] Ashworth listened to all these men at Square Chapel and what we know of them suggests that their doctrines were fully in accordance with those of Titus Knight. When James Scott died in 1783 the Academy was transferred to Northowram so that the students could be taught by Samuel Walker, one of Scott's most able former students who had been minister at Heywood's Chapel, Northowram since 1774. During 1785 and the early part of 1786 covered by Ashworth's second Diary the Northowram Academy was as successful as Scott's had been at Heckmondwike. However it was wound up in 1795 owing to The Northern Education Society, which funded both Heckmondwike and Northowram, losing confidence in Walker.[33]

Titus Knight was never very concerned with denominational differences. What mattered was Evangelical doctrine and so long as a preacher was sound in this respect Knight was happy. It is recorded that Knight remained on good terms with the Methodists whom he had left in 1762 and we know that Knight was accustomed to attend the Thursday Lectures in Halifax Parish Church when incumbents of the episcopal chapels of the parish preached.[34] In *Amyntas and Philetus* Knight wrote with obvious approval of the Evangelical revival in the West Riding where:

---

[30] J.Y.H. Briggs, 'Medley, Samuel (1738 – 1799)', *Oxford Dictionary of National Biography*, Oxford, Oxford University Press, 2004.

[31] J.G. Miall, *Congregationalism in Yorkshire*, London, Snow, 1868, pp.145-149 and p.164.

[32] For details of these men see Appendix.

[33] M. Pearson, *History of Northowram*, Halifax, King, 1898, pp.192-195.

[34] W. Knight, *Sermons and Miscellaneous Works of the Rev. Samuel Knight, A.M., to Which is Prefixed A Memoir*, Halifax, Whitley, 1828, p.xxiii.

> The Lord has been pleased to fix several eminent ministers, both in the
> established church and of the dissenters, most of whom seem to me to unite
> in one mind and judgement, (a few trivial things excepted.)………They seem
> to vie with a holy zeal to propagate the pure gospel, and to promote the
> interest of their common Lord.[35]

In this spirit of ecumenism Cornelius Ashworth was quite prepared to seek
out Evangelical preachers outside the Independent churches. On one
occasion he went to the parish church to hear Mr Allinson of Cross Stone
Chapel,[36] but more frequently he went to Pellon Lane, the first Baptist
chapel in Halifax, which had opened in 1763.

Ashworth's religion was no mere Sunday matter. He frequently attended
Titus Knight's Thursday lectures and went on several occasions to the
General Lectures, which were mid-week occasions when several
Independent ministers preached. He was present at other mid-week
religious gatherings too. For instance on Wednesday 11 June 1783 he was
present at the General Association of Baptists in Halifax when Thomas
Ashworth of Gildersome and John Fawcett of Brearley Hall were the
preachers. On Wednesday 10 August 1785 he went up to the Independent
Chapel at Booth to attend the ordination of John Toothill as the new pastor
and he heard sermons by both Joseph Cockin and Jonathan Toothill,
cousin of the new minister.

If Ashworth's religion was not confined to Sunday neither was it confined
to chapel. He frequently attended and sometimes hosted the week-night
cottage meetings, which were a feature of both the Baptist and the
Independent churches at this time. For example, on Monday 6 January
1783 he wrote in his Diary:

> Mr Knight Preached at our house from Pauls 1 Epistle to Timothy Chap: the
> 1st & later Part of the 15th verse.

On other occasions the minister was a Baptist, most frequently William
Ackroyd from Pellon Lane.

Clearly Cornelius Ashworth moved easily between the Independent and
Baptist churches and he seems to have maintained cordial relations with
both throughout the period covered by the Diaries. Towards the end of

---

[35] T. Knight, *Amyntas and Philetus or Christian Conversation*, Leeds, printed for the author, 1770, pp.20–
21.
[36] Diary, 3 August 1785.

1785 and at the beginning of 1786 he was attending Square Chapel in the morning and Pellon Lane Baptist Chapel in the evening. Perhaps this was a period of religious experimentation for Ashworth. Eventually his own belief seems to have undergone a significant change and he moved from Square Chapel to Pellon Lane where the church books record:

> Cornelius Ashworth was baptised, 17th April 1795, by William Hartley and added to the Church, 19th April.[37]

The baptism referred to here was full adult immersion, a ceremony conducted in the presence of the rest of the church. This was clearly a serious step and an indication that the spiritual journey from Square Chapel to Pellon Lane must have been of considerable significance for Ashworth. However it should be remembered that Ashworth's brother had his children baptised at the Baptist Chapel at Pellon Lane as early as 1779. Much remained familiar for at Square Chapel Ashworth had been a member of a Calvinist church and because Pellon Lane was a Particular Baptist chapel here too the doctrines were Calvinist. What prompted his migration from Independency to Baptistry is not known, but Ashworth was to remain a member of Pellon Lane Particular Baptist Church for the rest of his life (see *Figure 18*).

Going To Chapel

At Square Chapel and Pellon Lane Ashworth attended both the morning and the afternoon services. The reminiscences of Joseph Nicholl can provide a clue as to how Cornelius Ashworth passed the time between the two services. Looking back to the beginning of the nineteenth century, Nicholl recalled seeing people leaving Ovenden and Wheatley on a Sunday morning bound for Square Chapel:

> some with bread in their pockets for dinner, many of them went to the then well-known Inn, the ''Boar's Head'', and got a basin of broth or soup, and talked over the sermons to which they had just listened, and then adjourned to the afternoon service.[38]

---

[37] Quoted in T.W. Hanson, 'The Diary of a Grandfather', *Transactions of the Halifax Antiquarian Society*, 1916, p.244.

[38] J. Nicholl, *The History of Providence Chapel, Ovenden*, Halifax, Jackson, 1878, p.1.

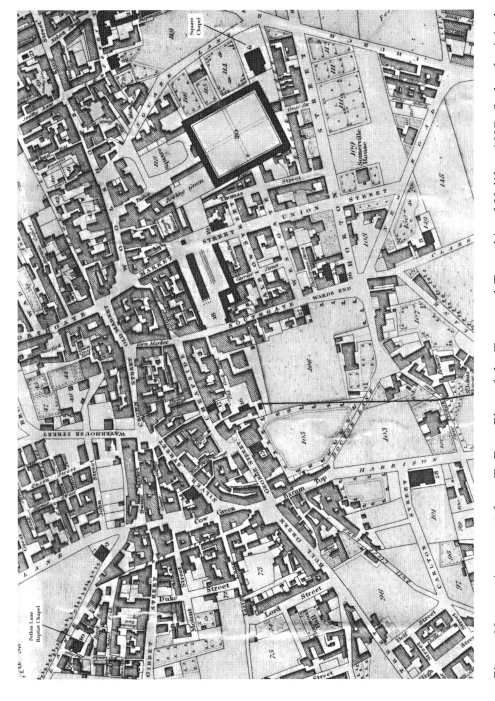

Figure 18   An extract from T. Day, Plan of the Town and Township of Halifax, 1827, Scale of original: twenty inches to one mile.

Throughout the period for which the Diaries survive Ashworth was remarkably conscientious in his attendance at chapel. In the twenty-eight months that the first two diaries cover, only five Sundays were missed: 'being sick in Body and therefore not fit to go anywhere'. He also stayed at home one morning with a wounded young heifer: 'I thought it work of necessity to get it dres,d Imediately'.[39]

Ashworth's careful record of all the Biblical texts on which sermons were preached must have had a purpose; there were sometimes even details from Sundays when Ashworth himself had not been able to attend. Did he re-read the texts at home to understand better their significance, or did he involve others as he sought out a more complete understanding? Perhaps his wife was a part of all this, but there is simply no evidence. Almost invariably Ashworth recorded: 'I went to Halifax and heard Mr Knight preach' or 'I heard Wm Acroyd preach both morning and evening'. Only once does Ashworth say that 'me & my wife heard Mr Lowell of Halifax preach'.[40] However his wife's family, the Marsdens, had certainly been touched by the Evangelical revival. Both Margaret Marsden's sons who lived in London sent their children back to Yorkshire to attend schools that met the highest Evangelical standards. Edmund Marsden, eldest son of Edmund and Ann Marsden, was sent to Ewood Hall School run by the Baptist minister John Fawcett. Hannah Marsden, daughter of Thomas and Susannah Marsden, was sent to the Moravian School at Gomersal, while like their cousin Edmund, her two elder brothers attended Ewood Hall School.

If we are to judge from the evidence of the Diaries for 1809 and 1815-1816, Ashworth's religious life as a member of William Ackroyd's Baptist congregation followed much the same pattern as it had when he belonged to Square Chapel. However because William Ackroyd was absent from his pulpit less often than Titus Knight, Ashworth experienced less variety of preaching there.

---

[39] Diary, 7 August 1785.
[40] Diary, 2 June 1785.

The two later Diaries show that Ashworth's attendance at cottage meetings increased and Walt Royd was used more frequently as the venue. Perhaps this is a reflection of the increasing use of cottage meetings being made by many dissenting denominations in the early years of the nineteenth century.[41] It is interesting to speculate as to whether meetings were deliberately held in cottages that were owner occupied. In 1809 there were ten cottage meetings held at Walt Royd. William Ackroyd and Joseph Cockin alternated every month from January to April. There appears to have been no meeting in May and then in June the preacher was Benjamin Sugden, minister of the Independent chapel at Skipton. In July William Ackroyd preached at Thomas Priestley's house near Illingworth and then for the rest of the year Ackroyd and Cockin alternated.

Something of the atmosphere of these cottage meetings can be gleaned from the testimony of William Hanson who was born in 1804 and attended prayer and experience meetings in Ovenden and Wheatley between 1826 and 1829. He wrote:

> I well remember the first experience meeting that I attended, which was at the house of Joseph Blagborough. There were present some old experienced fathers in Christ; and I was but a young disciple. And when it came my turn to speak I told my experience in a simple way, and when I had done, Mr Henry Mills said, "That is a thorough conversion;" to which they all assented. Oliver Blagborough, then a growing lad, was present and heard what they said about me. And in after years he referred to that meeting, and told me that he determined to watch whether I went back to the world or not; for according to his view of the doctrine of " the final perseverance of the saints," if I did turn back it would be proof that I had not been converted.[42]

Later in his autobiography Hanson relates how, at a cottage meeting, one of the Elders demanded an account from the new minister of his own conversion. Perhaps the meetings at Walt Royd were a little more deferential and less experimental but Hanson's account does have the ring of authenticity about it.

---

[41] D.W. Lovegrove, *Established Church, Sectarian People*, Cambridge, Cambridge University Press, 1988, Chapter 2.

[42] W. Hanson, *The Life of William Hanson Written by Himself*, Halifax, Whitaker, 1883, p.12.

In 1815 there were fewer meetings at Walt Royd and all were taken by William Ackroyd, but co-operation between Ackroyd and Cockin was maintained during those weeks when Square Chapel was closed for repairs. Ackroyd lent his pulpit at Pellon Lane so that for several weeks Cockin preached there at dinner time, between Ackroyd's morning and afternoon sermons. Predictably Cornelius Ashworth attended all three services.

Taken together the four Diaries provide remarkable testimony to a man trying to live out the religious life according to the tenets of the Evangelical revival. At first sight unrevealing about Ashworth's beliefs, the slender information they give is sufficient to reconstruct something of the thought–world that was his. And, of course, the keeping of the Diaries themselves with their laborious recording of how he spent his days was part of his religious discipline 'to redeem the time', words often on the lips of Titus Knight, Ashworth's first religious mentor.[43]

---

[43] *The Evangelical Magazine*, London, Chapman, September 1793, p.95.

Farming at Walt Royd

Ashworth farmed just over sixteen acres at Walt Royd. That does not sound a lot to modern ears, but in fact it was quite sufficient to provide the foundation of a decent living for Ashworth and his wife. In 1799 a rate book was compiled for the township of Ovenden that lists all the farms.[1] The farm sizes are expressed in terms of days' work, quarter days' work and perches.[2] There was, as might be expected, a considerable disparity in the size of the farms. The largest was Brookhouse, which had 206 days' work, three quarters and eight perches, but of the 235 farms listed only seven were over fifty days' work. At just over twenty-two days' work Walt Royd was almost exactly the average size for the township but it was unusual in being owner occupied.[3]

Cows were the main concern at Walt Royd but a quantity of oats was also grown. It was a compact farm as can be seen from the map and it had rights of grazing and turbary on the as yet unenclosed commons of Ovenden (see *Figure 19*).

The Diaries provide an interesting insight into operating a farm in the parish of Halifax at the end of the eighteenth and the beginning of the nineteenth centuries. What they do not do is provide a complete picture of the agriculture at Walt Royd. This is because Ashworth kept his Diaries as a record of his activity and his alone. Where Ashworth was involved in the work of the farm it is probable that the Diaries are a pretty complete record of what he did, even when he was undertaking a task as part of a larger group. However he never recorded the agricultural activities with which he was not involved. For example, the Diaries are silent about the daily feeding of the cattle and the milking of them. It is tempting to think that this was Margaret Ashworth's domain but there is simply no evidence.

---

[1] West Yorkshire Archive Service (Calderdale), HAS 198, *Township of Ovenden Rate Book, 1799.*
[2] One day's work in Halifax customary measure equals two roods and twenty-three perches. Alternatively one statute acre equals one day's work, two quarters and five perches in Halifax customary measure. There are 3136 square yards in a Halifax day's work and 4840 square yards in a statute acre. *Scale for Changing Statute Measure into Halifax Customary or Provincial Measure*, Halifax, Greenwood, 1847.
[3] West Yorkshire Archive Service (Calderdale), HAS 198, *Township of Ovenden Rate Book, 1799.*

Figure 19   An extract from the Plan of The Manor of Ovenden, 1817 showing Walt Royd. (West Yorkshire Archive Service, Calderdale)

Under the date Wednesday 31 May 1785 Ashworth wrote:

> I was this day employ,d in going to the Harwood well and all over Halifax
> Seeking for Piggs with intent to buy one

The following Saturday he was successful in making a purchase:

> I went to Halifax & Bo[t] a [a Swine] Hog the Price 1[£][S] & 1[s]

Ashworth was involved in killing the pig on 12 December when he recorded:

> we Killed our Hogg I assisted in killing it and Cleaning after &c

The Diaries record the killing of 'our Hogg' in 1809 and 1815. It is odd that the Diary for 1782-3 is silent on the matter of the pig. Was there in fact no pig kept, or is it simply that Cornelius Ashworth was not personally involved and therefore did not record the existence of a pig at Walt Royd in this period? The question cannot be resolved but should be born in mind when using the Diaries to reconstruct the farming practices at Walt Royd.

Cows were a very important part of Ashworth's agricultural regime at Walt Royd. Providing sufficient for them to eat was of prime importance. Critical to being able to feed the cattle through the winter was the provision of a plentiful supply of hay. Ashworth tended his ground carefully and was diligent in manuring his land including his hay meadows. The Diaries contain frequent references to 'laying up' his midden or dung heap and to spreading it on the land both during the summer and in spring. At the same time as the manure was spread, mole hills in the fields were also levelled and perhaps this is what Ashworth meant by the phrase 'Bursting lumps' which he used in 1783.[4] The Diaries contain several references to 'swilling' the fields. This is probably a reference to a practice often employed in situations where the land near the mistal could be fertilised by spreading liquid manure from the mistal across the fields below it using a system of shallow channels.[5] The topography at Walt Royd is well suited to this practice and it is significant that Ashworth mentioned a swilling dam and that it was near the farm.[6] In January 1816 Ashworth twice wrote that he was employed in 'Spreading Dung and Swilling'.[7] In addition to manure it is also clear that ashes were

---

[4] Diary, 5 April 1783.
[5] H. Cook and T. Williamson (eds), *Water Meadows: History, Ecology and Conservation*, Macclesfield, Windgather, 2007, p.59; W.B. Crump, *The Little Hill Farm*, London, Scrivener Press, 1951, p.51.
[6] Diary, 11 June 1785.
[7] Diary, 1 and 3 January 1816.

spread on the land in the spring. Sometimes the ashes were mixed with lime. On 14 March 1809 Ashworth recorded 'laying up' lime and ashes and eight days later they were spread on the land. 1809 was also a year when Ashworth sowed his hay meadow for on 12 May he noted:

To 3 days labour in Sowing Hay Seeds and Rolling our Oats   0 7 6

The hay was ready for cutting in July; in the dry year of 1815 the mowers started work on the 3 July but more usually it was ten days or more into the month before the grass was ready.[8] Haymaking occupied almost exactly nine full days in each of the years for which a Diary survives, although these were rarely consecutive days. Rain usually interrupted the process and of course haymaking never took place on a Sunday. In the Diaries for 1809 and 1815 Ashworth recorded that it cost fifty-four days' labour to get the hay in, excluding payments to the mowers. The cost had risen significantly in the five intervening years from 2/6 per man per day in 1809 to 3/- per man per day in 1815. This reflects the general rise in prices that took place towards the end of the Napoleonic War. In the two earlier Diaries for 1783 and 1785 Ashworth did not total up the days' labour required to get the hay crop in but he did record the number of men employed and the days they worked so it is possible to work out that in 1783 haymaking required thirty-nine days' labour and in 1785 forty-six days' labour. It rather looks as if the acreage laid down to hay was increasing. With that came an increase in the number of hay makers so that by 1815 as many as nine were employed on 12 July, the day that haymaking finished.

Haymaking involved cutting the grass, shaking it out, turning and spreading it out to dry, putting it up into haycocks and then bringing it in. Mowing appears to have been done by itinerant mowers because Ashworth reckoned the cost of 'Money & Boarding for Mowers' at £2 1s. 9d. in 1809 and 'Mowing Victuling and Wages' at £2 12s. 6d. in 1815.[9] In the latter year at least the haymakers, as opposed to the mowers, were local men and included Ashworth himself. Ashworth writes of housing 'bursdens' of hay, a reference to the practice of gathering four or five armfuls of hay into a pile and binding them up with a hay rope. This formed a 'burden' or 'burthen' of between forty-two and fifty-six pounds,

[8] J. Kington, *Climate and Weather*, London, Collins, 2010, describes the weather in the British Isles year by year from the first century BC to 2000 AD. The details for 1815 are given on p.339.
[9] Diary, 22 July 1809; 12 July 1815.

which was lifted by one man on to the shoulders of another by whom it was carried to the barn. In the barn the hay was spread evenly and trodden down on the balks to form the hay mow.[10] How long the hay lasted depended on how late in the year the cattle could be grazed outside. One way of increasing outdoor grazing was to allow the grass to grow in the hay meadows after they had been mown and then turn the cattle into the fields to eat this late growth of grass, which is known as eddish. Ashworth records doing this just once in September 1783 but it may well have been the regular practice of the farm.

By mid autumn grazing was getting sparse and the cows had to be brought into the barn and fed hay. In 1782 Ashworth recorded that he 'began Fodering the Cows once a day' on 20 October. In 1809 the cattle were brought in on 26 October, but in 1815 it was much earlier because in that year Ashworth wrote, 'Lay,d our Cattle in this Night' on 13 October. In 1783 Ashworth recorded that the cows were 'put to grass' on 19 April but this is the only time that he mentioned the date on which the cattle were turned out into the fields.

In order to maximise his grazing land Ashworth managed it intensively using the practice of water-furrowing. Early in spring the pastures by the Hebble Brook, which Ashworth called his 'Holms' were flooded with water, carefully regulated so that the new shoots of grass just showed through (see *Figure 20*). The water brought nutrients to the grass as well as slightly raising the temperature and the result was an early and abundant growth of grass on which the cattle could then be pastured. Water-furrowing required a weir to be built across the stream and a channel dug to take the water to the meadow where a series of secondary channels distributed the water over the land. These secondary channels were slightly raised above the level of the meadow so that, when blocked, the water would run over the land (see *Figure 21*).[11]

---

[10] W.B. Crump, *The Little Hill Farm*, London, Scrivener Press, 1951, pp.51-60 has a useful description of haymaking in the Halifax district. On p.53 is an illustration of a man carrying a burden of hay; on p.49 is an illustration of the hay rope used in making a burden.

[11] H. Cook and T. Williamson (eds.), *Water Management in the English Landscape*, Edinburgh, Edinburgh University Press, 1999 and H. Cook and T. Williamson, *Water Meadows: History, Ecology and Conservation*, Macclesfield, Windgather Press, 2007 provide useful information on the practice of water furrowing, although their emphasis is on southern England.

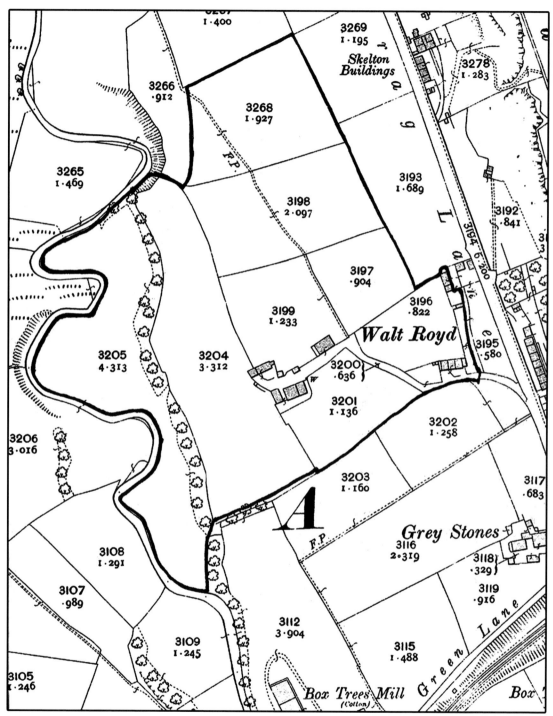

Figure 20   *An extract from the Ordnance Survey twenty-five inches to one mile map,*
Yorkshire (West Riding) sheet CCXXX 4, Revised 1905, published 1907,
with the boundary of the Walt Royd farm superimposed.

When T.W. Hanson was preparing his paper on Cornelius Ashworth, which he gave to the Halifax Antiquarian Society in 1916, he was shown the water-furrowing channels by the tenant of Walt Royd. The present editors have similarly been shown the channels, which can still be discerned albeit rather faintly, and the remains of the weir, which is much more clearly visible. These features have been sketched on to the twenty-five inch to one mile Ordnance Survey map of 1907 (see *Figure 22*).

In the eighteenth century many agricultural improvers regarded water-furrowing as a progressive technique and enthusiastically advocated its adoption. For example, Messrs Rennie, Brown and Shirreff visited the Crow Nest estate in Lightcliffe in 1793 during the course of gathering material for their report to the Board of Agriculture:

> Waited upon William Walker, Esq; at Crow-nest near Halifax, and examined his improvements, which are executed with singular taste and ingenuity. Mr Walker waters his ground with great success, which is all laid off for that purpose. All his inclosures are in perfect order, and his farm offices are in the neatest condition.[12]

In fact, although Walker had clearly brought the technique to a high state of perfection, he was building on local practice. He wrote that in the vicinity of Halifax:

> Great advantages are found to result from overflowing the meadows at proper seasons, and particularly in time of floods.[13]

The historian of Halifax, John Watson, corroborated this view, observing that watering or water-furrowing was a traditional practice in the locality:

> The parish abounds with common springs, as most hilly countries do: These it has been customary, time immemorial, to turn over the meadow and pasture grounds, which keeps many of them green all winter, and enriches them almost beyond description. This is performed by making small drains in different directions, and letting the water run out of these drains by little openings here and there, as occasion requires; thus, by degrees, a large space of ground will be benefited; for it is not suffered many days to run in the same direction, for fear of its starving the land, or making it rushy. This custom is not so proper for cold wet land, but any other it is sufficient manure for, and perhaps, upon the whole, is equal to any other method.[14]

---

[12] R. Brown, *General View of the Agriculture of the West Riding of Yorkshire*, Edinburgh, Watson, 1799, Appendix, p.17.

[13] Brown, *General View*, Appendix, p.17.

[14] J. Watson, *The History and Antiquities of the Parish of Halifax*, London, Lowndes, 1775, pp.17-18.

Figure 21   *A cross section of water-furrowing channels. (A.J.Petford)*

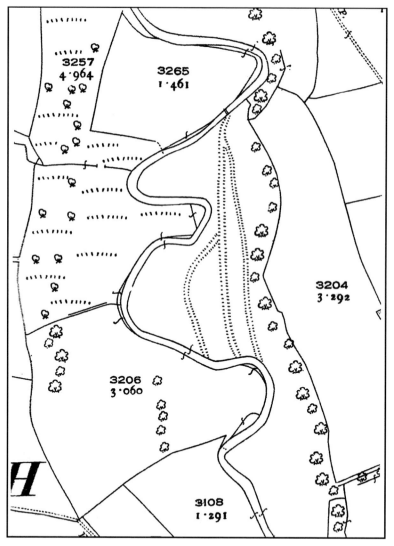

Figure 22   *An extract from the Ordnance Survey twenty-five inches to one mile map of 1907 with the lines of the water-furrowing channels sketched on.*

Presumably, therefore, Cornelius Ashworth was not unusual in watering his holmes, which bordered the Hebble Brook. The process usually began in March, although in 1815 Ashworth did not start until 3 April. First of all the ditches in the holmes had to be opened up. In 1783 Ashworth and George Town began ditching on 23 March. Three days later they returned to the task, and Ashworth recorded 'Ditched in the holms & Got the water into them'. The next task was to open the ditches and allow the water to flood the field. On April 4 Ashworth wrote:

'a Bright warm day I and 3 men Harrow,d till 5 O clock and began Water furrowing after'.

The next day the work was complete and Ashworth was able to record: 'I and 3 Men finished Water furrowing & bursting lumps'. This last stage of flooding the holmes was quite labour intensive and on 9 April, 1785 Ashworth recorded:

a Fine warm droughty day we had 5 Men this day Water furrowing and breaking Clods till 3 O clock and work,d in the Holms after

Nowhere does Ashworth mention how many cattle he possessed but in 1783 the Diary records the names of three of his cows, Tulip, Young Madam and Young Wibsey, and all had calves during the year. The Diary for 1809 is equally informative, as Ashworth noted taking Brear, Old Brear Red Brear and Pritchet and a little cow to the bull, the last two on two occasions. In the same year Ashworth's black cow calved and he bought a heifer in December. In 1815 a heifer and five cows are mentioned; a dark coloured cow, a light coloured cow, a red cow, and a young cow which were all put to the bull, the first one three times, and the red cow also had a calf.

In 1809 and 1815 Ashworth paid a shilling for putting a cow to the bull. In the Diary for 1815 Ashworth mentions the annual meeting of a Cow Club at Illingworth, which was probably a mutual benefit society whose members were entitled to payment in the event of a cow falling sick or dying.[15] It is not clear from the Diary entry whether Ashworth was a member or not.

---

[15] Diary, 7 August 1815.

Calving was often a serious business. On 18 January 1783 Ashworth: 'was Employed in Preparing a Calf Stall' which was required only two days later when:

> the Cow named young Madam Calved her first Calf about 6 O clock at night.

It was not an easy calving for Young Madam required much attention the following day and on the next evening Ashworth went into Halifax to buy medicine to help her to clean. Happily this was effective and the next day Ashworth:

> gave young Madam her medicine at 8 O clock in the Morning & she Cleaned in 5 or 6 hours after

The calf was not so fortunate and died on the last day of the month.

Only in 1785 does Ashworth mention the produce of his cattle; in that year he recorded that he churned on eighteen occasions. Thereafter he is silent on the matter, and we can only assume that someone else did the churning. Milking is never mentioned nor is the regular task of feeding the cattle in winter and again these must have been tasks that were undertaken by others.

As was the case with many small farmers in the parish of Halifax, Cornelius Ashworth grew a modest acreage of oats. He prepared the ground by the process of graving. John Watson reported that this practice was common in Halifax parish in the latter part of the eighteenth century and gave a useful description:

> The way of preparing the ground for the reception of the seed, is not always by plowing, but very frequently by what is called graving, which is performed by one man's cutting the ground in a right line, to a certain depth, with a spade contrived for the purpose, and another's pulling the earth over with an instrument called a hack, and so making a furrow. This is the only method which can be used on the very steep sides of some of the hills.[16]

Watson mentions that special spades were used for graving and some of these have survived in the Halifax area. Two are preserved at Shibden Hall Museum and they are characterised by their stout square section shafts and footrests to enable the digger to apply extra force to the cutting action of the spade (see *Figures 23* and *24*).

---

[16] J. Watson, *The History and Antiquities of the Parish of Halifax*, London, Lowndes, 1775, p.9.

Figures 23 and 24   *Two graving spades in the collection at Shibden Hall, Halifax.*
The spade in Figure 24 came from Upper Saltonstall. (A.J.Petford)

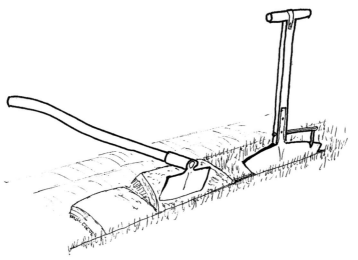

Figure 25   *The process of graving. (A.J.Petford)*

By the early twentieth century, when W.B. Crump was investigating traditional agrarian techniques in the district, this practice was confined to the breaking up of hitherto uncultivated land, but the method seems to have been the same and he described how it was done:

> …two men worked together, one with the graving spade, the other with the hack, having a longish blade, set like an adze or hoe; and together they trenched the ground. Starting with a long trench some 18 inches wide along the low side of the field, the graver then started the line of the next trench above it. He wore heavy iron-shod clogs to drive the spade down deeply, and he pushed forward, while the man with the hack, the 'putter-owr', pulled the sod so as to drop it upside own in the bottom of the open trench. Then more material was cleared out of the new trench and thrown on to the sods lying in the first one; at the same time stones of any size were put on one side for dry walling (see *Figure 25*).[17]

Certainly two men were employed in graving at Walt Royd for on March 29, 1785 Ashworth recorded

> John Town and Jonathan Priestley Finished Graving our wheat field for this year.

In 1809 Ashworth himself helped with the work and he therefore recorded the process in more detail. The work began on 15 March:

> I was Employed in Pulling Over and Brother Jnᵒ and Abraham in Graving after 1 O clock.

In that year graving took the three men four full days and there was some additional hacking. Ashes and lime were then spread and the seed sown. On two occasions Ashworth recorded the type of oats he sowed. In 1785 he noted that 'in 55 Hattocks of freez land Oats had 72 Strikes of Oats'.[18] Some contemporary observers suggested that Friezland oats yielded more highly than ordinary varieties but that was not Ashworth's experience as he had higher yields in previous years.[19] On 19 March 1809 he bought: '8 Bushels of Oats Called Poland Oats to Sow in Wheat Field' for which he paid £2 8s. 0d. William Marshall was not very complimentary about Poland Oats, remarking that it had:

> A short, plump grain; but the thickness of its skin seems to have brought it into disrepute among attentive farmers.[20]

---

[17] W.B. Crump, *The Little Hill Farm*, London, Scrivener Press, 1951, pp.43-44.
[18] Diary, 19 March 1785.
[19] J. Bailey and G. Culley, *General View of the Agriculture of the County of Northumberland*, Newcastle, Hodgson, 1797, p.85. For Ashworth's yields in 1782 see below p.54.
[20] W. Marshall, *The Rural Economy of Yorkshire*, Vol.2, London, Cadell, 1788, p.18.

In 1784 Ashworth had sown Friezland oats which were reckoned to produce a better yield and indeed the Diary records that fifty-five hattocks had yielded seventy-two strikes of oats.[21] Sowing occupied only part of a day but harrowing rather more, and Ashworth reckoned that the whole cost of the operation in 1809 was:

Graving and pulling over	16½ days' work	£2 1s. 3d.
Hacking	5½ days' work	13s. 0d.
Harrowing	8 days' work	£3 0s. 0d.[22]

The account for 1815 is rather less detailed, and only hacking and harrowing are recorded, although in that year Ashworth purchased fourteen bushels of seed oats at a cost of £2 12s. 6d.

Harvesting the crops was one of the major operations of the farming year and the timing of the operation could vary considerably. In 1782, an exceptionally cold, wet year, Cornelius Ashworth was still harvesting on 11 October; by contrast in the very warm summer that followed, harvest was finished by 16 September.[23] In 1785 Ashworth began harvest on 26 August, in 1809 harvest was finished by 11 September and in 1815 Ashworth recorded that the reapers finished on 20 September. Because of the incompleteness of the Diaries in places it is neither possible to say how long the harvest took, nor what the yield was, for every year for which the Diaries survive. However in 1782 eleven and a half days' labour was required to cut the corn in Pomfret field, which Ashworth recorded as yielding 118 hattocks. In the following year eighty-six hattocks were cut as a result of almost ten days' labour. Although Ashworth did not record the yield in 1815 he did note that eighteen days' labour were required to cut the oats and that it cost three shillings per man per day. Ashworth himself usually participated in cutting the crop and up to six other men were employed. Where the names of the reapers are recorded, and they usually are, they are local people, some of them Ashworth's near neighbours, so in contrast to haymaking, itinerant labour does not seem to have been employed.

Once the oats had been cut, the sheaves were stacked in hattocks or stooks which consisted of between eight to twelve sheaves. The hattocks then had

---

[21] Diary, 19 March 1785.
[22] Diary, 23 and 25 March 1809.
[23] J. Kington, *Climate and Weather*, London, Collins, 2010, pp.313-4.

to be brought in to the barn or, as Ashworth said 'housed', a process that took several men, usually including Ashworth, several days.

With the oats safely housed threshing could begin. This seems to have taken place either immediately after harvesting or in the winter time. Thus on Friday 18 October 1782, on the afternoon of the day the corn was finally housed, Ashworth and George Town began the work of threshing. Threshing and winnowing occupied the two men all day Saturday and the following Monday and Tuesday. On the next Saturday Ashworth wrote:

> A verry droughty day Made at the Mill in forenoon in 54 Hattocks 98 Strikes of Oats 31 Strikes of Shilling 3 Packs of Meal. [24]

From this it appears that threshing fifty-four hattocks had yielded ninety-eight strikes or forty-nine bushels of oats. The ninety-eight strikes of oats were, no doubt, the product of the threshing earlier in the week. At the mill the oats were ground. Ashworth never speaks of it, but almost certainly the oats would have to be dried before grinding as the husk is not easily removed unless it has been made harder and more brittle by the heat of the corn-drying kiln. On this occasion Ashworth brought home from the mill thirty-one strikes of 'shilling'. Shilling is shelled oats i.e. oats with the husks removed. Oats could then be put through a second pair of millstones to grind them into meal and it appears that Ashworth paid for a portion of his oats to be treated in this way, which produced three packs of meal. A pack of meal weighed fifteen stones, almost two hundredweight. No doubt the oatmeal was to be used for making oatcakes and other food at Walt Royd, whilst the shilling was for cattle feed. The next occasion when Ashworth threshed his oats was in the following January when forty-four hattocks were threshed to produce fifty-four strikes of oats[25].

The first two Diaries make no mention of potatoes but in the third Diary, on 12 April, Ashworth recorded: 'I was Employed in Picking Pottatoes for Setting'. On 27 and 28 of the month Ashworth and his two brothers in law spent the whole day in setting potatoes. Ashworth hoed the potatoes twice in June and once in the following month. In October Ashworth and several other men lifted the potatoes on three consecutive days, at the end of which the Diary records:

> 5 days labour in Getting Pottatoes   0 12 6 [26]

---

[24] Diary, 26 October 1782.
[25] Diary, 31 January 1783.
[26] Diary, 19 October 1809.

In 1815 the potatoes were lifted at about the same time but on this occasion six days' labour was required. If, as seems probable, potatoes had been introduced at Walt Royd some time between 1785 and 1809, Ashworth was certainly not in the van of progress for both William Marshall writing in 1788 and Rennie, Brown and Shirreff in the *General View of The Agriculture of The West Riding of Yorkshire* of 1799 observed that potatoes were a common crop throughout the Riding.[27]

During the thirteen months from January 1815 to February 1816 covered by the last Diary Ashworth's world changed dramatically. The Ovenden Enclosure Act received the royal assent on 27 May 1814 and Cornelius Ashworth was present on 17 August when the Commissioners, Thomas Gee and John Watkinson, held their first meeting at Illingworth.[28] Two days later the Commissioners gave notice that all getting of peat from the commons should cease immediately.[29] How far this affected Ashworth is not clear because he made only one reference to getting peat and that was in his first Diary on 8 July 1783 when he recorded:

> A Bright [Warm] hot day I was that day Employ,d in Churning helping To fetch the Turfs home & housing them & other Jobbs

It may be that by 1814 Ashworth had ceased to exercise his right to take peat from the common and it is possible that in later years the peat was running out or getting more difficult to find. On 16 January 1815 Ashworth recorded:

> I went to Halifax to a Meeting Concerning the Inclosing the Waste lands in the Township of Ovenden

The Commissioners' minute book recorded the business of the meeting at the White Lion Inn:

> ......we attended this Day and heard Evidence on objected Claims for Cottages[30]

It rather looks as if Ashworth's visit to the Commissioners concerned the cottage property he held. On 13 November Ashworth attended another meeting of the Commissioners when they met to hear objections to the

---

[27] R. Brown, *General View of the Agriculture of the West Riding of Yorkshire,* Edinburgh, Watson,1799, p.99; W. Marshall, *The Rural Economy of Yorkshire,* Vol.2, London, Cadell, 1788, p.56.
[28] Yorkshire Archaeological Society, MD 225/7/8, *[Draft of] Ovenden enclosure award with copy of Act [1814], sales particulars, news cuttings relating to roads, and Commissioner's minutes,* 1817.
[29] Yorkshire Archaeological Society, MD 225/7/8.
[30] Yorkshire Archaeological Society, MD 225/7/8.

setting out of the new roads. Unfortunately the Diary only records Ashworth's visit, not his reason for attending. As a landowner in Ovenden Ashworth had to pay his share of the cost of enclosure which amounted to £6 2s. 10d. When the final award was made on 12 May 1817 he received one acre and two roods of land on Page Hill to the south east of Walt Royd (see *Figure 26*). However the enclosure map records that this had been bought by a Mr Gibson and indeed Walt Royd itself had been sold to Samuel Dean.[31]

If Ashworth's time at Walt Royd had ended by 1817 his mode of farming was long-lived in the Halifax district. When Walt Royd was visited for the National Farm Survey in 1942 the farmer there was still farming exactly the same acreage of land as Cornelius Ashworth had done. He rented no other land and was using the land in a very similar way to Ashworth and his wife. One acre had been sown with oats in the previous year, doubtless due to the demands of Britain's war economy. He had nine milking cows, two cows in calf and five calves.[32] It is a remarkable testimony to the longevity of the farming regime that Ashworth knew so well.

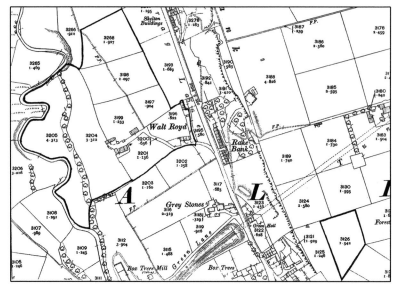

Figure 26   *The land at Page Hill allotted to Cornelius Ashworth in the enclosure award of 1817, shown in the south-east corner of the 25" OS Map of 1907.*

[31] West Yorkshire Archive Service (Calderdale), HAL 510, *Plan of The Manor of Ovenden, 1817.*
[32] The National Archives, MAF 32, *Ministry of Food: National Farm Survey, Halifax County Borough.*

Handloom Weaving

Winter was the time for weaving at Walt Royd. Every working day in December 1782 Cornelius Ashworth was at his loom. In 1783 there were only six working days in January, two in February, one in October and three in November when he did not sit at his loom. It is not possible to speak about December because unfortunately the Diary does not cover that month for the year 1783. But although weaving was especially concentrated in the winter months when the demands of the farm were less, it certainly was not confined to the winter season.[1] Indeed Ashworth found himself at his loom or employed about the textile business on no fewer than seventeen days during August 1783. Although Ashworth wove on only eleven days in May and nine in July, no month of the year was entirely free of textile activity. In the twelve months beginning on 13 November 1782, when Ashworth began to record his textile activity, he wove, or prepared warps for weaving during 268 days out of the available 311 working days in that period. Ashworth never worked on the Sabbath or on Christmas day. Clearly for the period when Ashworth was engaged in textiles, the industry was an important part of his life.

It is not known when Ashworth first began to weave. The first volume of the Diary begins on 4 October 1782 but the first textile related entry comes only on 14 October when Ashworth wrote:

Carried a Piece & Wove 4¾ Y^{ds}.

Clearly he had woven this piece before the Diary began or in the ten days preceding October 14, when he was keeping his Diary but had not recorded the fact. From October 14 onwards however Ashworth appears to be meticulous in recording his weaving activity until the first Diary ends on 23 November 1783. The second Diary shows Ashworth still busy at his loom. On 5 January 1785 he noted 'I Carried a Piece'. Since he had only recorded weaving twelve and a half yards since the year began, it is reasonable to infer that he had been weaving late in 1785. From 3 January 1785 the second Diary records steady weaving activity until 4 February, when Ashworth wrote that he had woven six and a quarter yards.

---

[1] D. Gregory, *Regional Transformation and Industrial Revolution: A Geography of the Yorkshire Woollen Industry*, London, Macmillan, 1982, pp.82-84, has shown how Ashworth's weaving was fitted into the rhythm of the agricultural year.

Figure 27 J.M.W.Turner, 'Leeds From Beeston Hill', 1816. (Yale Center for British Art, New Haven, USA)

This is the last time that Ashworth recorded weaving at Walt Royd. Indeed only once more did he record weaving at all and that was on 20 October when he:

Wove Tamy in Charles Crowther Loom

What caused Ashworth to stop weaving is not known, although it may be significant that he became ill on 4 February 1785, the day he last recorded weaving at Walt Royd and for five weeks he was too ill to do any work. Only on Thursday 17 March did he venture into the barn and help his father and George Town by shaking straw while they threshed corn.

Because Ashworth records when he 'carried his piece' as well as the amount he wove each day it is possible to work out the scale of his cloth production. For the sixty-three weeks during which Ashworth records weaving he produced twenty-eight pieces of cloth, although there is a strong suspicion that on at least two occasions he failed to record having 'carried his piece'. Even without the two possible extra pieces Ashworth's output averaged just less than half a piece of cloth per week. Usually the pieces were just over thirty yards long. This accords well with twenty-six yards which was the standard length of a kersey, bearing in mind that some extra length was required both to finish the ends and to leave in the loom to enable the next warp to be knitted in. On those days that Ashworth wove, the average length of cloth produced was five and a half yards. The least he made on any one day was half a yard and the most was thirteen and three quarter yards that he wove on 10 April 1783, but he produced over ten yards or more in one day on four occasions. Only once does Ashworth's entry permit a calculation of his hourly rate of production. On 16 January he recorded that he wove four yards between nine in the morning and three in the afternoon, which gives an average production of two feet of cloth per hour, but he could probably produce some cloth more rapidly than this: otherwise he would have found it difficult to produce his record thirteen and three quarter yards, or even his ten yards in a day. Not that he was necessarily constrained to working in daylight hours, for on 4 January 1783 he recorded:

I wove 1 Y^d in the morning before day light

Later in the year, on 4 November, he wove two yards in the evening by which time it must have been dark. It also seems probable that he wove on into the twilight on those occasions in 1785 when on two consecutive January afternoons he produced five and six yards.

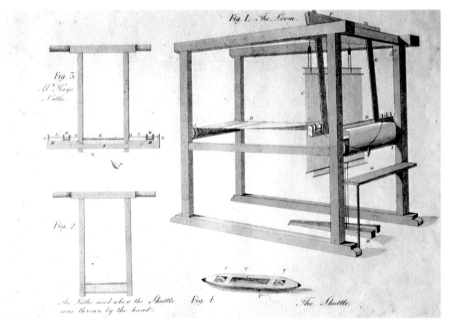

Figure 28   A Handloom similar to that used by Ashworth. (R. Guest, A
             Compendious History of The Cotton Manufacture, Manchester,
             Pratt, 1823)

Figure 29   Detail of J.M.W.Turner, 'Leeds From Beeston Hill', 1816,
             showing a figure apparently carrying a piece of cloth over his
             shoulders (Yale Center for British Art, New Haven, USA)

On 4 October 1783 Ashworth recorded:

> I and Jonathan Cockroft was empl^oy'd in fitting my Loom to weave double Stuffs Called Two Picks

Presumably, therefore, he wove double stuffs from that time onwards. Double stuffs were a kind of worsted cloth, that is cloth woven from yarn made from 'tops' produced by combing wool to remove the short fibres. We do not know what type of cloth Ashworth had woven prior to October 1783 but it is very likely, given the pre-eminence of Halifax in the worsted trade, that it was another variety of worsted. This supposition is given some weight by the fact that the conversion of Ashworth's loom to weave double stuffs only took him and Jonathan Cockroft a single day. A more radical alteration of the loom, for instance, from a woollen to a worsted fabric might well have been more complex and time consuming as well as involving rather more effort on Ashworth's part than appears to have been the case.[2] On the Monday afternoon following the Saturday that his loom had been converted Ashworth was able to produce two yards and by the following Monday had woven a complete piece of twenty-nine and a quarter yards. This speed of production was comparable with his normal productivity for this time of year. In fact the average daily length of cloth Ashworth produced after changing to double stuffs remained exactly the same as before; speed of production was clearly not a reason for the change. Why Ashworth altered the type of material he was weaving must remain a matter of speculation but it is likely that he was responding to the changing demands of the market. Back in August 1783 Ashworth noted that John Crowther had started to weave double russells,[3] another worsted fabric, and on 1 November he recorded that John Crowther had begun to weave grograms,[4] yet another variety of worsted. Interestingly Ashworth recorded that he wove a little on John Crowther's loom just nine days after Crowther had changed to weaving double russells; perhaps he was experimenting with a view to making the change himself (see *Figure 28*).

---

[2] Just how difficult it was for a weaver to change from woollen to worsted production may be inferred from the rather plaintive letter written by a woollen weaver being asked to weave worsted fabric:

'sir I think [I ca]nnot manage those saxtonise that you sent me for we never have been used to worstit sir I will thank you to let me go on at old sort sir I will thank you to send me 1 warp an 6 piece wefts

Arthur Bradley

Thornton'

West Yorkshire Archive Service (Bradford), WYB24/9/5/1, *Business records of T and M. Bairstow, Sutton in Craven,* undated letter in wages book in the pages relating to 1838. We owe this reference to P. Longbottom of Sutton in Craven.

[3] See Glossary.

[4] See Glossary.

Ashworth records 'carrying his piece' but we do not know to whom he was carrying it, or indeed where he was carrying it. It has sometimes been assumed that Ashworth was carrying his cloth to the Halifax Piece Hall but there is no evidence for this and on a number of occasions when he had carried his piece he records going into Halifax as if that was a separate journey. When Ashworth recorded 'carrying his piece' it is very likely that he meant that he had literally carried it on his back. We know that this was often done at this period. Joseph Greenwood, a fustian weaver, writing in the 1880s, recalled carrying pieces on his back from Hebden Bridge to Halifax in the earlier years of the nineteenth century:

> The goods when woven had to be carried to the manufacturers' places, and under the pressure of these circumstances I had to carry my father's piece. This to me was a happy juncture of affairs, and although a youngster, I was sharp and strong, very willing for the tough job. The distance was eight miles over the hills, and with the worsted piece strapped across my back I was to go in company with a most cheerful woman, a neighbour's wife, named Sutcliffe...[5]

In the 1840s Robert Howard recounted the experience of a woman who had regularly carried pieces on her back weekly between Heptonstall and Denholme, a distance of about ten miles.[6] Interestingly, J.M.W. Turner's well-known picture of Leeds, painted in 1816, is full of textile references and includes a figure in the foreground who appears to be carrying a piece of cloth over his shoulders (see *Figures 27* and *29*).

What does seem clear is that Ashworth was concerned only with weaving. He never mentions spinning and it appears that he was supplied with his yarn, perhaps by the merchant to whom he carried his piece. This specialisation of labour was more common in the worsted trade than in the woollen industry and, of course, pre-dates any spinning factories in the industry. Indeed the earliest worsted-spinning mill in the country, at Dolphinholme near Lancaster, was not built until 1784.[7] The first in Yorkshire, at Addingham in the Wharfe valley was not opened until 1787.[8]

---

[5] J. Greenwood, 'Reminiscences of sixty years ago', *Co-partnership*, 1909, 15(September), 131-132 at p.131.

[6] R. Howard, *A History of the Typhus of Heptonstall Slack...during the winter of 1843-4*, Hebden Bridge, Garforth, [1844], pp.65-67.

[7] E.M. Sigsworth, *Black Dyke Mills, A History*, Liverpool, Liverpool University Press, 1958, p.3.

[8] C. Giles and I.H. Goodall, *Yorkshire Textile Mills 1770-1930*, London, HMSO, 1992, p.79.

Frequently we find Ashworth preparing his yarn for the loom immediately after he had carried his piece. This was quite a time consuming procedure. First the warp had to be sized to strengthen it. Ashworth seems to have sized his warps outside where he was subject to the vagaries of the weather. On 19 December 1782 he complained that he and Charles Crowther had each sized a warp but there were heavy showers of rain and:

> for that reason our warps was sorely loss,d and littile drid.

Fortunately the next day was 'more droughty' and they:

> laid out my warp & got it a little drid

The process of sizing the warps outside was part of a process known as stretching. An equally important aspect of the process of stretching was to arrange the warp threads ready for putting on to the loom. We can amplify Ashworth's brief entries by several accounts of stretching. Ben Turner, later to become M.P. for Batley, wrote about helping an old handloom weaver stretch his warps in the neighbourhood of Holmfirth in the later years of the nineteenth century:

> He would get about forty poles, eighty inches long, stick one end into the wall on the lane side, and, with the poles a few feet apart, stretch his warp over them and dry it with the sun and the air, and also dress the warp by having each set of four or more ends drawn through a "raddle" and from there, put it on to a beam or roller and then take it to the loom ready for weaving.[9]

This picture is corroborated by John Longbottom who, at the end of the nineteenth century, talked with an old handloom weaver in the Luddenden valley who explained to him how he had used the stretcher-gate which can still be seen on the east side of the valley between Stocks Lane and Sentry Edge (see *Figure 30*). This explanation is worth quoting at some length.

> Very stout ash sticks were used, of which one end was stuck into a crevice in the wall, the other end resting on the top of one of the stones and fitting into the groove cut thereon…. Intermediately were shorter and thinner sticks, one end of each being fixed into the wall only and not resting on a stone at the other. And so on with all the short sticks. The large and small, or stout and thin, sticks being then fixed in position, the "warp-bag", or "piece-pooak", as my friend called it, was opened and in it was the warp brought hither to be stretched and sized. At each end of the warp and attached to it was another strong stick called a "raddle". One of these raddles was fixed firmly into the wall, and then the warp was "paid aat" (unrolled) along the tops of the projecting sticks or rods, until the other "raddled end" (other end

---

[9] B. Turner, *About Myself*, London, Toulmin, 1930, p.35.

of the warp) appeared, when that was also, after the warp had been tightly pulled or "stretched", firmly fixed in position......when the warp was ready for sizing, each handloom weaver having to find his own size in at the price paid for weaving. When this operation was completed the warp was left to dry, after which the raddles were re-rolled, again placed in the "piece-pooak", and taken home to be transferred by the weaver on to the beam of his loom......[10]

The Luddenden valley stretcher-gate allowed warps to be stretched either side of the track. Others were less capacious, the stretcher-gate in Midgley only allowed the warps to be stretched on one side of the path and this may have been the more normal plan. A single stretcher-gate, albeit for woollen yarn, can be seen at Holme where the wall has capping stones with holes in for the sticks that do not appear to have been supported in any other way (see *Figures 31* and *32*). Interestingly, in the only known contemporary illustration of stretching, the wall is of this type *(see Figure 33)*. Ashworth never says where he stretched his warp but it seems quite likely that he used the lane above his house. This lane runs in a straight line for thirty five yards and, while not so long as the communal stretcher - gates at Holme and in the Luddenden valley, which were intended to accommodate many warps, would have been quite long enough for a single warp (see *Figures 19* and *20*).

As Ashworth found to his cost, rain could interfere with the process of stretching a warp and Longbottom's informant had vivid memories of this as he recounted:

> Of course it goes without saying that a fine day was necessary for such work. If a sudden shower came on, all labour was thrown away. Then, as my friend said, "ther' wor some hurry-skurryin' amang us to get t'warps rolled up ageean an' into t'piece-pooaks, afooar t' rain made 'em run up".[11]

Once the warp was safely inside it could be transferred on to the warp beam on the loom, a process known as winding on or beaming. To take the new warp through the healds and reed of the loom it was usual to knit it in to the ends of the old warp (see *Figure 34*). Ashworth refers to this part of the process as 'healding' or 'knitting in'.

---

[10] J. Longbottom, 'Warp-stretching and hand-loom weaving', *Transactions of the Halifax Antiquarian Society*, 1950, pp.49-60 at p.53.
[11] Longbottom, 'Warp-stretching and hand-loom weaving', p.53.

Figure 30   *The stretcher-gate in the Luddenden Valley looking down from Sentry Edge to Stocks Lane. (A.J.Petford)*

Figure 31   *The stretcher-gate at Holme. Notice how the wall is set back at the far right of the photograph to accommodate the stretcher-gate which ran along the grassy verge to the right of the lane. (A.J.Petford)*

Figure 32   Detail of the Holme stretcher-gate showing a capstone with two holes in it to receive the poles or sticks which supported the warp. (A.J.Petford)

Figure 33   Warp Stretching. (R. Guest, A Compendious History of The Cotton Manufacture, Manchester, Pratt, 1823)

The whole process described was known as warping and Ashworth refers to it as such. It usually seems to have taken the better part of a day to complete.

The yarn for the weft required rather less elaborate preparation merely needing to be repackaged onto pirns ready for the shuttle.[12] This was accomplished by a pirn wheel, which was, in fact, a simple spinning wheel. Ashworth never mentions this process. Indeed he only once mentions a shuttle when he had to take it to be mended by Matthew Hiley.[13] What Ashworth does mention in 1785 is that he was scouring or washing the weft, something he had not mentioned at all in 1782-3. Perhaps this was a result of weaving a different kind of cloth.

It is difficult to determine how much the pieces produced by Ashworth were worth, not least because we do not know what kind of cloth he was weaving up to October 1783. After that date we assume that he was producing double stuffs for which no prices have been found. However we do know that the double russells which Ashworth's friend John Crowther was weaving sold for between 41 shillings and 115 shillings in 1791-2, while the grograms, which Crowther also wove, commanded more modest prices of between 36/6 and 42/- in the same period.[14] Some twenty years earlier, in 1771, John Sutcliffe of Holdsworth, in Ovenden township, had quoted 35/- as the cost of manufacturing one piece of stuff and prices had modestly declined since then.[15]

It is not known if Ashworth wove again after his last mention of weaving in February 1785. All that can be said is that he did not record weaving again in 1785 or in any of his later Diaries. It is significant that once Ashworth had stopped weaving his other work increased and we find him variously engaged with building, quarrying and hop dealing. For Ashworth, as for many of his contemporaries, weaving was only one of the ways to augment the income provided by agriculture.

---

[12] A pirn is a type of bobbin on which yarn is wound for use as weft. It is inserted into the shuttle.
[13] Diary, 1 January 1783.
[14] F. Atkinson, *Some Aspects of the Eighteenth Century Woollen and Worsted Trade in Halifax*, Halifax, Halifax Museums, 1956, p.59.
[15] J. Bischoff, *A Comprehensive History of the Woollen and Worsted Manufactures*, Vol.1, London, Smith Elder, 1842, p.185.

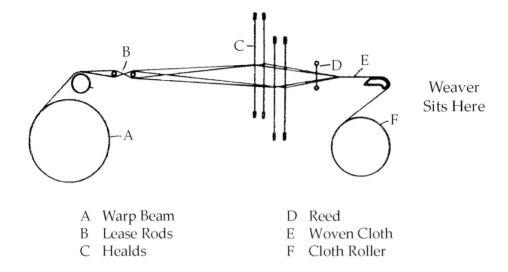

Weaver
Sits Here

A Warp Beam   D Reed
B Lease Rods   E Woven Cloth
C Healds   F Cloth Roller

Figure 34   *Cross-section showing the principal parts of a handloom*

Ashworth's Other Occupations

Building and Quarrying

In addition to his work on the farm and at the loom Ashworth seems to have sought casual employment as a semi-skilled labourer. In 1783 he helped to build a coal house for James Charnock. His involvement began on 5 September when he recorded:

I pick up stones in the forenoon for to build Jas Charnock a Coal house.

This may be a reference to the practice of using 'day stones', that is stones lying on the surface of the land, for the purpose of building. The use of stones of this type also had the advantage of clearing the land. A week later Ashworth was digging the site of the building and five days later he built part of the wall. His last recorded labour on this project was to assist:

The Mason & Joiner in building a Coal house for Ja[s] Charnock[1]

This job seems to have been fitted in amongst Ashworth's weaving and harvesting. By contrast, when he helped with the building of a coal house for Nancy Priestley, Ashworth spent four consecutive days on the job.[2] Perhaps this was because the coal house was built opposite Ashworth's own back door and Nancy Priestley may in fact have been one of his tenants who lived in the cottages at Walt Royd.

Of all the years for which a Diary survives 1785 and 1786 were the years in which Ashworth was most frequently employed as a labourer. On Friday 15 August he noted in the Diary;

I was at Jumples Mill most of the afternoon Charles Crowther undertook [dig]

the Cleaning & inlarging the above Mill [day] Dam and I assisted in [the work]

For the next seven days, with the exception of Sunday 21, and Wednesday 24 which was wet, Ashworth laboured at Jumples in spite of the fact that his own corn was being harvested during this period. On Saturday 27 August he and five others harvested at Walt Royd but the following Monday Ashworth returned to Jumples Mill. Unfortunately there are no entries from the end of August to 14 October so it is not possible to know the extent of Ashworth's work at Jumples Mill in this period. However he was labouring there again on 17 October when he:

---

[1] Diary, 4 November 1783.
[2] Diary, 6-9 November 1809.

went twice to Whealy [to] and Jumples Mill in the forenoon and assisted in
Measuring Stone &c.

Ashworth worked at Jumples Mill on one day in November and on three consecutive days at the end of December. In 1786 Ashworth was employed again at Jumples Mill and worked there for three days until on 14 January he recorded:

I work'd at Jumples Mill and it wa Reer'd that Day & the Reering Feast was at Savil Green that night.

This suggests that the work had now moved into a second phase involving considerable construction at the mill itself. During the time that this phase of the Jumples Mill project was drawing to a conclusion Ashworth was also working on a job near Hebble Bridge but he recorded no more details about this work.

In February 1786 the work at Jumples Mill entered a third phase. Ashworth noted on Friday 3 February that:

I began working at Jumples Mill along with John Town Ric^d Longbottom Timothy Walsh &c in enlarging a Mill Day (sic) 8 Person worked

Ashworth was engaged full time on this work for the next two weeks and perhaps for longer but unfortunately a leaf of the Diary is missing at this point making it impossible to know exactly the extent of Ashworth's employment. It is significant however that on 8 March, the next surviving entry, Ashworth recorded that he worked at Jumples in company with ten other men. Ashworth never stated the nature of his employment but one Diary entry suggests that he may have been a kind of foreman. On 11 February he wrote:

I work,d at Jumples Mill in the fore & went to Halifax in the afternoon with Richd Longbottom to Mr Cha^{r}les Houdson for Money to Pay the Man we their Wages with

Ashworth's work at Jumples Mill was part of an ambitious enlargement of the fulling mill. On 10 September 1785 Charles Hudson, who was operating the mill, had signed a contract by which he was to pay Joseph Mitchell of Honley £200 to install a water wheel and four fulling stocks at the mill.[3] The work was specified in a drawing that has survived (see *Figures 35* and *36*). According to the contract, the work was to be completed by 13 February 1786.

---

[3] West Yorkshire Archive Service (Calderdale), RP: 779/1, *Memorandum of an Agreement between Joseph Mitchell and Charles Hudson 10 September 1785*.

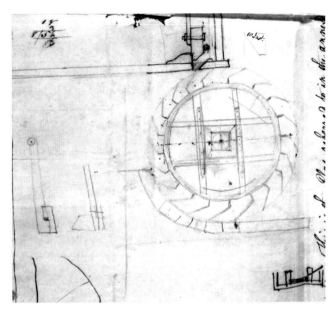

Figure 35   Sketch of the water wheel installed at Jumples Mill from the contract drawing of 1785. (West Yorkshire Archive Service, Calderdale)

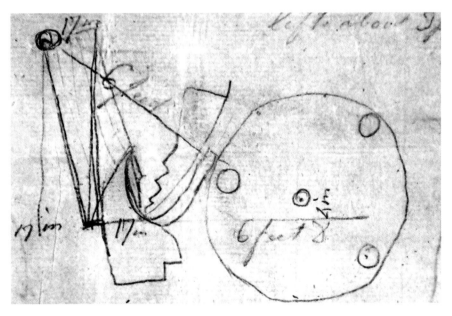

Figure 36 Detail of the fulling stocks installed at Jumples Mill from the contract drawing of 1785. (West Yorkshire Archive Service, Calderdale)

It was to provide the water for this wheel that Ashworth was involved in cleaning out and enlarging the mill dam. The second enlargement of the mill dam in February and March 1786 may indicate that more water was required to turn the new wheel than had originally been anticipated.

The Diary for 1785 also records Ashworth actively seeking other building work. On 29 November:

> I went with Charles Crowther John Sheard & Isaac sharp to the Triangle beyond Sowerby Bridge to to vew a Place whe a Mill was to erected

Nothing came of this but Ashworth was already engaged in getting stone for another building project. On Monday 14 November he had recorded that:

> I began working in Wheatly edge with James Hains[worth] who was getting Stones to Build a House for John Smith

Lying just to the east of Ashworth's home, Wheatley Edge was a convenient place for him to work and he spent the next fortnight on this job. In March the following year he helped Richard Longbottom, with whom he had worked at Jumples Mill, to quarry further down the Wheatley valley at Leebank Shroggs.[4]

It is significant that it is the Diary for 1785 and 1786 that records the majority of Ashworth's building and quarrying activity. This work seems to have replaced weaving in Ashworth's economy for he stopped weaving at Walt Royd on 4 February 1785. Like weaving, building and quarrying work was usually undertaken in those parts of the year when agricultural work was light.

Dealing in Hops

The first time Ashworth mentioned hops in his Diaries was on 13 December 1785 when he recorded:

> went [H] Salter Hebble Warf in the afternoon for a Paket of Hops

The next day he went to Halifax again and weighed out the hops. By 1792 he was being described as a hop merchant[5] and that is how he was

---

[4] Diary, 10 and 11 March 1786.
[5] West Yorkshire Archive Service (Wakefield), *West Riding Registry of Deeds*, Vol. DK, p.63, Deed 94, 1792.

described in the key to the Ovenden Enclosure Award of 1817.[6] If, however, the public perception of Ashworth was as a hop merchant the Diaries give scant evidence of it. There is a single reference to hops in the third Diary and only a handful of entries mention hops in the Diary for 1815.[7] What they do make clear is that the volume of hops that Ashworth was dealing in by this time was considerable. On Monday 2 January 1815 he brought home nine packets of hops from Salterhebble and the following day delivered six of them to three customers. Later in the year he and his brother in law:

> went to Warley Town with half a Pocket of Hops and Brother John assisted me in carrying them[8]

Where the hops that Ashworth collected from Salterhebble Wharf came from is not known but it is tempting to think that they might have passed through the hands of his stepson Edmund Marsden who worked in the business owned by William Swaine, Ashworth's brother-in-law, who was a hop factor living in Southwark.

It rather looks as if Ashworth was dealing in hops in two ways. In the case of the six pockets of hops he delivered to three people in January 1815 he was clearly acting as a wholesale merchant. A pocket of hops weighed from one and a quarter to one and a half hundredweight. To brew five gallons of beer would require very roughly an ounce of hops so it is clear that those purchasing two pockets of hops were brewing on a more than domestic scale. However it may be that Ashworth also sold hops in small quantities to people brewing on a domestic scale. This is perhaps what is implied in his Diary entry for 4 October 1815:

> I went to Carry Hops & Collect Money to Ovenden Moorside in afternoon.

The relative paucity of Diary entries relating to Ashworth's hop dealing activities is puzzling and can perhaps be explained only by assuming that Ashworth did not undertake much of the work himself.

---

[6] West Yorkshire Archive Service (Calderdale), WYC 1361/1/2, *Ovenden Enclosure Award*, 1817.
[7] Diary, 27 September 1809; 4 January 1815; 4 and 7 October 1815.
[8] Diary, 7 October 1815.

'Jobbing About the Farm'

If Ashworth was not skilled enough to undertake building or quarrying on his own account then it is clear that he was a very practical man. He frequently recorded doing jobs at Walt Royd. He mended items as diverse as a rake and a chest while on one evening in 1782 he settled down to make a coal box.[9] In May 1783 and in the same month again in 1785 he recorded painting the doors and gates around his house.[10] And he was prepared to tackle more ambitious jobs: for example he recorded that on 16 May 1785 'Charles Crowther and I thatched the ashes Hous.' Incidentally, this is an interesting dialect use of the word 'thatch' to mean put a roof on a building. It would not have been of straw but, almost certainly in this case, have been made of stone slates or 'thakstones'.

In 1786 Ashworth 'Jobbed up Stairs in the great Chamber and Put window Shutters in little Chamr'.[11] On 6 May 1783 he 'helped the Joiners & other jobs about the lathe' and later in the year he helped the mason who was working in the kitchen.[12] Just before Christmas 1809 he 'assisted Job Hasleden in Setting Our Oven and Boiler'.[13]

In the later Diaries he records doing a number of jobs on properties around Walt Royd. It seems likely that they were the cottages that Ashworth and his wife owned and he was maintaining them. In December 1809 he paid 1s. 3d. for a lock for Nancy Priestley's house and in the same month he recorded 'Paid for Mossing William Charnocks House   0 2 [3]0'.[14] This is a comparatively late reference to the practice of packing moss in the gaps between the stone flags on a house roof to render it more weather tight.

Sometimes his neighbours must have paid Cornelius Ashworth to do odd jobs because on 21 August 1815 he noted:

> I was Employ,d in the afternoon in pruning the thorns on which our neighbours hang their Linen to dry   ½ Days labour in the above   0. 1. 3.

---

[9] Rake: Diary, 11 July 1783; Chest: 18 October 1785; Coal box: 14 December 1782.
[10] Diary, 17 May 1783; 14 May 1785.
[11] Diary, 6 January 1786.
[12] Diary, 21 June 1783.
[13] Diary, 21 December 1809.
[14] Diary, 4 December 1809.

Travel

Cornelius Ashworth lived at a time when a revolution in transport was underway. The Railway Age lay in the future, but a canal system now linked all the important industrial and agricultural districts of England, and new turnpike roads had been built in most parts of Britain too. Halifax benefited significantly from these developments. The town's approaches were steep in almost every direction. Range Bank, Lee Bank, Southowram Bank and similar routes were little more than packhorse tracks which heavy wagons and stage coaches could not negotiate, and the River Calder was unnavigable.

The volume and nature of traffic in Halifax was changing dramatically during Ashworth's lifetime. Roads heading west into Lancashire via Hebden Bridge and Sowerby Bridge were greatly improved during the second half of the eighteenth century when Turnpike Trusts were established, whilst to the north of the town the Keighley Turnpike was opened. Thereafter easier access to the Bradford, Leeds and Wakefield roads was eventually provided when the New Bank was constructed.[1] And Ashworth would surely have admired the new North Bridge across the Hebble Brook that opened in 1774 and made this particular development possible (see *Figure 37*). Meanwhile John Smeaton's Calder and Hebble Navigation was completed during the 1770s, and some thirty years later the Rochdale Canal from Sowerby Bridge finally established a link between the Humber and the Mersey.

Cornelius Ashworth's home at Walt Royd lay some two and a half miles from Halifax. He went there regularly, most particularly on Sundays when he attended morning and afternoon services at Square Chapel, and subsequently at Pellon Baptist Chapel. Quite often, however, no reason for his visit is indicated.

---

[1] Two Turnpike Acts 1824: 1827 led to improvements between Godley Lane Head and Northowram Green. A deep cutting and an embankment made the road more manageable. 'A stupendous feat' as Anne Lister of Shibden Hall observed. J.A. Hargreaves, *Halifax*, Edinburgh, Edinburgh University Press, 1999, p.74.

Figure 37 Nathan Fielding: 'View of Halifax From Haley Hill'. Late Eighteenth Century. (Calderdale MBC Museums and Galleries)

His route would have taken him along the lower reaches of the Hebble Brook, which he crossed at Lee Bridge, before walking up Cross Hills to Northgate (see *Figure 43*). This must have been a pleasant walk, taking less than an hour, and there were few signs of industry along the way in the 1780s, but there would be many changes over the next forty years.

The earliest surviving Diary covers the period when Ashworth was busy at his loom. During a two-week period in November 1782 he wove over sixty yards of cloth, and he would complete his 'piece' within five or six days. The identity of the merchant or clothier who bought the cloth is not known but he must have lived nearby, because on 6 December 1782 Ashworth recorded that he: 'went with my Piece and Twice to Halifax after'.

When Ashworth began to deal in hops he collected them in 'pockets' from Salterhebble Docks, the nearest point on the Calder and Hebble, which lay almost five miles from Walt Royd. The Diaries record journeys in 1809 and 1815 around Ovenden township and out to Warley delivering hops. Longer journeys are mentioned. In May 1783 Ashworth went to Keighley, in February 1785 he visited a doctor in Hebden Bridge and in December he went to Bingley to a Justices' meeting. He made regular family visits to Birstall and Gomersal on the outskirts of Leeds and Bradford. His step-granddaughter Hannah was at the Moravian School in Gomersal and his step-grandson Edmund attended Ewood Hall School near Mytholmroyd. Only in the very last entry in the Diaries, on 28 February 1816 is there evidence of Ashworth making a more ambitious journey when he wrote: 'I set off for London by way of Leeds'.

This one reference to a journey beyond Yorkshire is a reminder that Ashworth had little cause to travel far,[2] but acquaintances, like the Reverend Titus Knight and various members of the Ashworth family, were not so constrained. For many years Knight served as a visiting Minister at chapels in Tottenham Court Road and Woolwich, and the Swaines and the Marsdens travelled to and from London quite regularly via Manchester or

---

[2] He was still expected to pay Composition Money to the Surveyor of Roads in Ovenden Township. He records two payments of 18 shillings in 1809. These payments were an alternative to Statute Labour, which in earlier times had been the intended means of keeping the roads under repair.

Leeds.[3] Improved roads meant that long distance travel was not as burdensome as it once had been. On 22 June 1815 Ashworth noted that he:

> went to Hal[x] to Meet my Doughter Marsden Tho[s] Marsden's wife who had Traveled from London to Leeds in a Stge Coach in 23 hours.

By 1830 there were over twenty departures daily from the White Swan in Crown Street, just one of Halifax's several coaching inns, and the cross-country mail from Liverpool to Hull took just twelve hours. Much had changed since December 1782 when Ashworth had recorded:

> Mary Cooper Set off in the wagon for London.

Set against this background, one crucial question remains. Did Cornelius Ashworth own a horse? The evidence certainly seems to suggest that he did not have a working horse. In all four Diaries there are references to work done on the farm. On 24 March 1783 Ashworth recorded that:

> I and George Town & Jame Riley with his Cart & Two horses led mainer into Long field in forenoon & in after lead Earth into Do & Stones into little field for the use of making a Drain.

In March 1785 he noted that:

> we had … George Armitage and his Mother's Horse and Cart leading dung and Ashes.[4]

Three men, a cart and two horses were employed in leading ashes in March 1809,[5] whilst on 1 March 1815 Ashworth employed:

> 3 Men 1 Cart and 2 Horses Leading Ashes in the Morning and 1 Horse in the afternoon
>
> Expense of Ashes Leading   0. 15. 0.

There are regular references in the Diaries to cows that Ashworth owned, and the expense he had in buying and keeping them. Cows were bought and calves were sold and he makes a note whenever a cow has been covered. He records their injuries or illnesses. A black cow cost £7. 5s. 0d. in June 1809, and £12. 7s. 0d. was paid for a young heifer in December.

---

[3] E. Webster, 'Cornelius Ashworth of Walt Royd, Wheatley', *Transactions of the Halifax Antiquarian Society*, 1985, 30-48 at p.46, wonders if Brother Swaine planned to sail to London when he set off via Liverpool in December 1809, but this seems rather unlikely.
[4] Diary, 24 March 1785.
[5] Diary, 9 March 1809.

At the end of the year Ashworth lists £10. 2s. 0½d. in his accounts as the cost of 'Waiting on the Cow all the past year'.[6] This sort of expense and more would have been inevitable if he had kept his own horse, but the Diaries are silent on this matter.

Some of Ashworth's journeys would have been quite demanding if he did not have a horse. On 21 May he: 'went to Keig^hly with Mr Swaine & Came back that night', eight days later: 'Mr Swaine & I went to Bradford & Returned'.[7] In the same month he 'went to Cleckheaton… & Returned that night'. He: 'went to Bingly along with John Smith and James Hains^worth' on 1 December 1785 but was employed in husbandry at Walt Royd the following day. He would have covered between fifteen and twenty miles on these occasions. Only twice, however, did Ashworth say how he travelled. On 16 December 1809 he wrote: 'I walked to Farsley in the afternoon' and three days later he recorded: 'I walk from Farsley to Home before 5 O clock in the Evening'.

It is interesting to note that when family or acquaintances came to Walt Royd with horses a special mention was deemed to be appropriate. On 23 November 1782:

> Joseph [&] Cordingly & Joseph Clough & Nancy Cordaly came to our hous with each of ym a horse

And on 19 June 1815:

> Mrs Rhodes Senr Came to our house on a visit her son Schechaniah Came with her on Horseback

Some of the distances Ashworth travelled would seem unmanageable to almost everyone today. The condition of many roads and footpaths would be an issue too. But his regular trips around Halifax and district would not have been too difficult, even when 'carrying his piece' or the hops he traded in.

---

[6] Diary, 29 December 1809. Is this his Cow Club subscription (see above p.49)? Ashworth recorded the meeting of the Cow Club at Illingworth in August 1815 but it is not clear if he was a member so this may have been money paid separately to a 'Cow Doctor'.

[7] It seems that John Swaine, Ashworth's brother-in-law, owned a horse at least. On 28 October 1782 Ashworth recorded: 'I went to Gildersome about Bro^r Swaines Horse'.

In over four years' Diaries spread over thirty-four years Cornelius Ashworth never once mentions owning or riding a horse. But before conclusions are drawn, one last point deserves consideration. During his time as Overseer for the Poor in Ovenden Township between November 1780 and April 1781 Ashworth went to Cottingley to meet Justice Wicken. A girl called Rebekhah Naylor was with him, and it seems likely that an indenture was signed. Accounts record that 'Wages for self and horse' were claimed.[8]

---

[8] E. Webster, 'Cornelius Ashworth of Walt Royd, Wheatley', *Transactions of the Halifax Antiquarian Society*, 1985, p.42.

Cornelius Ashworth: The Man

Nowhere in any of the four extant Diaries does Cornelius Ashworth express an opinion. At one level they are a deeply unrevealing testimony and one might despair of ever finding the man behind the carefully noted details of his daily occupations.

However a cursory examination of the Diaries soon reveals a man deeply interested in religion, a loyal and active member of the two churches to which he belonged and wholeheartedly committed to their evangelistic mission.

The daily record of his Diaries suggests a methodical and hard-working man who rarely wasted a moment of the day. He was clearly trusted by others, witness his journey to Halifax in March 1786 to collect the money to pay his fellow workmen at Jumples Mill.

Ashworth's willingness to walk frequently into Halifax, sometimes undertaking the journey twice a day, suggests a man in good health. It is true that the Diaries note his illnesses in some detail and there may be an element of hypochondria in this but perhaps he viewed his ailments and his recovery from them as part of God's dealings with him. This is perhaps the point of his Diary entry for Tuesday 23 September 1783:

> At night had a sore fit of sickness thought to be Occation,d by eating some Wheat Loaf a little at 5 and a little at 8 O clock in the Evening and was very Ill from 9 till 11 O clock I vomited 3 times 2 twice before and once after taking a quantity of Oil which the lord Cause to work for good in that Reespect as it was Supposed the above bread had Pot Ashes in it.

Ashworth had a serious bout of illness early in 1785. At the end of the first week he went to Hebden Bridge for some medicine which, he recorded was 'of use to me through the Blessing of god upon it',[1] nevertheless he was not well enough to go out for another month. Ashworth was ill 'with Pain in My back Head and Knees' for a week in February 1809 and again

---

[1] Diary, 10 February 1785.

for a few days in October. [2] The same complaint seems to have afflicted Ashworth early in 1815 for he recorded on Sunday 12 February:

> I was much better in health but not fitt to go out as I had Only been out once for 10 Days past.

Only twice does Ashworth mention anything to do with his own appearance. On 25 March 1785 he recorded: 'I began wearing a wig' and on 11 June of the same year he noted:

> Went Halifax in the Evening and Bought A new hat for my self at 12/- Price.

This seems an extraordinarily high price for a hat given that only the day before Ashworth had paid 12/9 for half a load of wheat, a load being forty bushels. Perhaps the wearing of a wig and the purchase of expensive headgear are a measure of just how prosperous Ashworth was at this period.

Marrying a woman considerably older than himself with three children in their teens cannot always have been easy, yet his step-children often returned to Walt Royd and he seems to have had a good deal of responsibility for his step-grandchildren when they were sent north for their education. Indeed the epitaph on Cornelius Ashworth's gravestone recorded that he was 'very much esteemed' by his relations.[3] Further evidence comes from a letter written in 1819 by a young clergyman, Edward Ramsden, to his mother at Jumples, who had just let one of her cottages to Cornelius Ashworth:

> It gives me great pleasure to find Mr Cornelius Ashworth has taken the cottage, I trust he will be a good, & respectable neighbour, we could not have had a better.[4]

---

[2] Diary, 12-15 October 1809.

[3] T.W. Hanson, The Diary of a Grandfather, *Transactions of the Halifax Antiquarian Society*, 1916, p.247.

[4] West Yorkshire Archive Service (Calderdale), RMP 54, *Letter from Edward Ramsden to his mother*, 13 March 1819.

Cornelius Ashworth: The Diarist

Many entries indicate that Ashworth did not write his entries each day. Indeed, like many diarists, it appears that he wrote his Diary up weekly. Take, for example, his entry for Monday 26 December 1785:

> Thos Marsden Went to Gomersal and Stay'd till Wednesday.

Such an entry could only have been made retrospectively. Writing up his Diary for Thursday 12 January 1786 he began: 'a Bright frosty' but then crossed out the phrase and recorded: 'Dull Soft day day (sic) I work.d near Hebble Brigd '. Again it is clear that Ashworth was writing up the Diary some days later. In this case he either altered the entry as he remembered the weather correctly or began to copy up the weather from a rough note but got the wrong day. Perhaps it is significant that he recorded the following Saturday 14 as 'a Bright frosty day'. When Cornelius Ashworth recorded the burial of his step granddaughter he initially recorded it as having taken place on Monday 20 February 1809 but then crossed that part of the entry out and wrote for the following day:

> Hannah Marsden was Buried this day in the Afternoon at Baptist Chappel in Halifax

Only the retrospective writing up of his Diary could explain the confusion in Ashworth's account of this event (see *Figure 38*).

Many entries Ashworth made have words or letters missing which suggests, perhaps, that he was copying his Diary up from rough jottings, possibly late in the evening when he was tired and prone to make mistakes. These mistakes should not be taken to mean that Ashworth wrote only with difficulty. This is clearly not the case; he wrote with ease and had mastered the difficult art of writing with a quill, producing a pleasant copperplate hand that, at its best, is very elegant.

Probably Ashworth wrote his Diary up on a Sunday. There are certainly fewer errors and erasures in his entries for Sundays and on average they are longer than for any other day of the week. If Ashworth did indeed write up his Diary for the week on a Sunday this might suggest that Ashworth's motive for keeping his Diary was primarily religious.

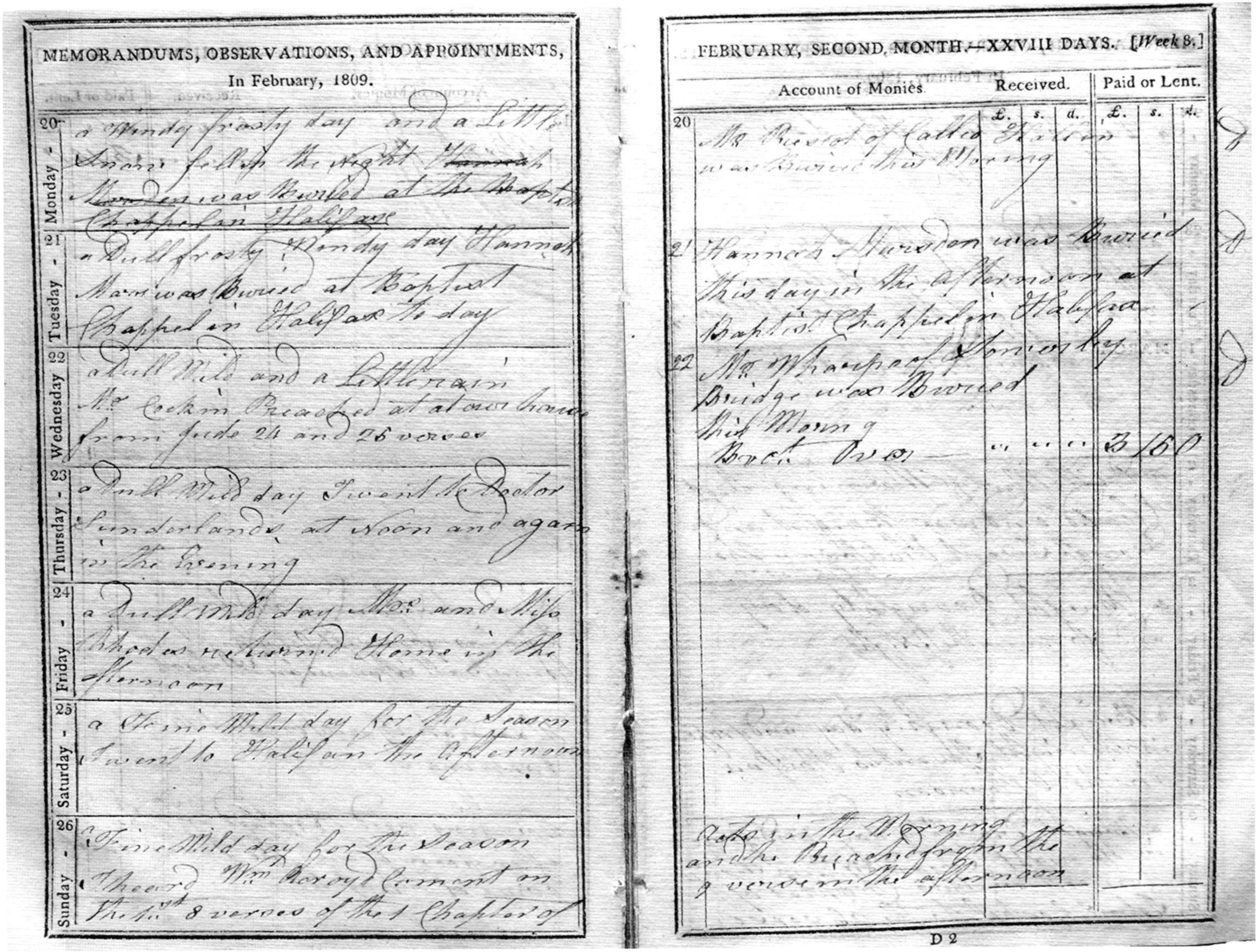

MEMORANDUMS, OBSERVATIONS, AND APPOINTMENTS,

In February, 1809.

20 Monday - a Windy frosty day and a Little Snow fell in the Night ~~Hannah Marsden was Buried at the Baptist Chappel in Halifax~~

21 Tuesday - a Dull frosty Windy day Hannah Marsden was Buried at Baptist Chappel in Halifax to day

22 Wednesday - a Dull Mild and a Little rain Mr Cockin Preached at at our house from Jude 24 and 25 verses

23 Thursday - a Dull Mild day I went to Doctor Sunderlands at Noon and again in the Evening

24 Friday - a Dull Mild day Mrs and Miss Rhodes returned Home in the Afternoon

25 Saturday - a Fine Mild day for the Season I went to Halifax in the Afternoon

26 Sunday - Fine Mild day for the Season I heard Wm Aeroyd Comment on the 1st 8 verses of the 1 Chapter of

FEBRUARY, SECOND MONTH.—XXVIII DAYS. [Week 8.]

	Account of Monies	Received £	s.	d.	Paid or Lent £	s.	d.
20	Mr Priestley of Catton was Buried this Morning						
21	Hannah Marsden was Buried this day in the Afternoon at Baptist Chappel in Halifax						
22	Mr Wharf of Sowerby Bridge was Buried this Morning						
	Bot. Oven	..	..	..	3	15	0
	Acts in the Morning and he Preached from the 9 verse in the afternoon						

D 2

Figure 38 The Diary 20-26 February 1809

Ashworth must have been aware of the published diaries of George Whitefield and John Wesley that had first issued from the press in 1738 and 1740 respectively. Equally he probably knew of the religious Journal written by John Nelson, the Methodist stonemason and well-known local preacher, which John Wesley had edited and published in 1767. Keeping a diary had long been regarded as an aid to the spiritual life, especially amongst the nonconformist denominations, and it may well be that was why Ashworth began to keep his own Diary.

However by no stretch of the imagination could Ashworth's Diary be described as a work of spiritual introspection. It is a plain record of how he spent his time, which sermons he heard, and what the weather was like. In this respect it is not dissimilar to the diary kept by Peter Walkden, an Independent minister in the Forest of Bowland earlier in the eighteenth century, who wrote that his diary was to be:

> An account of my daily Transactions with a true account of where, in what, and how I Spend my Time Every day

Walkden declared this record was:

> Done as a merror to review my Life and actions in, y^t I may know how to walk, and to humble my self before ye Lord; and when to reioyce in ye Experiences of his divine Love and favour[151]

Ashworth was never so forthcoming about the purpose of his Diary but his record could well have been a means to ensure that God-given time was properly spent. The daily record of the weather may be more than just a farmer's obsession; it might have been noted down as daily evidence of the dealings of God with men. Certainly Ashworth's lists of those who died, frequently with comments about the manner of their demise, can be seen in this light as well as being a warning to prepare for the day of judgement. It has already been noted that Ashworth's entries for Sunday are more detailed than for other days and it is interesting that whenever he went on any week-day journey connected with church business Ashworth also wrote in greater detail than normal.

---

[1] P. Walkden, *A Diary from January 1733 to March 1734*, Otley, Smith Settle, 2000, p.171.

It is not known when Ashworth began to keep a Diary. Quite possibly he began the practice when he became a member of Square Chapel. However the first of the extant Diaries begins on Friday 4 October 1782 and it is not until 27 October that Ashworth settled down to his subsequent practice of recording his attendance at chapel and the texts the preacher used (see *Figure 39*). It is therefore possible that the first extant Diary is the first that Ashworth actually wrote. As to the remaining three Diaries there is no way of knowing whether they are just three survivors from a series of Diaries covering many years or whether they represent all that Ashworth kept. It is clear, however, that Ashworth was not absolutely consistent in keeping his Diary because he made no entries for the period from 11 to 22 April or from 29 August to 15 October in 1785. In 1815 Ashworth wrote no Diary entries from 27 November to 11 December.

The Diaries

By the early twentieth century the Diaries had come into the possession of Miss Edith Blagborough of Moorlands Place, Halifax who allowed T.W. Hanson to consult them when he was preparing his paper on Cornelius Ashworth.[152] This was printed in the Transactions of the Halifax Antiquarian Society for 1916. It appears that Hanson eventually acquired the Diaries himself and gave them to the Antiquarian Society.[153] They were certainly in the possession of the Society by 1960 when J. Wilson recorded that they were in the Society's collections at Bankfield.[154] In 1964 they were deposited in the Halifax Borough Archive Service. This archive became part of the West Yorkshire Archive Service in 1983 and today the Diaries are in the collections of the Calderdale office of the West Yorkshire Archive Service.[155]

---

[2] West Yorkshire Archive Service (Calderdale), MISC 139, *Notebook belonging to T.W. Hanson containing notes on Cornelius Ashworth.*

[3] E. Webster, 'Cornelius Ashworth of Walt Royd, Wheatley', *Transactions of the Halifax Antiquarian Society*, 1985, 30-48 at p.30.

[4] West Yorkshire Archive Service (Calderdale), MISC 139, *Notebook belonging to T.W. Hanson containing notes on Cornelius Ashworth,* note by J.Wilson.

[5] West Yorkshire Archive Service (Calderdale), HAS 300-303 (761-764), *Cornelius Ashworth, Diaries 1782-1816.*

The details of the four Diaries and the periods they cover are as follows:

4 October 1782 to 23 November 1783, written in a note book measuring 4" x 6¼"

1 January 1785 to 11 March 1786, written in a note book measuring 4" x 6¼"

1 January 1809 to 31 December 1809, written in a note book measuring 4" x 6¼"

1 January 1815 to 28 February 1816, written in a note book measuring 4" x 6⅜"

In the first two notebooks Ashworth has written his Diary first on the left hand page and then on the right hand page of a blank note book, writing the date and day on the right hand of the page and ruling off after each entry (see *Figures 37* and *38*). These two Diaries have rather attractive decorative covers which seem to have been popular at this time (see *Figure 40*).[156] The third Diary was written in a leather bound copy of *The Daily Journal or Gentleman's, Merchant's, and Tradesman's complete Annual Accompt-Book…for 1809* where the day and date were already printed (see *Figure 42*). The use of this printed diary seems to have occasioned a slight change in Ashworth's method of keeping a diary. In the first two Diaries he had simply recorded the weather, what he had done and the sermons he had heard but the printed Diary has a heading for accounts on the right- hand page and Ashworth used it for this purpose so that his Diary takes on the additional function of an account book. In the last Diary Ashworth continued to note accounts down in a column he ruled on the right hand side of the right-hand page. In this Diary Ashworth wrote each entry right across each double page spread (see *Figure 41*). This Diary has lost its cover and the name Hariot Priestley is written on the flyleaf several times.

---

[6] P. Cooksey, *Joseph Wood 1750-1821: A Yorkshire Quaker*, York, Quacks Books, 2010, front and rear endpapers, reproduces a selection of similar notebook covers.

Figure 40   *The cover of The Diary for 1 January – 11 March 1786.*

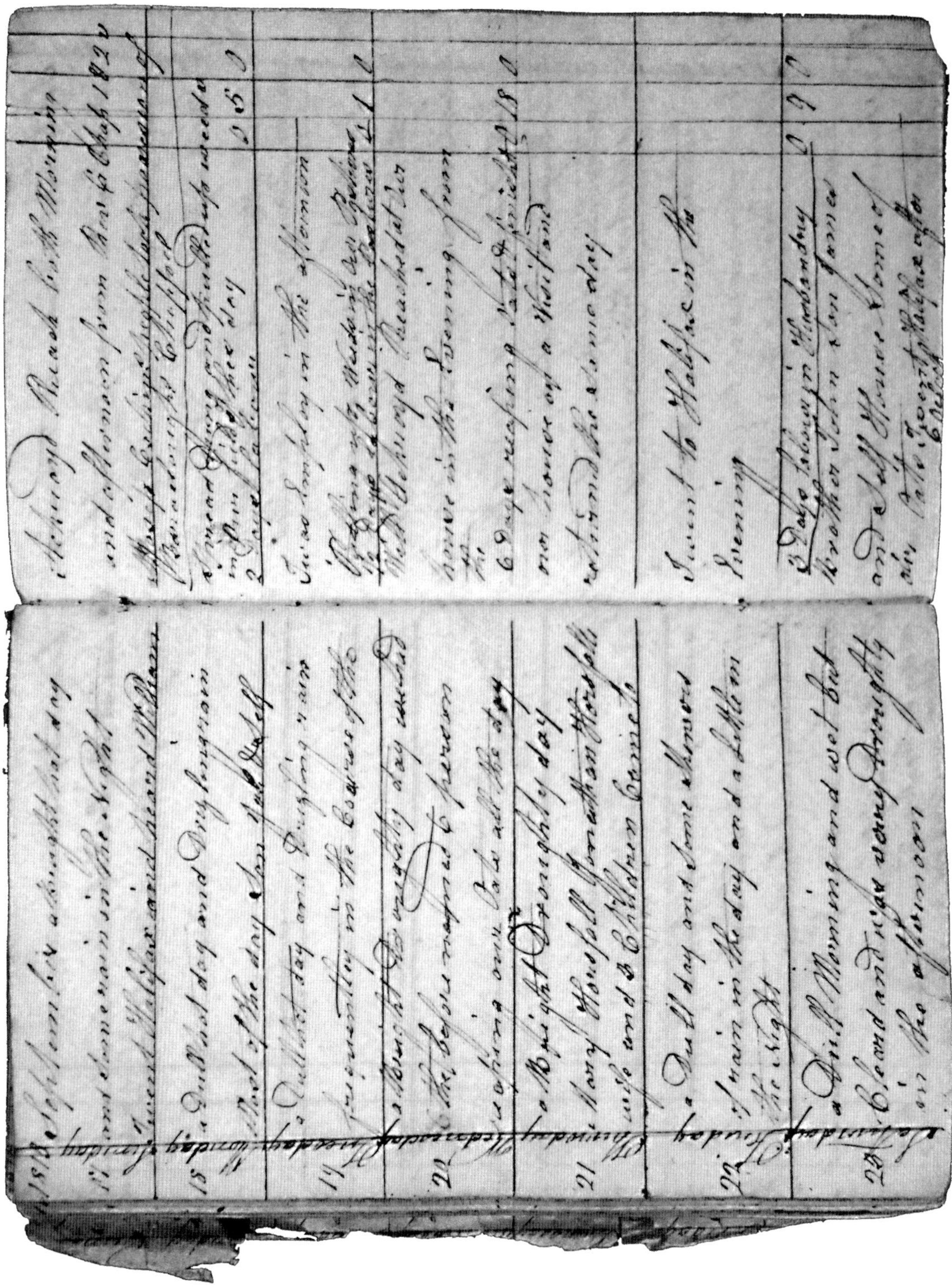

Figure 41 The Diary 17 - 23 September 1815

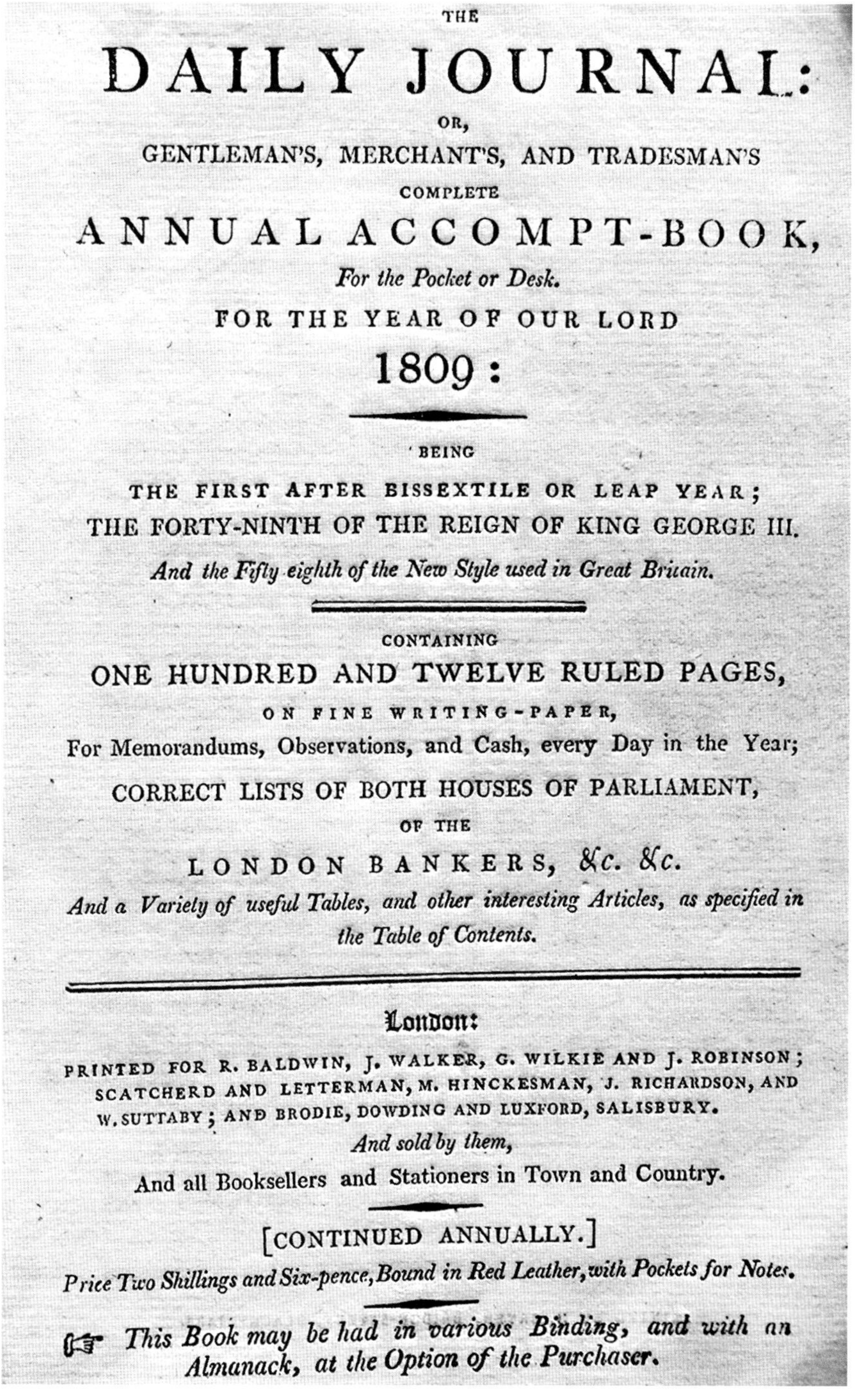

THE

DAILY JOURNAL:

OR,

GENTLEMAN'S, MERCHANT'S, AND TRADESMAN'S

COMPLETE

ANNUAL ACCOMPT-BOOK,

For the Pocket or Desk.

FOR THE YEAR OF OUR LORD

1809 :

'BEING

THE FIRST AFTER BISSEXTILE OR LEAP YEAR;

THE FORTY-NINTH OF THE REIGN OF KING GEORGE III.

And the Fifty-eighth of the New Style used in Great Britain.

===

CONTAINING

ONE HUNDRED AND TWELVE RULED PAGES,

ON FINE WRITING-PAPER,

For Memorandums, Observations, and Cash, every Day in the Year;

CORRECT LISTS OF BOTH HOUSES OF PARLIAMENT,

OF THE

LONDON BANKERS, &c. &c.

*And a Variety of useful Tables, and other interesting Articles, as specified in
the Table of Contents.*

===

London:

PRINTED FOR R. BALDWIN, J. WALKER, G. WILKIE AND J. ROBINSON;
SCATCHERD AND LETTERMAN, M. HINCKESMAN, J. RICHARDSON, AND
W. SUTTABY; AND BRODIE, DOWDING AND LUXFORD, SALISBURY.
And sold by them,
And all Booksellers and Stationers in Town and Country.

[CONTINUED ANNUALLY.]

Price Two Shillings and Six-pence, Bound in Red Leather, with Pockets for Notes.

☞ *This Book may be had in various Binding, and with an
Almanack, at the Option of the Purchaser.*

Figure 42   *The title page of The Diary for 1809.*

The Diaries

Editorial Method

We have attempted to be as faithful as possible to Ashworth's manuscript. The following principles have been adhered to in making our transcription of the Diaries:

i) The spelling, capitalisation and punctuation of the manuscript have all been faithfully preserved.

ii) Abbreviations have not been expanded.

iii) We have been careful to retain the many erasures and alterations in the Diary because they can sometimes illuminate Ashworth's thought process. Words erased or crossed through in the manuscript are indicated in this transcription by being enclosed in square brackets.

iv) Words inserted above the line in the manuscript have been indicated by printing the insertion in superscript.

v) Where Ashworth wrote over a word to correct or alter it we have treated the overwritten word as an erasure and printed it in square brackets followed by the correction Ashworth made as normal text.

vi) Ashworth frequently missed out a word, or sometimes a phrase, by accident. In many cases it is obvious what the omission was intended to be, but this is not by any means true in all cases. We have resisted the temptation to conjecture missing words or letters, leaving readers to come to their own conclusions rather than being led into error by our surmise.

vii) On many occasions Ashworth annotated his Diary with a capital letter. These appear to signify: B for birth, D for death, M for marriage and V for visit.

viii) Editorial notes on the text are printed in italic type and enclosed in round brackets.

ix) Footnotes have been provided to explain the text for each volume of the Diary.

Volume 1

4 October 1782
to
23 November 1783

In the manuscript of this Diary Ashworth ruled a margin on the left hand of each page in which he wrote the day and the date of the entry. In the interests of making the printed text more intelligible we have placed this information at the beginning of each entry while retaining the original spelling.

Ashworth usually wrote the month at the top of each page. Because the pagination of this edition does not correspond to the manuscript we have omitted this feature, which makes little sense in the printed text. We have also omitted the lines by which Ashworth ruled off each entry, preferring to separate the entries in the printed text simply by a space.

On verso of cover
Cornelius
Cornelius Ashworth Book Sep[tm] 25th 1782
Edmund Marsden Set off for London the above mention,d Day[1]

On fly leaf recto
Cornelius   Cornelius Ashworth
                          Cornelius
Ashworth

Friday Oct 4
a fine [da] Cold day froze hard at Night Samuel Sheard Killed [or so hurt] [o] in the quary above James Gledills.

Saturday 5
a darkish day with some rain in the Afterno[on]

Sonday 6
a fair day bu Coldish for the Seson

Monday 7
A darkish day with some Drizling rain in Afterno[on]

---

[1] Edmund Marsden was Ashworth's eldest stepson. See above p.12.

Tuesday 8

a dull day with some drizling rain in the Afternoon Samuel Sheard's body Was buried at Illinghworth I share[2] 4 Hattocks[3]

Wedenesday 9

a dull day I share 3 Hatt[ks] In the Evening

Thursday 10

a dull morning with soome rain In the forenoon Hannah Town died between 9 & 10 O clock in forenoon – droughty in the After[noon] 4 Men this day share 54 Hattks

Friday 11

a dull morning with some rain at noon but verry fine in the After noon this day 6 Men share 57 Hattock in all 118 large Hattocks in Pomfret[4]

Saturday 12

a fine droughty[5] morning but Brisk Showers in Afternoon

Sunday 13

a fine Clear droughty day Hannah Town was buried

Monday 14

a dull Soft[6] day Several Showers a Carried a Piece[7] & Wove 4¾ Y[ds]

Tuesday 15

a Soft Morning but a moderate Droughty day Wove 9 Y[ds]

---

[2] Share: to cut or shear.

[3] Hattock: a stook or shock of corn.

[4] Pomfret was the name of one of Ashworth's fields, on 2 November 1809 it is called Pontefract.

[5] Droughty: dry.

[6] Soft: calm, balmy weather.

[7] Ashworth records carrying his piece many times. He appears to mean that he carried it to the merchant on whose behalf he had woven it. Who this merchant was remains a mystery but it would appear that he lived near to Walt Royd, Ashworth's home, and not in Halifax because on several occasions Ashworth records carrying his piece and then going to Halifax. A good example of this is Ashworth's entry for 6 December 1782. Although it has often been assumed that Ashworth patronised the Piece Hall in Halifax, there is no evidence for this.

Wedenesday 16

a dull day with some little rain in the Afternoon 2 Men and my self housed[8] 40 Hattock of Corn and thrasht corn

Thursday 17

a fine Clear droughty day I and George Town[9] thrasht Corn

Friday 18

a verry High wind With rain Drizling rain most of the day 3 [men] & my self and Tho[s] Marsden[10] Hous,d 78 Hattocks of Corn between 7 O clock and a little past 9 O clock in the forenoon I and George Town Mooed before noon and thrast in the Afternoo[n]

Saturday 19

a verry high wind with heavy Showers of rain and Hail I & G. Town Winow,d[11] 3 quarters of Oats – it froze verry hard at Night

Sunday 20

a Cold windy day with some Showers of rain I heard Mr Langdon[12] Baptis minister from Leeds Preach in the Baptist Chappel at Halifax from Cor: [2 of] Chap: 2 & verse began Fodering the Cows once a day[13]

Monday 21

a Cold high wind I and George T. Thrash,t

Tuesday 22

a Windy day with some rain I and G. Town thras[ht] winow,d 3 quarter in after

---

[8] House: to get under cover, to bring in.
[9] George Town was a neighbour and tenant of the Ashworths. See above p.12.
[10] Thomas Marsden was Ashworth's second stepson.
[11] Winnowing: process of separating the grain from the chaff after threshing. This was done traditionally by putting the threshings in a cloth. Two men held the cloth, one at either end, shaking it up and down so that the breeze would catch the chaff and carry it off. Often this process took place in the centre of a barn on the threshing floor with both doors open to create a draught.
[12] Rev. Thomas Langdon, minister of the Baptist chapel in St Peter's Square, Leeds, 1781 – 1824.
[13] Fodering: feeding.

Wedenesday 23

Showers in the forenoon Droughty in the Afternoon I worked out till 3 O clock Wove 2 y[ds] before Sun set Clouted my Coal[14] in the Evening

Thursday 24

Moderate fine [fore] noon but heavy Showers in the Afternoon Sally Rhodes came to our House with Sarah Crowther Who had been nursing her mother Mrs Rhodes [3 weeks]

of her laying in of her doughter Rhoda[15] I Churned till 10 o clock wove 6 ½ y[ds]

Friday 25

Rained almost all the day Wove 8½ y[ds]

Saturday 26

a verry droughty day Made at the Mill in forenoon in 54 Hattocks 98 Strikes[16]of Oats 31 Strikes of Shilling[17] 3 Packs of Meal[18] Share at James Rileys in After[noon]

Sunday 27

a verry mild day I went to Halifax heard Mr Knight[19] in forenoon Comment on Hos: Chap 11 In Afternoon Preach From Hebrews Chap 9 & verses 16 & 17

Monday 28

a Soft morning but Cleard & was a verry fine day I went to Gildersome about Bro[r] Swaines Horse[20] & came back that Night

---

[14] Clouting: breaking up with heavy blows.

[15] Susannah Rhodes, nee Swaine, was Ashworth's sister-in-law. She had married Shechaniah Rhodes and had several children of whom Sally and Rhoda were the eldest girls.

[16] A strike of oats: a measure equal to two bushels in the West Riding, although it could vary from half a bushel to four bushels in other districts.

[17] Shilling: grain, especially oats, which has been freed from the husk.

[18] Pack of meal: this may be an indefinite quantity or a pack of 252 lbs, which was a recognised measure of meal.

[19] Rev. Titus Knight, minister of Square Chapel, Halifax, 1773–1793. Ashworth was admitted as a member of the church in July 1771 at the age of nineteen and well before his marriage to Margaret Marsden in 1775. West Yorkshire Archive Service, (Calderdale), SC 3, *Square Chapel Church Membership Book.*

[20] Brother Swaine was Ashworth's brother-in-law William Swaine.

Tuesday 29

Several Showers of rain did Sunday Jobs and went to Halifax Wove 3 ¼ Y^ds froze verry hard at Night

Wedenesday 30

a Moderate fore but a very rainy afternoon & Night wove 4 yds & Carried a Piece

Thursday 31

a Cold high wind with freque^nt Showers of rain the forenoon More moderate in Afternoon Wove 9 ¼ Y^ds

Friday 1 November

a fine frosty clear droughty day Sized a warp[21] and Churned in the forenoon In the Afternoon Wove 5 yd

Saturday 2

a fine frosty morning Snowd from 7 O clock till then began rain^ing and rained till ^mostly midnight & Disolvd the Snow Woved 6 yds

Sunday 3

a Windy wet morning but Cleared in the forenoon went to Halifax heard Mr Knig^ht in forenoon Comment 8 & 9 verses of 11th ^Chap of Hos: in The Afternoon Preach from the 28 verse of the 11 Chap of Matt:

Monday 4

a fine frosty droughty day Wove 6¾ Y^ds

Tuesday 5

a fine frosty morning but overcast & was dull went with my Piece went to Halifax Loomed a Warp[22]

Wednesday 6

a fine bright day & frosty Wove 3¼ Y^ds [a b]

---

[21] Sizing a warp: treating a warp with a glutinous liquid made from animal bones to strengthen it.
[22] Looming a warp: putting the warp onto the loom.

Thursday 7
a bright frosty day wove 6½

Friday 8
Frosty some showers of snow in the forenoon Sally Rhodes went home Churned till After 10 O clock & off again from 12 to 3 O clock went to Halifax in the Evening Wove 2¼ Y^{ds}

Saturday 9
a Mild frosty day John Casson was buried Wov 6½ ^{yds}

Sunday 10
a Mild frosty [day] morning but Soft in the Evening Went to Halifax heard Mr Knight in the forenoon Coment^t on the 10 &11 verses of 11 Chap of Hos: In the Afternoon Preach from the 28 verse of the 11 Chap: of Matthew

Monday
a Soft fore but fine Afternoon Wove 6½ Y^{ds}

Tuesday 12
a darkish fair fore but drizling rain in the Afternoon froze hard hard at Night wove 9 Y^{ds}

Wedenesday 13
a fine bright frosty day wove 3¼ Y^{ds}

Thursday 14
a dull day I went to John Illingworth ☞ [23] Matt: Sheards Matt: Hilups & Laid up the Miding till 3 O clock wove 3¼ Y^{ds}

Friday 15
a verry rainy day Went in Ov^{n}den & to Halifax in fore but wove 4½ Y^{ds} in Afternoon

---

[23] This symbol, or a variation of it, often occurs in connection with John Illingworth. At present its meaning is unknown.

Saturday 16

a fine bright frosty day froze hard at Night I was Churning till 11 O clock wove 5¼.Y^ds

Sunday 17

a fine frosty day I went to Halifax heard Mr Knight Preach in forenoon from Hoshea Chap 11 & 11 verse in Afternoon Ezra

Monday 18

a fine mild day from 10 to Past 1 O clock wove 6 yds

Tuesday 19

a dull Soft day wove 7¼ yds

Wedenesday 20

a fine frosty day went my Piece went to Halifax & wove 2¼yds

Thursday 21

a bright frosty day went to Halifax heard Mr Langdon Baptist minister from Leeds Preach from Habakuck Chap & verses 17 & 18 4½ Y^ds

Friday 22

I George Town & James Riley led[24] mainer[25] with James Cart & 2 Horses a [s] Cold day

Saturday 23

I a verry Cold day & froze ^a wind & froze verry hard I & the above George & James lead mainer till noon o & in afternoon George & I Ditched in holme Joseph [&]Cordingly[26] Joseph Clough & Nancy Cordaly came to our hous with each of ym[27] a horse

---

[24] Led, to lead: to carry, cart or convey by cart.

[25] Mainer: manure. This spelling is frequently found in seventeenth-century inventories in the Halifax district.

[26] Joseph Cordingley was a cousin of the Diarist's wife.

[27] This is the only occasion where Ashworth has used the abbreviation 'y' for th.

Sunday 24

a verry Cold frosty day went to Halifax Heard Mr Knight in forenoon Coment on the 3. 4. 5. & 6 verses of the 12 Cha of Hoshea in afternoon ^P Preach from the 33 Chap: of Job & 29 & 30 verses

Monday 25

the frost Continued some Snow fell in the afternoo^n wove 6 Y^ds

Tuesday 26

a Bright frosty day Sised a warp & wove 4¾ Y^ds

Wednesday 27

a dull frosty day Wove 7¾ Y^ds

Thursday 28

a dull frosty day wove 7 Wove 6½ Y^ds

Friday 29

a dull Soft day with Several Showers of rain Carried my Piece ^wan,d on a warp in forenoon[28] in the Afternoon went to Henry Fowler's ^at edge end to John Earnshaws in Bradshaw to Noah Taylors at Swill hill end to Edward Bentlys at Foor in Northowram[29] Came back by Daniel Firths in Houldworth

Saturday 30

a dull Soft day Churn,d in the forenoon went to Mathew Sheards & Healded a warp in the afternoon[30]

---

[28] Winding on a warp; putting it on to the warp beam of the loom. See diagram p.68.
[29] This is almost certainly Ford in Northowram township which lies between Ambler Thorn and Queensbury. In the Census Enumerator's Returns for 1841 the district is called Foor, so Ashworth's spelling may well reflect the local pronunciation.
[30] Healding a warp: drawing the warp through the healds and reed and winding it on to the cloth roller. See above p.63-64.

Sunday 1

a dull Cold day froze hard at Night went to Halifax Heard in the forenoon Coment (*blank*)

In afternoon Preach from the 23 verse of the 6th Chapter of Daniel

Monday 2

a Bright frosty day I began of a warp wove 4 Y^{ds}

Tuesday 3

a dull frosty day wove 8 ½ Y^{ds}

Wedenesday 4

a dull frosty day wove 5½ Y^{ds}

Thursday 5

a dull frosty day wove 9 Y^{ds}

Friday 6

a dull frosty day wove 5 Y^{ds} in the forenoon went with my Piece and Twice to Halifax after

Saturday 7

a dull morning & Soft in Afternoo^n did sundry Jobbs about my Looms & wove 1½ Y^{ds}

Sunday 8

a dull misty ^{frosty} morning I went to Halifax head Mr Knight Preach in Forenoon from the 1st verse of the 13 Chap: of Hoshea in the Afternoon from 81 Psalm verse 15. 16. 17.

Monday 9

a very dull misty frosty morn^{ing} but clear'd a little I wove 6 yds Went to Halifax at night heard Mr Groves from Rotheram[31] Preach Deut Chap 32 verses 15. 16. 17 & 18

---

[31] Rev. Thomas Grove, Minister of Masbro' Independent Chapel, Rotherham, 1777-1793.

Tuesday 10
a dull frosty day wove 9¼ yds

Wedenes 11
a dull day rather Soft but fosty wove 8 Y^ds

Thursday 12
a dull day with some Drizling rain wove 9 Y^ds

Friday 13
a dull day with some rain in the Afternoon Carried my Piece &c till 2 O clock wove 4 Y^ds after Mary Cooper Set off in the waggon for London

Saturday 14
a dull day with frequent Showers of Snow and rain I wove 4¼ Yds made a Coal Box in the Evening it froze verry hard at Night

Sunday 15
a dull misty frosty day I went to Halifax heard Mr Knight in fore Comon on the 2. 3 & 4 verses of 13 Chap of Hoshea in Afternoon Preach from the 25 verse of the 7 Chap of Pauls Epistle to the Hebews

Monday 16
some Drought till 3 O clock when it began raining Driziling rain & rained frequently till midnight wove 8½ Yds

Tuesday 17
a dull Soft day I went to John Illingworths ☞ wove 7 yds

Wedenesd 18
18 a dull day ^high wind with frequent showers of rain wove 6yds Carried my Piece & went to Halifax

Thursday 19

a dull day with a high wind Some drought but intermixed with heavey Showers of rain (I & C sised each a warp) and for that reason our warps was sorely loss,d[32] and littile drid[33] I & C. Crowther got white Sand in the Afternoon heard Mr Knight Pre[ach] in the Evening from 132 & (*blank*) verses William Bowcock brought 14 sack Coals

Friday 20

a dull forenoon but cleared & was more droughty in aftern I & C. Crowther laid out my warp & got it a little drid we spread mainer in Afternoon till half Past 5 O clock

Saturday 21

a high wind but moderate Droughty I did Sundry Jobs till 2 O clock Loom,d a warp After it froze verry hard at [night]

Sunday 22

a Bright Droughty day I went to Halifax heard Mr Knight Preach in forenoon from Hoshea Chap: 13 & verse 9 in Afternoon from Genesis Chap: 41 & 55 verse

Monday 23

a dull day little drought I began of a warp & wove 3¼ y[d] Will[m] Bowco[ck] brought 7 Sacks of Coals

Tuesday 24

A high wind & moderate drought I wove 2 Y[ds] before 11 O clock I was laying in the Coal heap Sweeping the Roof & walls of the Kitchen & laying the muck miding[34] &c till 10 O clock at Night Tho[s] Came home to [make] [his] Christmas [holiday] [35]

Wedenesday 25

a moderate droughty day being Christmass day I went to Halifax heard Mr Knight Preach both forenoon & After from galations Chap: 4/ 4.5.6 & 7 [vs]

---

[32] Loss'd: wet through.

[33] From this entry it appears that Ashworth was preparing his warps outside, a process known as stretching a warp. See above pp.63-68.

[34] Miding: midden.

[35] Thomas Marsden, the Diarist's stepson, was apprenticed to a carpenter in London. See above p.13.

Thursday 26
a moderate Droughty day Cornelius & James Ashworth my nephews[36]
Came to our house - I wove 5¾ Y^ds

Friday 27
a dull wet morning but Clear,d & was moderate droughty wove 7 Y^ds

Saturday 28
a dull wet morning & raind drizzling rain most of the day my Nephews
went home Thos Marsden went to Gomersal to his Uncle Rhodeses[37] I
wove 5 Yds a high wind in Several Preceading days

Sunday 29
a dull day but some drought ^a high wind & wet in Evening I went to Halifax heard Mr
Knight Prech both morning and afternoon from Hebrews Chap: 2nd & 14 &
15 verses I saw 10 graves open in Halifax Church yard 9 of them for
Children & was informed that 110 Children had been inter,d in the above
yard in 4 week which died of the Small Pox [John Rawson ^a Child buried][38]

Monday 30
a dull wet morning but Cleard a little and was a little drought in Evening
froze verry hard at night I wove 5 ½ Yds

Tuesday 31
a Bright frosty droughty day wove 5 y^ds before 2 O clock Carried my Piece
After

Wedenesday Jan. 1 1783
January a Bright frosty day I went to Matthew Hiley,s with my Shuttle to
mend & did Sundry other Jobbs wove 4 ¼ ^yds Jonathan Acroyd Married

---

[36] Cornelius and James Ashworth were the eldest sons of Ashworth's brother John and his wife Elizabeth.
[37] His uncle was Shechaniah Rhodes who had married Margaret Ashworth's sister Susannah.
[38] These words are written in the margin.

Thursday 2

a Bright frosty day Misty in the Evening wove 3 ¼ yᵈˢ I went to Halifax at night Heard. Mr K. Preach from Deut: Chap 15 & last Clause of 2 verse

Friday 3

a dull frosty day with some little wet in the Evening I wove 7 Yᵈˢ

Saturday 4

a dull Soft day Began to rain a little in the Afternoon I wove 1 Yᵈ in the morning before day light & did Sundry Jobbs in the houseᵉ & out of doors till 1 O clock & went to Halifax Afterwᵃʳᵈˢ Thoˢ Marsden Came home from Gomersall & his Uncle Rhodes came with him

Sunday 5

a dull Soft day with some rain in the Evening I went to Halifax heard Mr Knigʰᵗ Preach ⁱⁿ ᶠᵒʳᵉⁿᵒᵒⁿ from Hebrews Chap: 13 & 5 vers in after from Matt: Chap 12 & 49 verse

Monday 6

a dull Soft day a high wind Sometimes with frequent Showers of rain Mr Knight Preached at our house from Pauls 1 Epistle to Timothy Chap: the 1ˢᵗ & later Part of the 15ᵗʰ verse[39]

Tuesday 7

a dull wet windy day with frequent Showers of Drizling rain Thoˢ Marsden Returned to his Master Christmas Holiday being over I wove 5 Yᵈˢ Benjamⁱⁿ Blagbrough at Illingwoʳᵗʰ Buried his Son Thomas

Wedenesday 8

a dull windy day & rain,d most of the day ˢᵐᵃˡˡ ʳᵃⁿ & the ʷⁱⁿᵈ was verry high af Sun set & heayer raⁱn I wove 4¼ Yᵈˢ John Irwin buried

Thursday 9

about 4 O clock in the morning a Storm of Thunder & Lightning follow,d by hail ⁶ Rain fair from day light till noon high wind f and rain from noon mostly till midnight the wind was verry hight after Sun Set I wove 5 ¾ Yᵈˢ

---

[39] This is the first time that Ashworth records a cottage meeting at his house.

Friday 10
a fine & droughty till 2 O clock then began to rain & was ᵃ verry Rough as there was frequent and heavy Showers of raⁱn with a very hight wind till ten O clock at night I carried my Piece & wove 2 ¾ Yᵈˢ and went to Halifax at Night

Saturday 11
a Windy droughty day I worked in the fields

Sunday 12
Some Thunder & rain in the Morning cleared about 9 O cloᶜᵏ & was fair & windy all the day the wind was verry ʰⁱᵍʰ at Night I went to Halifax heard Mr Knight in fore noon Comment on Hoshea Chap: 13 from the 11 verse to the end of the Chapter in the Afternoon Preach from Romans Chap: 7 & 13 verse

Monday 13
a dull windy day with frequent Showers of rain and Hail I wove 5 ½ Yᵈˢ

Tuesday 14
a dull day fair in the fore noon ⁱᵗ began raining at noon & was wet and windy in the Afternoon a verry high wind at Night I wove 5 ½ yds

Wedenesday 15
a Dull day with Several Showers of rain about noon & in the Evening I wove 6¾ ʸᵈˢ fell snow & froze at Night

Thursday 16
a fine bright frosty draughty day I was about Siseing a warp & from 9 O clock to 3 O clock I wove 4 Yᵈˢ

Friday 17
a fine frosty droughty day I wove 7 Yᵈˢ Carried my Piece & went to Haˡⁱfax in the evening

Saturday 18

a fine frosty day I was Employed in Preparing A Calf Stall Fetching the Tops of three Plain Trees home which grew in the Lane and was that day cut down & Sold to John Blagbrough

Sunday 19

a Fine frosty day I went Halifax Heard Mr Knight in the forenoon [Comment] Prech from Hoshe Chapter 14 & 1st verse in the afternoon from Mark Chap: 8 & 36 verse I saw 11 open Graves in Halifax Church yard 8 or 9 of them for Children Mr William Pollards wife was buried that day she died the Preceding Tuesday – In the Evening I Heard Mr John Hindle[40] who Statedly Preched[41] at Halifax Perticular Baptist meeting Place [42] Preach at Barnaby Blagbroughs from 1st (*blank*)

Monday 20

a Dull frosty day misty in the forenoon In the night the ground was Pretty Coverd with Snow I Loom,d a warp & wove ½ Yd the Cow named young Madam Calved her first Calf about 6 O clock at Night

Tuesday 21

a Dull frosty day with frequent Showers of Snow & Brisk gales of wind I went to Wheatley I wove 2¾ Yds the 1 Cow having Calved She required much attendance

Wedenesday 22

a Dull misty frosty day some Snow fell in the Night I wove 2½ Yds & went to Halifax in the Evening to buy a Medicine to Cause young Madam to Clean[43] after Calving

Thursday 23

a Dull frosty day with Some Showers of Snow I went to Wheatley &to John Illingworths ☞ I wove 3 Yds gave young Madam her medicine at 8 O clock in the Morning & She Cleaned in 5 or 6 hours after

---

[40] Rev. John Hindle, minister of Pellon Lane Baptist Chapel 1779 1789.
[41] Statedly: regularly.
[42] 'Perticular Baptist Meeting Place': Pellon Lane Particular Baptist Chapel, Halifax. The Particular Baptists were Calvinist and therefore believed in predestination as opposed to the General Baptists who were Arminian in theology and therefore advocated the doctrine of free will.
[43] To clean: to bring forth the after-birth.

Friday 24

a Dull day rain,d in the fore noon fair in the After but Continued thawing till after Sun set but froze very hard till the Morning I wove 5 Y^ds

Saturday 25

began thawing in the again some Showers of Snow rain & fore but verry Rainy in Afternoon & Thawed verry Swiftly but froze hard in the Night I wove 2 Y^ds ^and went to Wheatley and did Sundry Jobbs about the lathe[44] and in the Yard & wrote a letter in the Evening

Sunday 26

a Moderate clear day with Shower or two about noon I went to Halifax heard Mr Knight in forenoon Preach From Hoshea Chapter 14 & 2 & 3 verses in the Afternoon from the 62 Psam & Saw 7 open Grave in Halifax Church Yard

Monday 27

a Dull ^day with Several Showers of Rain I was 2 hours Jobbing in the Mistal & wove 7 Y^ds

Tuesday 28

a Fine droughty day Had George Town working in the fields I wove 10½^Yds News in our Paper of Peac with France & ^Spain [45]

Wedenesday 29

a Dullish day with a high wind I and G.Town thrashst verry wet & windy in the Night

Thursday 30

a very wet & windy day Especi^aly in the Morning and Evening I & George Town thrasht Corn

---

[44] Lathe: barn.

[45] During the American War of Independence France and Spain had allied with the American rebels. Peace between Great Britain and America had been made on 30 November 1782 but was not to come into effect until peace had been concluded between Great Britain, France and Spain. This was achieved on 20 January 1783. The Treaty of Versailles of 3 September 1783 settled the territorial arrangements at the end of the conflict, recognising the independence of the thirteen American colonies but requiring the restitution of most of the British territories acquired by France during the war.

Friday 31

a Dull day a high wind ^{Cold} with Several Showers of Rain I & George Town thrasht Corn in the forenoon & winnowed in the Afternoon in 44 Hattocks 54 Strikes of Oats – a Calf which young Madam Calverd died about midnight being 11 Days Old A

Saturday 1 February 1783

a Dull day a high wind and brisk Showers in Evening I was employ'd that day in laying up the miding working in the field & going to Illingworth finisht our hay which was on the Balks[46]

Sunday 2

a Dull day some rain in the afternoon I went to Halfax heard Mr Knight in forenoon Coment on Hoshea Chap: 14 4. 5. 6. & 7 verses in afternoon ^{Preach} from Isiah Chap. 52 and (*blank*) ver

Monday 3

a Bright fore but dull in the afternoon I wove 6 Y^{ds}

Tuesday 4

a Dull day fair till 10 O clock verry wet ^{mostly} after till midnigh I wove 6 ½ Y^{ds}

Wedenesday 5

very wet most of the day I made at the Mill in 30 Strikes of Oat 9 Strikes of Shelling[47] besides mooter[48] I was about making till 2 O clock wove 2 ¾ after

Thursday 6

A Bright day till 4 O clock then Overcast & rainy. I wove 8 ¾ Y^{ds}

Friday 7

^{a Dull} a fair day till ² O clock but very wet after Especialy after Sun set I wove 6 ¼ Y^{ds} Carried my Piece & went to Halifax in the Evening froze sometime in the night

---

46 A balk or baulk: the loft in the barn, often over the mistal, where the hay is stored.
47 Shelling: husks or chaff produced by threshing.
48 Mooter: toll paid at the mill.

Saturday 8
a Dull day fair till about noon in the afternoon was frequent Showers of Snow Hail & rain I Churn,d and went to Matt: Hileys John Hileys Willm Oddys and Benj Pages in mixenden and in ^{fore} Afternoo Work,d in the Barn & fields

Sunday 9 D
a Dull day with Showers of rain in the Morning & ^a bout noon & verry wet in the Night I went to Halifax heard Mr Knight in forenoon Coment ^{on} of Hosh: Chap: 14 & 8. & 9 verses in the afternoon Preach from Isiah Chap: 52 & 7 ver^{se} Charles Taylor was buried in the Evening

Monday 10
a Wet windy day I Wove 6 Y^{ds}

Tuesday 11
a Bright day & verry droughty but Some rain in the Evening. I wove 5¼ Y^d and Sised a warp

Wedenesday 12 D D
a wet windy forenoon but moderate fair in after a good Deal of Snow fell in the Night David Crabtree buried 2 Doughters of the Small Pox I wove 5¾ Y^{ds}

Thursday 13
a Dull day moderate droughty in fore but wet in the Afternoon I Wove 8¼Y^{ds}

Friday 14
a Dull & windy day with frequent & heavy Showers of rain & froze verry hard in the Night. Joseph Cordingly Came to our house & Stayed all night & went home the Next day following I wove 6¼ Y^{ds} and Carried my Piece

Saturday 15
a fine droughty day till 4 O clock Some rain afterwards and froze hard in the night I loom,d a warp and Jobb,d about the Barn

Sunday 16
a fine droughty day I went to Halifax heard Mr K. in fore Coment on Isi Chap 52 & 13. 14 & 15 verses in afternoon in the 107 Psalm 17. 18 & 19 verses Occation'd by C. Taylor Death

Monday 17
a Draughty frosty day misty in the Evening I began of a warp & wove 5 ½ yds

Tuesday 18 D
a Dull frosty day I wove 7 ¼ yds James Presly was buried Who died about 3 O clock of Sunday Afternoon aged 7 years & 11 months

Wedenesday 19
a Dull day & wet in the night I Churned & wove 5 ¼ Yds

Thursday 20
a Dull wet day I Wove 8 ½ Yds

Friday 21
a Dull wet day I wove 6 ¾ Yds Carried my Piece & went to Illingworth

Saturday 22
a Dull day with Drizling rain in the Morning & towards night I worked in the fields Shreading Swilling &c[49]

Sunday 23
a Dull day wet in the morning & a very heavy Showers of Rain in the afternoon Some Snow fell in the Night & froze hard I went to Halifax heard Mr Hough[50] In forenoon Preach from Isiah Chap: 53 & 1 verse In afternoon from Job Chap 22 & 21 verse Judith Wood was Buried Tulip Calvd about 1 O clock afternoon

---

[49] Swilling: the practice of spreading liquid manure from the mistal across the fields below it by using a system of shallow channels. See above p.43.
[50] No information has been found on Mr Hough.

Monday 24

a Dull frosty fair day till 4 O clock Some Snow fell after I was Jobbing till 11 O clock wove 5 ½ Y^ds

Tuesday 25 D

George Prestly died of Small ^Pox A fine frosty day till 4 O clo ^ck Some Snow fell After I was about going with Young Madam to Bull till 11 O clock wove 6 Yds after

Wedenesday 26

a fine frosty day Wove I Wove 7 ½ Y^ds

Thursday 27

a verry wet day b thawld verry finely[51] but froze hard at Night I wove 9½Y^ds

Friday 28

Dull frosty day with frequent Showers of Snow wove 3 ¾ Y^ds & Carried my Piece & went to Cattering Slack Moorside & Whithill

Saturday 1 March

a fine frosty day I was Churning &c till & wove 4 ½ Y^ds after

Sunday 2 D

a Dull frosty day I went to Halifax heard Mr Preach in forenoon frosty Isiah Chap 53 and 1 verse in the after [is] from Rev. Chap 19 & 9 verse Occation^d By Judith Wood's Death

Monday 3

a Dull frosty day with Frequent Showers of Snow I wove 8 Y^ds

Tuesday 4

a Fine frosty day I sised A Warp & wove 4 Y^ds

---

[51] Finely: considerably.

Wedenesday 5

a verry Cold windy frosty Day fair in the forenoon but Snow,d all the afternoon I went to Halifax & heard Mr Burnet[52] Preach from Genesis Chap the 5 & (*blank*) verse I wove 4 ¼ Y^ds

Thursday 6

a Dull frosty day Snow,d all the day I wove 9 ¼ Y^ds

Friday 7

a Dull frosty Snowey mor Till 9 Oclock then began to thaw – I carried my Piece In the morning Loom,d a warp After

Saturday 8

a Dull Soft day but froze hard at night – I went to John Illingworth,s ☞ began a warp & wove 1½ Y^ds & work.d 3 hours about the lathe

Sunday 9

a Dull Soft day but froze at night I went to Halifax heard M^r K Preach from Isiah Chap: 53 & 1 verse in the afternoon from Job Chap 19 & 23 verse

Monday 10 D

a Dull Morning ^but Cleard & was a fine bright droug^hty Day & froze hard at night I wove 7¼ Y^ds D/Ann Robertshaw of Fever

Tuesday 11

a very fine frosty day I was 2 hours about weigh^ing Hay for James Riley & wove 6½ Y^ds

Wedenesday 12

a Dull Soft day froze Hard at night – I went To Halifax and a general Lecture being at our Chap^el Mr Cocking[53] Preached From Eph: Chap 3 & 19 & Mr Moorhouse[54] from The 1. general Epistle of Peter Chap the 1 & 8 verse

---

[52] Rev. John Burnett, minister of Dagger Lane Independent Chapel, Hull, 1761-c.1782.
[53] Rev. Joseph Cocking, minister of the Independent chapel at Kipping, 1777-1791, subsequently minister of Square Chapel, Halifax, 1791-1828.
[54] Rev. William Moorhouse, minister of Highfield Chapel, Huddersfield, 1772-1823.

Thursday 13
a Dull Soft day & Continued Soft in the Night I wove 8 y^{ds}

Friday 14 D
a Dull Soft day with some Showers of Snow & Hail – wove 6 ½ y^{ds} & Carried my Piece Elizabeth Ingham in Wheatley Died of Fever froz in night

Saturday 15
a Fine droughty day with Some Showers of Snow & Hail – I Jobb,d in the house till 11 O clock worked in the fields after till night froze in the night

Sunday 16
a Fine droughty day froze verry hard at night – I went to Halifax heard Mr Knight in forenoon Preach from Isiah Chap:53 & last Clause of the 1 verse in the after from Job Chap22 & 24.25.26. & 27 verses

Monday 17
a Bright droughty day froze hard at night I Wove 5 ¾ y^{ds} and was off most of forenoon

Tuesday 18
a Bright droughty day I went to Henry Hooson's in the morning wove 8 y^{ds} after

Wedenesday 19
a Bright droughty day I Wove 6 ¾y^{ds}

Thursday 20
a Bright droughty day I wove 6 ¼ y^{ds} & went Halifax In Evening & heard Mr Knight Preach from Galations Chap. 6 & 6.7.& 8 verses

Friday 21
a Dull Morning Clear & droughty afternoon Wove 5 y^{ds} and Carri^{d} my Piece went Illingworth Joseph Cordingley Came & Stay,d all night

Saturday 22

a Fine Bright droughty day I & George Town ditching holme I went to Halifax in Evening began Graving[55]

Sunday 23

a Dull Cold droughty day a little wet in Evening a verry high wind in the night I went to Halifax heard Mr Tetley[56] from (*blank*) Preach in the forenoon from [Romans] Galations Gal Chap: 3 & 24 verse In the afternoon from Mark Chap: Chap: 10 & 47 verse

Monday 24

a Cold windy droughty day I and George Town & Jame Riley with his Cart & Two horses led mainer into Long field in forenoon & in after lead Earth into Do & Stones into little field for the use of making a Drain – it froze hard at night

Tuesday 25

a Cold windy day with some light Showers of snow & hail in forenoon heavy rain in the afternoon from 2 till 4 O clock I and G. Town Ditched in the holms & Got the water into them[57]

Wednesday 26

a Cold windy day I & G Town made a Drain in the little field

Thursday 27

a Cold windy day with heavy Showers of hail I went to John Illingworths ☞ & to Illingworth in the forenoon & worked in the little field and long field & wood field in the afternoon froze verry hard at night

Friday 28

a Cold frosty droughty day I worked in the fields froze verry hard at night

---

[55] For an explanation of graving see pp.50-52. Holme was one of Ashworth's fields by the Hebble Brook.

[56] Rev. James Tetley, minister of the Independent chapel at Ravenstonedale, Westmorland, 1766-1775.

[57] This is a reference to the practice of water-furrowing. See above pp.45-49.

Saturday 29

a Cold windy day began thaw^ing in the Evening I worked in the lathe Crost 4 hours & ^helped to Load Some Old wood & went to Halifax in the Evening I had gat a verry Sore Cold

Sunday 30

A Dull Soft Soft day misty in the morning – I went to Halifax heard Mr Knight in the forenoon Preach from Isiah Chap: 53 & 2. & 3 verses In the afternoon from Ephes^ions Chapter the 5 & 2.& 2 verses

Monday 31 D

A Dull Soft warm day I and 3 men hacked[58] in Pomfret Joshua Cockroft Daughter died of a fever

Tuesday 1 April D

April a dull Soft warm day I and 3 men Hacked [Betty Houldsworth died of a fever] Pickles of Pellon died of a fev^er

Wedenesdy 2 D

a Bright Warm day I and 3 men Hacked till 5 O clock John Crowther came home from Glasgow in Scotland being discharge from the 48 Reigiment of foot where he had Served 4 Years & about 3 Months Betty Houldsworth died.

Thursday 3 DD

a Bright warm day I and 3 men Harrow,d this day died ^also this Widdow Riley's son of Sodhouse Green of a fever and David Hirst's daughter of the Small Pox

Friday 4

a Bright warm day I and 3 men Harrow,d till 5 O clock and began Water furrowing after

---

[58] Hacking: breaking up the soil with the use of a hack.

Saturday 5 D
a Bright Cool day I and 3 Men finished Water furro^wing & Bursting lumps
This day
Matthe Wade was also buried this week

Sunday 6
a Bright droughty day I went to Halifax heard Mr Knight Preach in forenoon from Isiah 53 & 4.5 verses in afternoon from Ephes Chapter 5th and 2 & 3 verses

Monday 7
a Bright droughty day I was Employed in gathering Stones in long ^field
New of an earthquake in Sicily[59]

Tuesday 8 D
a Bright droughty day I was gathering and Walling up breaches John Priestly Son of Thos Priestly in wheat^ly died about noon of a Fever being about 12 years Old

Wedenesday 9 L
a Bright droughty day I was working in the fields the general Lecture a Huddersfield[60]

Thursday 10 D
a Bright warm day I wove 13 ¾ ^yds Jonas Varley buried a Child the above Varley lived in Birks Lane near lee Bridge

Friday 11 D
a Fine Bright droughty day I wove 4 y^ds & went with Tulip to Bull also to Halifax in the Evening Jonathan Priestleys wife in Bradshaw died of a fev^er

---

[59] In February and March 1783 Sicily and the southern tip of Italy were hit by a series of earthquakes. Massive destruction resulted, and an estimated 50,000 lives were lost.
[60] The general lecture at Huddersfield: Probably one of the monthly meetings of Independent ministers, held during the week, where they preached in each other's pulpits. They were organised in the Huddersfield district by Rev. W. Moorhouse. W. Moorhouse, *A Brief Memoir of the Life and Character of the Rev. William Moorhouse*, Huddersfield, William Moore, 1823, p.19.

Saturday 12

a Bright droughty day ^in forenoon I worked in garden & I & G Town worked in the afternoon

Sunday 13 D

a Bright droughty day I went to Halifax & heard Mr Knight Preach in fore from Isiah Chap: 53 & 4.5 verses & in the afternoon from Eph^s Chap 5 & 2 & 3 verses Cockroft Joshuas Daughter died of a fever

Monday 14

a Bright droughty day a little Softish in Evening I & George Town work in the garden

Tuesday 15

a fine Soft day of drizling rain I wove 5 y^ds the Newspaper gave the awfull Account of the Distruction of 60 thousand person ^at ^Messina the Island of Sicily in the Kingdom of Naples in Italy[61]

Wedenesday 16

a Bright droughty day Wove 5 ¼ y^ds

Thursday 17

a Bright droughty day I Sised a warp & wove 4 ¼ y^ds & went to Halifax in the Even^ing heard Mr Knight Preach from Lukes gospel Chap 24 & 46 verse was a little rain at night

Friday 18

a Dull droughty day with a little rain in the Morning I wove 9 ½ y^ds & carried a Piece

Saturday 19

a Bright droughty day I [worked] job'd in the house & worked in the fields till 5 O clock the went to Halifax after Put cows to grass that day[62]

---

[61] See Diary, 7 April 1783.
[62] The cattle were turned out to graze in the fields for the first time after the winter.

Sunday 20
a Dull day with heavy Showers of Hail & rain I went to Halifax heard Mr Knight Preach it being Easter Sunday from Romans Chap 14 & 9 verse in forenoon made Observations on the foregoing verses & in the afternoon Preached from 9 verse a high Cold wind

Monday 21
a ^dull^ day with frequent Showers of hail & rain I Put on a Pair of healds^63 loomed a warp & worked in the fields 2 hours ^in^ Evening

Tuesday 22
a high Cold wind with heavy Showers of hail I was 4 hours weighing hay & other Jobbs about the lathe & 4 hours Jobbing in the house & went to Halifax in the Evening & heard Mr Knight Preach from Col Chap 8 & 1. 2 verses

Wedenesday 23
a Cold windy droughty day wove 5 ½ y^ds

Thurs 24
a Cold windy droughty forenoon but milder in the after I went to Halifax heard Mr Knight Preach from Col Chap (*blank*) the & 3.4 verses

Friday 25
a Cold windy droughty day I wove 6 ½ y^ds and was weighing hay Several hour^s Miss Cloughs came to our house & stayed all night Mr Richard Bates of Skircoat hanged himself being luni^tick

Saturday 26
a Cold windy droughty day I was employed in working in the field laying up the miding going to John Illingworths ☞

Sunday 27
a Bright Cold droughty day I went to Halifax heard heard Mr Knight Preach in forenoon from Isiah Chap 53 & 4. 5. verses in afternoon from amos Chap 3 & 3 verse

---

63 Healds: lift the warp threads allowing the weft thread to be passed across and create the weave. See above p.68.

Monday 28
a Bright droughty warm day I went into Ovenden^wood into Mixenden into Bradshaw^w & to Swillhill end in forenoon worked in the fields & went to John Illingworth's in after

Tuesday 29
a fine droughty Cold day I wove 9 ½ y^ds

Wedenesday 30
a Dull warm day wove 8 ½ ^yd & carried my Piece

Thursday 1 of May
a Dull droughty day wove 9 ½ ^yds & went to Halifax heard M^r K Preach from Gal. Chap 6th & verse

Friday 2
a Dull day with Showers of rain ^in afternoon wove 9 ¾ ^yds

Saturday 3
a Fair droughty day wove 3y^ds in forenoon weighed hay & did other Jobs in & about the lathe in after

Sunday 4
a fair droughty day I went to Halifax & heard Mr Turner from Leeds[64] Preach in forenoon from the 119 & 49 verse in afternoon from the 1st of Peter 3 Chap & 18 verse

Monday 5
a fair droughty day I wove 4 y^ds in afternoon went to Southowram & Skircoat green and Halifax in the after

Tuesday 6
a windy droughty day I helped the Joiners and other Jobbs about the lathe

---

[64] Perhaps Rev. W. Turner ordained at Pudsey, 1783.

Friday (*Wednesday*)**7** [65]
a Dull windy day with frequ^ent Showers of Snow & hail & fell a good deal of Snow fell in the night & froze hard Worked in the field a

Saturday (*Thursday*) **8**
a Bright droughty day I Jobbed about the House and lathe all the day

Friday 9
A Bright drought windy day I but very wet in the night I jobbed abou^t the house wove 1 y^d in the forenoon & in after went to Southowram Skircoat Green and Halifax

Saturday 10
a Bright droughty day I Jobbed about the house and lathe

Sunday 11
a droughty day I went to Halifax heard M^r K Preach from Isiah Chap. 53 & 4. 5verse In forenoon & in after from Matt: Chap: 22nd & 42 verse

Monday 12
a droughty windy day with Several Showers of rain I worked in the fields

Tuesday 13
a droughty day with some rain at night I worked in the fields

Wedenes 14
a Bright droughyt day I went to Northowram and general Lecture being there Mr Gallen from holmfirth[66] Preach from Romans Chap (*blank*) & verse and Mr Toothill from Hopton[67] Preach from the 2nd Epistle to Timothy Cap: 2nd & 2 verse

Thursday 15
a [Dull] Bright droughty with Some rain in the night I wove 7 y^ds

---

[65] Ashworth got his days mixed up at this point and entered Friday instead of Wednesday and, in the next entry, Saturday instead of Thursday. He resumed the correct day and date with his entry for Friday 9 May. The text preserves Ashworth's error noting the correct day in brackets.
[66] Rev. Robert Galland, minister of Lane Independent Chapel, Holmfirth, 1779-1801.
[67] Rev. Jonathan Toothill, minister of Hopton Independent Chapel, 1768-1826.

Friday 16
a Dull drought day wove 8 y^ds

Saturday 17
a Bright droughty day I wove 2 ¾ y^ds in the morning Sised a warp & Jobbed about the house asisting in Paint^ing the gates doors &c Some rain the night

Sunday 18
a Windy Cold day with Some drizling rain I wen^t to Halifax heard M^r K Preach from Isiah Chap 53 & 6 verse in forenoon & in the after from Matt Chap the 8 & 19 verse & in the Evening heard Mr John Toothill Preach at John Thomas house in Mixenden from the 4th Chapter & 6 verse of Pauls Epistle to the Philipians

Monday 19
a Cold windy day with frequent Showers of drizling rain I was Employed in going into Bradshaw to Illingworth & to Halifax & Jobbing in the lathe I was ^informed this day by the Sexton at Ilingworth that the Mortality had been so great in the Neighbourhood that since the beginning of January last he had dug 49 or 50 Graves in the above Chappel yard

Tuesday 20
a droughty Bright day I wove 4 ¾ y^ds Mr John & ^his wife Mrs Sarah Swaine our Bro^ther & Sister from London Came to our house this Evening[68]

Wedenesday 21
A Cold wind droughty day I went to Keig^hly with Mr Swaine & Came back that night

Thursday 22
M^r & ^Mrs Brother & Sister Rhodes Came with their daughter Rhoda a Cold droughty day I wove 2 y^ds & went to Halifax heard Mr Knight Preach from (*blank*) Mr Swaine went to Bradford and Returned that ^night a fine Shower of rain in afternoon

---

[68] John Swaine was a London hop factor and Ashworth's brother-in-law.

Friday 23

a Cold windy droughty day Mr Swaine went to Halifax

Saturday 24

a cold droughty day Exceeding Cold in the Evening Mr Swaine & I went to Halifax & Returned that Evening

Sunday 25

a Cold droughty day I went to Halifax & Heard Mr Knight Preach in forenoon from Isiah Chap 53 & 7 verse In Evening from Isiah Chap (*blank*) Mr Swaine went Halifax in the Evening & Retu^{rned}

Monday 26

aCold droughty day I went to John Illingworths ✆ Richard Garforths & to Halifax & again into Lee Bank Mr Swane went to Gomersal Stainclif haall Leeds &c & Returned on Wedenesday next following Mrs Swaine & Mrs Rhodes wen Halifax

Tuesday 27

A Cold droughty day I wove 3 y^{ds} young Wibsay Calved

Wedenesday 28

a verry Cold windy droughty ^{day} I went to Halifax in forenoon Mr Joseph Thompson of Southowram Mr James Thompson of Staincliff Hall near Dewsbury and Mr Shechan^{i}ah Rhodes $^{our \; Broth}$ of Gomersal[69] & Mr John Hamilton of Halifax Came to our house in forenoon & Returned that night

Thursday 29

a Cold droughty day till about 8 O clock at ^{night} when the wind fell & began Light^{n}ing about 10 & began raining ab^{out} 11 & rained till 10 O clock in the morning that ^{day} Mr Swaine & I went to Bradford & Returned

---

[69] Shechaniah Rhodes was a wealthy merchant who had married Margaret Ashworth's sister Susannah.

Friday 30
a Warm day rained till 3 O clock in afternoon M^r & Mrs Swaine Set out from our house went to Gomersal that night with M^r & Mrs Rhodes I went to Cleck Heaton along with them & Returned that night

Saturday 31
a Warm droughty day I Jobbed about the house & getting White Sand &c

Sunday June 1
a Warm droughty day I went To Halifax heard Mr Knight Preach ^in fore from Isiah Chap: 53 & 8 verse in afternoon from genes^is Chap 24 & 31 verse

Monday 2
a Warm droughty day I Jobb,d in the House in the morning and Set off to Halifax
^at 10 o clock [Set off] at 2 O clock left Halifax wet to Bir^stal and Gomersal & Returned home that night

Tuesday 3
a Warm droughty day I wove 1 ½ y^ds Carried my Piece & loom,d a warp

Wedenesday 4
a dull day fair [in] till 3 clock Rain,d afterward Several hours I began of a warp wove 2 y^ds & worked 4 hours in the fields

Thursday 5
a fine warm day I wove 5 y^ds & worked 1 ½ hours in the fields I bruisd my forefing^er so that I could not weave Several days

Friday 6
a Fine warm day I work,d the garden & went to Halifax In the Evening

Saturday 7

a Fine Warm day I went to Halifax and worked in the garden there was a mob at Halifax that [day][70]

Sunday 8

a Fine Warm day I went to Halifax & heard M[r] Knight Preach in forenoon from (*blank*) Chap: (*blank*) & (*blank*) vers In afternoon from 1 of Corin Chap 15 & 58 verse

Monday 9

Whitmanday

a Bright droughty warm day I worked in the garden till 6 O clock M[r] Knight Set off [for London][71]

Tuesday 10

a Fine warm day began to rain about 4 O clock & rain till bed time & a good Deal in the night

Wedenesday 11

[wove 2 yds in the forenoon] a warm day there fell a good Deal of rain both in fore & after[noon] I went to Halifax in afternoon & there being a general Sociation of Baptists M[r] Ashworth from gildersome[72] Preached from Isiah Chap: 58 & 13 & 14[vers] & M[r] Fawcet of Brearley hall[73] Preach Ephesians Chapter 6 & 2 verse

---

[70] The mob demanded a reduction in the price of grain. Grain prices had increased dramatically in 1783, for example, the average price of oats in the United Kingdom rose from 15s. 7d. per quarter in 1782 to 20s. 5d. per quarter in 1783 (B.R. Mitchell and P. Deane, *Abstract of British Historical Statistics*, Cambridge, Cambridge University Press, 1962, p.488). There were grain riots in several West Riding towns. The Halifax mob led by Spencer and Saltonstall demanded that Mr Anderton of The Boars Head Inn, where a good deal of grain was stored, should sell it at what they considered a fair price. The price they demanded was 30 shillings per load for oats and 21 shillings per load for wheat i.e. 6 shillings per quarter for oats and just over 4 shillings per quarter for wheat. Anderton refused the demands of the mob. The mob then went on to sell the grain from wagons and carts standing in the town. Spencer then ordered the mob to commandeer wagons on the roads leading to Halifax that had turned back from the town in an effort to avoid the mob. Many wagons and carts were taken and their contents disposed of by the mob. T. Knight (ed. H. Martin), *Christian Conversation*, Halifax, Martin, 1845, p.201; J. Crabtree, *A Concise History of the Parish and Vicarage of Halifax*, Halifax, Hartley and Walker, 1836, p.148. See below, Diary entry 16 August, for the execution of Spencer and Saltonstall.

[71] Titus Knight went to London for two months each year to preach in the chapels of Whitefield's connexion. On this occasion he returned from London on 8 August .

[72] Rev. Thomas Ashworth, Baptist minister of Gildersome.

[73] Rev. John Fawcett, Baptist minister, resident at Brearley Hall in Midgley from 1776 where he conducted a school. In 1796 he moved his residence and school to Ewood Hall.

Thursday 12

a Fine warm day [with a good] & began to rain about 8 O clo^{ck} in the Evening & rain,d a good Deal in the night I helped a Mason & went to Halifax with a Calf in the Evening

Friday 13

a Warm day with a good deal of rain in the morning before 7 O clock and in Evening after 8 O clock & in the night I worked in the new house in our yard

Saturday 14

a Warm rained most of the day I Churned & other Jobbs till 10 O clock & wove 4 y^{ds} after

Sunday 15

a verry warm day with a Deal ^{of sun} in the morning & Evening I went to Halifax heard M^{r John} Toothill from ^{Booth 74} Preach from the 1 Epistle to the Corin: Chap 15 & 19 verse in afternoon from Psalm 46 & 1 verse & In the Evening heard Mr Cooking Preach near Illingworth from Isiah chap 50 & 1 verse

Monday 16

a Warm day & wet till 10 O clock fair after till night I wove 6 y^{ds} & worked 2 hours ^{out} of doors in fields

Tuesday 17

a Dull Warm day with Several Showers of Rain I wove 6 y^{ds} & was Jobbing 2 ^{hours}

Wedenesday 18

a Dull warm day with Several Showers of Rain I wove 8 y^{ds} M^{iss} Clough Came to our house & Stayed all night

Thursday 19

a Dull warm day with a little rain I wove 2 y^{ds} & carried my Piece went to John Blagbroughs Churned Weeded garden^{etc}

_____

74 Rev. John Toothill, minister of Booth Independent Chapel, 1783-1787.

Friday 20

a Dull warm day I wove 7 ½ ^{yds} & was Jobbing 2 hours

Saturday 21

a Dull warm day I Cut the Hedges helped the Mason in the kitchen from 9 unto 10 at ^{night}

22 Sunday

a fine warm day I went to Halifax & heard Mr (*blank*)[75] from Morley in forenoon Preach from the 46 Chap of Isiah & part of the 17 verse & in the afternoon from the 31 Psalm & 7 verse

Monday 23

a fine warm day I wove 6 ½ ^{yds} & was jobbing 2 hours in Even^{ing} Miss Clough flitted[76] from Southowram to Keighley Jas Riley with his Convey,d her Furniture thither & our Thos Marsden went a long with them

Tuesday 24

a Dull warm day I went to Halifax & did other jobbs in fore & wove 4 ½ ^{yds} in after^{noon}

Wedenesday 25

a Dull warm day I wove 9 y^{ds} F

Thursday 26

a Bright warm day I Churn,d wove 3 y^{ds} Carried my Piece & went to Visit Thos Houlden the young^{er} of Illingworth who was Sick of a fever

Friday 27

a Bright warm day I wove 8 ½ y^{ds} & went my Fathers in Evening[77]

---

[75] Rev. Thomas Morgan at Morley Old Chapel was considered too moderate in his Calvinism and many ceded from his congregation to form a new church, which built Rehoboth Chapel in 1764. In 1783 the minister at Rehoboth was Rev. Joseph Sowden, about whose orthodoxy there was no question, so it was probably Sowden who supplied the pulpit at Square Chapel that day.

[76] Flitting: moving house.

[77] Abraham Ashworth, the Diarist's father, must have lived near Walt Royd, although exactly where is not at present known.

Saturday 28
a Dull warm day I wove 8 y^{ds} & went Twice into Ovenden wood Once to John Illingworths ☜ & Once to Joseph Hindles

Sunday 29
a Dull warm day I went to Halifax heard Mr Tap from Pontefract[78] Preach both forenoon and afternoon Isiah Chap 45 & 25 verse

Monday 30
a Dull warm day misty in the morning but Cleard & was verry hot I wove 8 y^{ds} ☞ Brothers John & William ashw^{orths} wifes Came to our house Jas Charnock took Possession of the new house

Tuesday 1 July
a Dull misty morn^{ing} but Cleard & was hot I wove 5 ½ y^{ds} E Churned & other jobbs after

Wedenesday 2
a Dull day verry hot with a good Deal of Thunder & a little Rain in the afternoon I carried my Piece went to Halifax & into wheatley in fore and Sised a Warp in the after but did not get it dried weeded garden & then ^{jobbs}

Thursday 3
a Dull ^{day} with a little Rain I went into wheatly & made Rope Shacles & other jobbs in forenoon got my warp dried and Sised it over aga^{in} & Loomed Part of it in afternoon

Friday 4
a Bright warm day I loomed a warp & wove 4 ½ y^{ds}

Saturday 5
a Dull warm day with Some Rain if forenoon I wove 3 y^{ds} in fore & helped Jas Charnock to flit in afternoon

---

[78] Rev. William Tapp, minister of the Independent chapel at Pontefract, 1782-1790.

Sunday 6

a Bright Warm day I went to Halifax & heard Mr Jon: Toothill from Hopton Preach in forenoon from Acts Chap 20 & 21 verse in afternoon fro^om Ephesians Chap 2 & 12 verse

Monday 7

a Bright hot day I wove 6 ½ y^ds & was Jobbing Several hours ☞

Tuesday 8

a Bright [Warm] ^hot day I was that day Employed in Churning helping To fetch the Turfs^79 home & housing them & other Jobbs

Wedenesday 9

a Bright hot day I wove 5 ½ y^ds and was Jobbing Several hours ☞

Thursday 10

a Dull hot day and at night the was a Terrible Storm of Thunder & Lightning which began at 10 O clock and Continued till Past 1 on friday morning there was verry little Rain I wove 10 y^ds

Friday 11

a Dull hot day with a good deal of Thunder & lightning In the night and Soon on [Friday] ^Saturday morning also a good deal of heavy Rain I wove 2 y^ds & Carried my Piece mended Rake &c

Saturday 12

a Dull hot day with a good deal of Thunder in the afternoon I went to John Illingworths ☞ & worth husbandry &c Aunt Cordingly & Joseph^80 Came to our house Joseph went home the next day following

Sunday 13

a Bright hot day I went to Halifax heard Mr Turn^er from Leeds^81 Preach from the 89 Psalm & 15 both fore & afternoon at Heard Mr Cocking from kiping Prea^ch from Revelation Chap 6th & 15 16 & 17 verses

---

79 This is a reference to getting turf or peat, presumably for use as fuel. As Walt Royd had common. rights on Ovenden Moor it is probable that Ashworth got the turf from this moor.
80 Aunt Cordingley was Margaret Ashworth's aunt who had married Eli Cordingley in 1744.
81 Possibly Rev. W.Turner who was ordained at Pudsey in 1783.

Monday 14

a Bright hot day we began mowing this day I mo^wed all day had 2 hay makers Susee Crossley died

Tuesday 15

a Bright hot windy day we had 5 hay makers

Wedenesday 16

a Dull day but moderate drought till 5 or Six O clock began Raining about 7 O clock we had 6 hay makers housed about 2 days work of hay Aunt Cordingly went home Susee Crossley was buried

Thursday 17

a Dull wet forenoon Cleared about noon & was moderate droughty in afternoon I Jobbed in the fields to 5 O clock & went to Halifax in the Evening & heard Mr Cocking Preach from the 1st general Epistle of Peter Chapter 2 & 3 verse

Friday 18

a Dull wet day I worked in Pulling up weeds in Summer Pastur^e

Saturday 19

a fine droughty forenoon but wet in the after we had 6 hay makers employ in the hay til 4 O clock afterwards in Pull^ing up weeds & Spreading Dung in the Summer Pastures

Sunday 20

a Dull ^warm day with a good deal of Rain in the afternoon I went Halifax heard Mr Meldram from Brighouse[82] Preach from the 1st general Epistle of John Chap: 3 & 24 both morning & even^ing

Monday 21

a Dull Wet day with a little Thunder & a good deal of Rain in the afternoon & in the night I was employed in weeding Garden getting Cherries &c

---

[82] Rev. John Meldrum, minister of Bridge End Independent Chapel, Brighouse, 1785-1786.

Tuesday 22

a Dull wet morning but Cleard about 10 O clock & was moderate droughty till 6 O cl^ock we had 5 haymakers ^in afternoon worked in ^the hay till 4 O clock weeded Corn ^in long field [l]in[y] grass in Pomfret ^after

Wedenesday 23

a Dull forenoon but Cleard [about 10 O clock] & was a windy droughty afternoon we had 7 hay makers

Thursday 24

a Dull warm day with frequent Showers of Drizling Rain but moders but moder betw^een Showers I went to Halifax July & heard Mr Cocking from Galatians Chapter 6 & (*blank*) vers was employ this day in waiting on the mo^wers and other work in the hay and &c

Friday 25

a fine droughty day only a little Drizling in the afternoon about 4 O clock but verry fin after we had 6 haymakers that day

(*The following entry has been written on a slip of paper which has been sewn onto this page*)

Saturday 26

a Dull forenoon but bright afternoon we had 3 hay makers ☞

Sunday 27

a Bright hot day I went to Halifax & heard Mr Moorhouse from Hudder^sfield Preach in the forenoon from Pauls Epistle to the galation: Chap: 6 & in after from genesis Chap. 30 & 13 verse Henry Swift who died of a Conswmption was buried at our Chappel
[Elkanah Garforth was Married][83]

Monday 28

a verry hot bright droughty ^day we had 6 Six hay make and got all our hay ^in Except 3 Burdens of Rakeings[84]

---

[83] These words have been added in the margin.
[84] A burden: a load of hay gathered up and tied with a rope so it could be carried on a person's back. The rakings were the last remnants of hay.

Tuesday 29
a Dull day but moderate droughty till 4 O clock a little Rain after I got in Rakeings in fore but Jobbed in the house and in the fields in afternoon

Wedenesday 30
a Dull but Moderate droughty till 4 O clock & a little rain after I wove 5 y^ds

Thursday 31
a Dull hot droughty day I wove 7 y^ds

Friday 1 August

a fine hot day I wove 6 y^ds and was of my weaving several hours ☞

Saturday 2
a Verry hot day with some Thunder and a little Rain in the afternoon I wove 7 ½ y^ds

Sunday 3
a Fair hot day till 5 O clock then began to rain and rain Pretty heavily in the night and on Monday morning - I went to Halifax & heard Mr Galland from Holmfirth Preach in the forenoon from the Epistle of James Chap: 1 & 18 verse and in the after from the 1 Book of the Kings Chap 14 & later Part of the 13 verse

Monday 4
a Dull hot day with frequen^t Showers of Rain I Churned wove 4 y^ds & carried my Piece ☞ Brother Sheepaniah Rhodes Called to see us

5 Tuesday
a fine warm Day I wove 6 ½ ^yds and was Several hours ^of ☞ [my] our Mother Ashworth[85] Came to see us & went home that night

---

[85] Her name is not at present known.

6 Wedenesday

a fine Warm day wove 5 ½ ^{yds} & went to Halifax in the Evening & heard Mr Bruce from Liverpool[86] Preach from St Johns Gospel Chapter 4 & Part of the 45 verse

7 Thursday

a Fine warm day I and John Wiglesworth with his one Horse lead mainer into the holm

Friday 8

a Dull warm day with frequent Showers in the forenoon I Spread mainer Mr Knight Returned from London

Saturday 9

a Dull ^{warm} day with frequent Showers in afternoon Especia^{ly} I and George & John Town Share 14 Hattocks in forenoon I Spread mainer & other Jobbs in the afternoon

Sunday 10

a Dull day with & a good Deal of Rain in the night I went to Halifax heard Mr Knight Preach in forenoon
from Isiah Chap 53 & 9 verse in the afternoon from Isiah Chapter 48 & 17 verse and in the Evening hear Mr John Toothill Preach near Illingworth from Romans Chap 8th & 5 verse

Monday 11

a Dull day with Several Showers of Rain I and G: Town Share 20 Hattocks & was both hindered by the Rain above an hours

12 Tuesday

a Moderate droughty day [w]then it was fair but was frequent Showers of Rain Especialy in the afternoon I Share 5 hattoc^{ks} in forenoon and work,d in garden in the after

---

[86] Rev. David Bruce, minister of Newington Independent Chapel, Liverpool, 1787-1808.

Wedenesday 13

a Fine Warm droughty day I went to Booth and a general Lecture being there I heard Mr Tap from Pontefract Preach from the 1st Epstle of John Chap 3 & ^{verse} 1 Mr Walker[87] of Northouram from Acts Chap 70 & Part of 59 verse [wove 2 ½ ^{yds}][88]

Thursday 14

a Fine Warm day I wove 6 y^{ds} & went to Halifax in the Evening & heard Mr Knight Preach from Isiah Chap 45 & 17 verse

Friday 15

a fine Warm droughty day I wove 10y^{ds} Nancy Akroyd & Joseph Firth Came to our house

Saturday 16

a Fine Warm droughty I Churned Sised a warp in the morning Went to Halifax & Saw Two Men hanged on Becon Hill the^{i}r Names Thos Spencer and Mark Soltanstall having been Tried at York assizes and found guilty of being active in a Riot in and about Halifax in June last they was Sentenced to be Executed on the above hill[89] We housed 38 Hattock in afternoon

Sunday 17

a Fine hot day I went to Halifax & heard Mr Knight Preach in forenoon from Isiah Chapter 53 & Part of the 10 verse In the after from Galatians Chapter 3 & 13 verse Nancy Acroyd & Joseph Firth went home

Monday 18

a hot droughty day I and George Town thrashed Corn

Tuesday 19

a Dull hot day with a heavy Storm of Thunder and light$^{ning\ in\ afternoon\ \&\ at\ night}$ a heavy shower of Rain which Continued from [a little Past] $^{7\ O\ clock}$ almost 2 hours I and G Town ^{Thrasht} Corn there was a Verry great flood in the Brook blow our house

---

[87] Samuel Walker, minister of Heywood Chapel, Northowram, 1774-1793. From 1782 to 1795 Walker also conducted the Independent Academy at Northowram.

[88] These words have been added in the margin.

[89] Thomas Spencer and Mark Soltonstall were hung on Beacon Hill, Halifax for inciting a riot on 6 June, see Ashworth's entry for that day. These were the last such public hangings in Halifax.

Wedenesday 20

a dull hot day with a good deal Thunder and lightning and a good deal of Rain in the night I an G Town winow,d in forenoon worked in garden in after

Thursday 21

a Dull hot day & thunder in after I went to Illingworths ☞ Carried my Piece and wound on a warp went to Halifax in the Evening & heard Mr Knight Preach from Genesis Chap: 28 and 12. 13 verses

Friday 22

a Dull hot day I loom,d a Warp and was off my loom in half the day E Marsden Turner was taken Sick

Saturday 23

a Dull warm day with frequent and heavy Showers of Rain I went to Illingworth Churned and wove 3 yds

Sunday 24

a Dull hot day with a good Deal of Rain I went to Halifax heard Mr Knight Preach from Isiah Chap: 53 & Part of the 10 verse in forenoon & in after from St Matthews gospel Chap 15 & 12 & 13 verses

Monday 25

a Dull day with some Rain in the morning I made at the Mill in the forenoon and in 38 Hattocks thrahst had 59 Strikes of Oats 20 Strikes of Shilling 31 Stone Meal and in the afternoon wove 2 yds a did Sundry Jobbs

Tuesday 26

a Dull drough day I wove 4 yds

Wedenesday 27

John Crowther began weaving double Russels[90] a Dull droughty forenoon but wet in the afternoon I Share Corn in forenoon but wove 2 yds in afternoon

---

[90] Double Russels: Russell is a ribbed or corded cloth made with a cotton warp and woollen weft. A double cloth is where two fabrics, each with its own warp and weft, are woven simultaneously on the same loom and held together by interweaving a certain number of the warp threads. The purpose of weaving doubles is to produce a heavy cloth with a fine face.

Thursday 28

a Dull day fair till 6 o clock but a verry wet night I Share till 5 O clock & went to Halifax and heard Mr Knight Preach from Pauls Epistle to the Romans Chapter the (*blank*) and (*blank*) verse

Friday 29

a Dull day & rained verry heavily most of the day Especially from 6 O clock in the morning to 1 O clock in the afternoon I wove 5 y^ds & was off my loom Several hours *☞*

30 Saturday

a Dull warm day with heavy Showers of Rain I Churned went to Illingworth & other Jobbs till 11 O clock wove 4 y^ds in afterwards

Sunday 31

a Dull warm day I went to Halifax heard Mr Knight Preach in forenoon from Matt: Chap 7th & from the 24 verse to the end of the Chapter and in the afternoon Mr Toabman from Gainsborough Linconshire[91] Preached from St: Lukes gospel Chap the 3 & 11 verse and in the Evening from Prov: Chap 13 & 19 verse

Monday 1 of September

a Dull warm day I wove 5 y^ds

Tuesday 2

a Dull warm day and was a good deal of heavy Rain before day break I wove 7y^ds ½

[Wedenesday 3]Thursday 4

[a Dull warm day moderate droughty in the forenoon but very wet in the afternoon]

a Dull Cool wet day I wove 2 ¾ y^ds in the forenoon In the ^after heard Mr Hindle Baptis Preach in ^Houldsworth from the Acts of the apostles Chap 2 & 37 verse and in the Evening went to Halifax & heard M^r K Preach from St. Matthews Chap 12 & 49 verse

---

[91] No reference to Mr Toabman from Gainsborough has been found.

Wedenesday 3
a Dull warm day [I ca] moderate droughty in forenoon but verry wet in the after I Carried my Piece in the fore and Share 3 hours and in the after wove 2 ½ y^{ds}

Friday 5
a wet windy day I pick up stones in the forenoon for to build Jas Charnock a Coal house with and in the after wove a little in John ^{C} ^{looms}

Saturday 6
a very wet windy day I wove 3 y^{ds} and was Jobbing 4 hours

Sunday 7
Bro^r abrams wife was $^{Delivered\ of\ a\ Daughter\ 92}$A Dull windy day with frequent and verry heavy Showers of Rain I went to Halifax & heard Mr Knight Preach in forenoon from Isiah Chapter 53 & Part of the 10v. and in the afternoon from the 66 Psalm & 16 verse Mr John Wesley Preached at Halifax^{93}

Monday 8
a Dull windy wet day I wove 4 ¾ y^{ds}

Tuesday 9
a verry wet forenoon but Cleard ^{a} ^{little} and was fair a moderate droughty most of the afternoon I wove 4 ½ y^{ds}

Wedesnesday 10
a verry wet morning but moder^{ate} droughty in the afternoon till 6 O clock I wove 2 ⅛ y^{ds} in fore but work in the afternoon

Thursday 11
a Dull day with frequent and Show^{ers} of Rain I wove 5 ½ y^{ds}

---

92 Abraham Ashworth's daughter was called Susan after her mother.
93 T.W. Hanson in 'The Diary of a Grandfather; Cornelius Ashworth of Walt Royd, Wheatley', *Transactions of the Halifax Antiquarian Society,* Halifax, 1916, 233-248, p.243 correctly recorded the fact that Wesley did not mention this visit to Halifax in his *Journal.* However he did refer to it in his *Diary.* The entry reads: 'Sunday 7. 4 Prayed; letter. 7 Philippians 1:21! necessary business; tea, religious talk; prayer. 9.30 chaise; 11 Birstall; writ notes. 12 Dinner, religious talk. I Matthew 8:2! Chaise. 4.30 Halifax; tea 5 Romans 8:33! Society! Prayed; supper, religious talk; prayer; 9.45.' W.R. Ward and R.P. Heitzenrater (eds.) *The Works of John Wesley* Vol. 21, *Journal and Diaries VI (1776-86),* Nashville, Abingdon, 1995, p.460.

Friday 12

a Dull day with heavy Showers of Rain 3 Men Share 3 hattocks Part of the afternoon & worked in Removing Earth in Ja^s Charnock Coal house stead the other Part of it

Saturday 13

a Wet forenoon but a verry fine droughty afternoon 4 men share 20 Hattocks after 2 O clock our Cows began eating our Eddish[94]

Sunday 14

a Bright droughty day most of the day Except a heavy Showe^r of two in the afternoon I went to Halifax & heard Mr Knight Prea^ch in forenoon from Isiah Chapter 53 & last Clause of the 10 verse and in afternoon from the 33 Chapter and 16 verse of the same Prophesy Mr Joseph Knight Preached at Halifax Chu^rch[95]

Monday 15

a Fine droughty day Except a heavy Shower Between 3 & 4 O clock in afternoon 5 men Share 50 Hattocks

Tuesday 16

a verry Bright droughty day I and G Town finish our Shar^ing Share 13 Hattocks and Thrasht Remaining Part of the day

Wedenesday 17

a verry Bright droughty G Town & I Thrash.d Corn in fore but wall,d Part of Ja^s Coal house in afternoon

---

[94] Eddish: grass that has grown after the field has been mowed.

[95] Perhaps Ashworth made a mistake about the Christian name. Titus Knight's eldest son by his second marriage, Samuel, was ordained in the Church of England in March 1783 and was appointed curate of Winteringham, Lincolnshire, in April 1783 so it may well be he who preached in the parish church. After being appointed first incumbent of Holy Trinity, Halifax in 1798 Samuel Knight became Vicar of Halifax in 1817, a position he retained until his death in 1827. J. Knight, *Sermons and Miscellaneous Works of the Rev. Samuel Knight, A.M. To which is Prefixed a Memoir by the Rev. William Knight, A.M.*, Halifax, Whitley, 1828.

Thursday 18

a Dull morning but Cleard and was moderate droughty in the afternoon I and G. Town housed corn and mooed it[96]

Friday 19

a Dull misty morning but Clear and Droughty aftenoon I and G: Town Thrasht Corn

Saturday 20

a fine droughty day I and G. Town Thrasht Corn till 3 O clock and winow,d Corn after

Sunday 21

a Little Rain in the morning and a very Slight wind in the night& Rain I went to Halifax I [went] & heard Mr Knight in forenoon from Isiah Chap 53 and Part of the 11 verse and in the after from the 4th Psalm and 1st verse

Monday 22

a Bright droughty windy day I and G. Town winow,d corn till 10 O clock and in 44 Hattock had 77 Strikes of Oats I went to the Mill wove 1 ¼ yds and Carried my Piece and did Several other Jobbs afterwards

Tuesday 23

a Moderate droughty day with several [Rain] Showers of Rain I wove 4 ¾ yds and at night had a sore fit of sickness thought to be Occation,d by eating some Wheat Loaf a little at 5 and a little at 8 O clock in the Evening and was very Ill from 9 till 11 O clock I vomited 3 times 2 twice before and once after taking a quantity of Oil which the lord Cause to work for good in that Reespect as it was Supposed the above bread had Pot Ashes in it

Wedenesday 24

a Fine Bright droughty day I did no work except Sewing a little

Thursday 25

a Dull day moderate droughty I did no work except Sewing a little

---

[96] 'housed corn and mooed it': to house corn is to put it in a stack or to put it in a barn. To moo corn is to put it up into a mow by stacking it.

Friday 26
a Dull warm day I wove 4 ¼ y^d

Saturday 27
a Fine warm droughty day I wove 1 ½ y^ds in forenoon but Poorly I walked about in after

Sunday 28
a Dull Cool day for the Season I went to Halifax & heard Mr Knight Preach in forenoon from Isiah Chap 53 & part of 11 verse and in the after from the 57 Chapter of the same Prophesy and 18 verse

Monday 29
a Warm droughty day I wove 4 ¾ y^ds

Tuesday 30
a Dull warm day I wove 4 ¾ y^ds

Wedenesday 1 October
a Warm droughty day I went I went into Ovenden to Moorside & wove 3 ½ y^ds

Thursday 2
a Bright warm day I wove 6 y^ds

Friday 3
a Windy warm day verry windy and wet in the night I wove 2 y^ds and made at the Mill and Carried my Piece and in 44 Hattocks had 77 strikes of Oats 21 Strikes of Shilling besides Moolter and 35½ Stones of Meal

Saturday 4
a windy drouhgty day I and Jonathan Cockroft was empl^oy'd in fitting my Loom to weave double Stuffs Called Two Picks[97]

---

[97] Double Stuffs called two picks: a worsted cloth woven double.

Sunday 5
a very windy day with a good deal of Rain I went to Halifax heard Mr Knight Preach from Isiah Chap: 53 and part of the 13 verse in forenoon and from Pauls Epistle to the Romans Chapter the 5th and 14 verse

Monday 6
a Dull day moderate droughty I went to Halifax and into Ovenden in the fore in the afternoon began weaving Double Stuffs and wove 2 y^{ds}

Tuesday 7
a Dull day with a good Deal of Rain I wove 6 y^{ds}

Wedenesday 8
a Dull Cool day with frequent Showers of Rain I wove 6 y^{ds}

Thursday 9
a Dull day with frequent Showers of Rain I wove 6 y^{ds}

10 Friday
a Moderate droughty day I wove 4 ½ y^{ds} and went to Halifax in even^{ing}

Saturday 11
a Bright droughty day I wove 4 ¾ y^{ds}

Sunday 12
a Fair droughty day I went to Halifax heard Mr Knight Preach in fore from Isiah Chapter 53 and Part of the 13 verse and in the afternoon from the 119 Psalm and 75 verse and in the ^{Evening} heard Mr Hindle Preach at Moses Elsworths from the 49 verse of the same Psalm

Monday 13
a Fine warm day I Carried my Piece and wove 4 ¾ ^{yds}

Tuesday 14
a fine warm day for the Season I wove 6 y^{ds}

Wedenesday 15
a Fine warm day for the Seson I wove 6 y^{ds}

Thursday 16

a Fine warm day I wove 7 y^{ds}

Friday 17

a Fine warm day I wove 6¼ y^{ds} and Carried my Piece

Saturday 18

a fine warm day I wand a warp and Knitt in Part of it[98] and did Several Jobbs about my Loom and about the house

Sunday 19

a Dull misty day with Some Rain both in the morning and in the Evening I went to Halifax $^{&}$ heard Mr Knight Preach in forenoon from Isiah Chap 53 and Part of the 13 verse and in the afternoon from the Acts of the apostles Chapter 4th & Part of the 25 & 26 vers

Monday 20

a Dull Soft day I Knitt in Part of my warp did Severall other Jobbs & wove 4 y^{ds}

Tuesday 21

a Bright day and moderate droughty I wove 7 yd^s

Wedenesday 22

a Dull windy day & wet in the afternoon I went to John Illingworths ☞ & wove 6 yd^s

Thursday 23

a Dull day and moderate droughty I wove 8 y^{ds}

Friday 24

a Dull day with a good deal of Rain I wove 5 y^{ds} and Carried a Piece and went to Halifax in the Evening

---

[98] Knitting in: to tie the threads of a new warp to the ends of the old warp as the old warp is finished. This facilitates the winding on of the new warp through the healds and on to the front or cloth roller thus enabling a new piece of cloth to be started.

Saturday 25
a Fine fine Cool day not much drought I went Halifax and to Jacob Towns in forenoon & Laid up the miding and other Jobbs in after

Sunday 26
a Cool Dull day some Rain in the night I went to Halifax & heard Mr Knight Preach in the forenoon from Genesis Chap: 6th & (*blank*) verse & in after from (*blank*)

Monday 27
a Dull Cool day with frequent showers of Rain I Jobbed in most the forenoon and wove 5 y^{ds} in that [of] day

Tuesday 28
a Dull Cool day with several showers of Rain I went to Moorside $^{\&}$ Halifax with a box to be Carried to London by the waggon & wove 5 y^{ds} that day

Wedensday 29
a Dull Cool winday day with several showers of Rain I Helped to Churn Wrote a letter &c in fore and wove 3½ y^{ds} in aftern^{oon}

Thursday 30
a Dull Cool day with seve^{ral} showers of Rain I wove 9 y^{ds}

Friday 31
a Dull day with sever^{al} showers of Rain I wove 7½ y^{ds} and Carried a Piece

Saturday 1 of November
a Fine mild day Moderate droughty I Jobb,d about the lathe in fore & beamed a Warp and Knitt in Part of it John Crow^{ther} Began Weaving Grograms[99]

Sunday 2
A Dull misty day with some Rain at night I went to Halifax & heard Mr Knight Preach in forenoon from Genesis Chap 6th & Part of the 9 verse and in after of Peter Chap 1 & (*blank*) verse Jonathan Swifts ^{wife} was Buried that night

---

[99] Grogram: a coarse cloth made from a mixture of silk and wool.

Monday 3

a Dull misty mild day I began of warp and wove 5¼ Y^{ds}

Tuesday 4

a Dull mild day I asisted the Mason & Joiner in buildin a Coal house for Ja^s Charnock & wove 2 Y^{ds} in the Evening

Wedensday 5

a Dull day mild and mode droughty I wove 7 Y^{ds}

Thursday 6

a Dull Soft day I wove 8¾ Y^{ds} Hannah Crowther & Luke Hemingway was married

Friday 7

a Bright droughty day I wove 7 Y^{ds} and Carried my Piece & went to Halifax in the Evening

Saturday 8

a verry Fine Bright mild droug^{hty} day I went to Illingworth helped to Churn went Halifax &c

Sunday 9

a Dull mild day I went to Halifax & heard Mr Knight Preach in forenoon from Genesis Chap 6 & Part of the 9 verse and in after from John's Gospel Chapter 19 & 26 verse

Monday 10

a Dull wetish day I wove 5¼ Y$^{ds\ it}$ froze at night

Tuesday 11 D

a Dull day with several Showers of Rain I went to Halifax by Wheatley and to John Greenwoods & Benj Rigleys at Hayley hill and Came back by my Fathers and little Braconbed Elkanah Garforth in Mixend^{en} was so burnt in the morn^{ing} that he died in the Evening I wove 5½ Y^{ds} tha day froze in the night & a little snow fell

Wedenesday 12

a Fine frosty drough day I wove 6¼ Y^{ds}

Thursday 13

a verry Dull wet day and a high wind and a deal of Rain in the night I wove 8¼ Y^{ds} that day

Friday 14

a Fine Bright droughty day a good deal of Snow fell in the night I wove 4¾ Y^{ds} Carried my Piece & went to Halifax

Saturday 15

a Brighty Fair forenoon But Dull and wet after 3 O clock and thawed so that most of the snow was gone on sunday morning

Sunday 16

a Dull Soft day and a verry wet windy night I went to Halifax and heard Mr Knight Preach in the forenoon from Jon: Chap 6 & Part of the 9 verse and in after from Acts Chap 26 & 18 verse

Conelius ashworth Book 1783

Monday 17

a Dull windy day with with some Rain in the afternoo^{n} I Wove 3¾ Y^{ds}

Tuesday 18

a Dull windy day & wet in the aftern^{o}on I went to Halifax &c in forenoon & wove 3¾ Y^{ds} in after

Wedensday 19

a Dull wet windy day I wove 6½ Y^{ds}

Thursday 20

a Dull windy day with some Rain I wove 6½ Y^{ds}

Friday 21

a Fine frosty day I wove 9½Y^{ds}

Saturday 22

a Fine ᶠʳᵒˢᵗʸ Bright day I wand in a warp & Jobb,d a bout the lathe & went to
Halifax

Sunday 23

a Fine Bright day I went To Halifax & heard Mʳ Knight Preach in forenoon
from gen: 6 ᶜʰᵃᵖ & Part 9 verse and in after from 2 of Peter & 2 Chap 2 &
verse

(*On recto of back cover*)

S

Volume 2

1 January 1785
to
11 March 1786

In the manuscript of this volume of the Diary Ashworth ruled a margin on the left-hand of each page in which he wrote the day and the date of the entry. In the interests of making the printed text more intelligible we have placed this information at the beginning of each entry while retaining the original spelling.

Ashworth usually wrote the month at the top of each page. Because the pagination of this edition does not correspond to the manuscript, we have omitted both this feature and the page numbers which Ashworth wrote at the top of the first few pages, which make little sense in the printed text. We have also omitted the lines by which Ashworth ruled off each entry, preferring to separate the entries in the printed text simply by a space.

Usually Ashworth's entries under one date simply run on as continuous text but occasionally he deliberately began a new line and this feature has been preserved in the printed text.

Saturday 1ˢᵗ January
a Dull frosty day I went to Halifax and did some Jobbs of husbandry

Sunday 2
a Dull frosty day I went to Halifax and heard Mʳ K. Preach in the forenoon from the 1ˢ Peter Chapter 2 & 25 verse in the after from the 2 of Cor: Chap the 9 & 15 verse

Monday 3 D [1]
a Dull thawing day I wove 6 yᵈˢ Elizabeth the wife of John [died] Farror died

Tuesday 4
a Dull misty thawing day a Deal of Snow & Rain fell in the afternoon I wove 6 ½ yᵈˢ

Wednesday 5 B
a Dull day thawed in the fore but froze in the afterⁿᵒᵒⁿ I carried a Piece and went to H Towler Sale & into Mixenden Jon: Priestley Daughter ʷᵃˢ ᵇᵒʳⁿ

---

[1] On this and subsequent occasions Ashworth used a capital letter **D** for a death, **B** for birth, **M** for marriage and **V** for visitor.

Thursday 6 B
a Bright frosty day I wove 4 ½ y^{ds} and went Halifax in the Evening & heard Mr K. Preach from the 13 Chapter of St Lukes Gospel 6. 7. & 8 verses Jon: Priestley had daughter born about 1 this morning

Friday 7
a Dull frosty day I wove 5 y^{ds} and Went to Halifax in the Evening

Saturday 8 2D 3D 4D
a Dull misty Rainy thawing ^{day} I wove 3 ½ y^{ds} & did some Jobbs of husbandry Mr Joseph Hoult of Halifax died this Morning Matty Spencer of Swillhill and Joseph Hargeaves^{wife} o Kitten Clough near Mount Pellam was Buryed this Week

Sunday 9 5D
a Dull frosty day I went to Halx & heard Mr K. Preach in the forenoon the 3rd Chap of the 2 Epistle of Peter from the 1st to 8 verse and in the from Hebrews Chap 2 & Part of 3 verse
a Child at Mark Cockroft was Drow'd in the Brook in Ov[d]enden near the Place called Lordship

Monday 10
a Dull thawing day I was employ'd in Husbandry that day

Tuesday 11 B
a Dull frosty day I wove 7 y^{ds} John Crowther had a Daughter about 3 O clock in the Morning

Wednes 12
a Dull frosty day I wove 7 y^{ds}

Thurs 13 6D
a Dull frosty day I wove 4 y^{ds} and Carried a Piese Thos Hoyle of Halifax was buried this week week

Friday 14
a Dull frost day I wand on a warp Scoured my weft laid up the dung hill
&c had violent Pain in my Teeth in the afternoon and night

Saturday 15 7D 8D
a Dull frosty day I Jobbed about the lathe and knitt in a warp
Robt Kelly,s son of Halifax and Jane Harrod of Ovenden workhouse was
buried this week

Sunday 16
a Dull frosty day I went to Halifax and heard Mr K. Preach in the forenoon
from the 1st Epistle of Peter Chap the 3 from the 8 to the 12 verse in the
after a Funeral Sermon was Preached for John Farrars wife in Mixenden
from Mic^{ah} Chap 7th 18 & 19 verses

Monday 17 9D
a Dull thawing day I work'd Husbandry in the forenoon and wove 3 ½ y^{ds}
in the after Mary the Widdow of James Smith of Illingworth died

Tuesday 18
a Dull Soft [day] morning but Clear'd and was moder^{ate} droughty I was
employd about Husbandry in the fore but wove 5 y^d in the afternoon Thos
Snowden fetched a Calf ^{19 days old} from our house which always lame
therefore did not thrive verry well

Wednes 19 B
a Dull Soft day I wove 6 y^{ds}
John Midgley the younger of Illingworth had a Daughter born

Thursday 20 B
a Dull Soft day I wove ⁵ y^{ds} & Went to Halifax in the Evening and heard M^r
K. Preach from Rev: Chap:6 and from 9 verse to the end of the Chapter
John Crossley had a son born this day

Friday 21
a Dull mild day I wove 7 y^{ds} froze in the night

Saturday 22 10D 11D 12D B
Went to John Illingworth ☞
a Dull soft day I went to Halifax and worked Husban^dry this day William Etenfield and Betty Pye of Halifax and Mary Smith of wheatly died this week Thos Longbottom had a son born

Sunday 23
a Dull mild day for the Season I went to Ha^lifax and heard M^r [Knight] Oulton one of Mr Walker's Pupils of Northouram[2] Preach in the morning from Heb 3 & 3 in the afternoon from the Acts of apos Chap 26 & 28 verse

Monday 24
a Bright mild day for the Season I Jobb'd about the House in the fore and Wove 6 y^ds in the afternoon

Tuesday 25
a Bright mild day I Carried a Piece and Scour'd a weft in fore and worked in the Wood in the afternoon

Wednes 26 13D
a Dull ^Soft day I wove 5 y^ds a Jobb'd a little in Husbandry Mary Cooper was buried this day

Thursday 27 14D
a Dull soft day & verry wet and windy in the night
I wove 5 y^ds and went to Halifax in the Evening and heard Mr K. Preach from Rev^n Chap 7th from the 1st to the 13 verse
Aron Sutcliff's wife in wheatly died in the Morning of about 10 Days Sickness of a Fever & was buried in the Evening of the same day

Friday 28 15D
a Soft Windy day I wove 7 y^ds Thomas Green's wife of Halifax was buried this day

---

[2] 'Mr Oulton' is probably Joseph Houlton, one of Scott's pupils who transferred with the Heckmondwike Academy when it moved to Northowram to be under the tutelage of Samuel Walker, minister at Heywood's Chapel, Northowram.

Saturday 29
I wove 4 y^ds a Dull frosty Snowy but began thawing sometime in the night

Sunday 30
a verry wet day of snow and Rain till almost midnight but froze exceed^ing
^hard ing ^hard afterwards -- I went to Halifax that ^day and heard Mr Knight
Preach in the forenoon from the 2 of Peter Chap the 3 & 12 verse and in the
after he Preached a funeral sermon for William Etenfield from Micah Chap
7 & verse 7th James Charnock had his 3^d Daughter born in the ^afternoon

Monday 31
a Bright frosty day I wove 6 ½ y^ds

Tuesday 1 February
a Bright frosty
I wove 5 y^ds and Carried my Piece Scour'd my Weft &c

Wednes 2 16D
I work,d a little Husbandry Swilling &c a Bright frosty day I wove 5 y^ds
William Whitely of Halifax was buried at Illingw^orth

Thursday
a Dull frosty day I wove 6 ¾ y^ds

Friday 4
a Bright frosty day I wove 6 ¼ y^ds I was verry much Pain,d in my Bowels
this day

Saturday 5
a Bright frosty day I was verry Ill of the above Compla^int

Sunday 6
a Dull frosty day and some snow fell in the afternoon I was sick therefore
stay'd at home Mr Knight Preached at his H his own Chappel in the
forenoon from the 1st of Peter Chap 3^d & 13.14 & 16 verses and in the after
Preached a Funeral Sermon for the wife of Thos Green deces'd from Isiah
Chap 54 and 11 & 12 verses

Monday 7
a Bright frosty day

Tuesday 8 M
a Bright frosty day Willm Clayton Was Married that day

Wednes 9
a Dull frosty day Williams Bairstow,s wife in Ovenden was buried this day

Thursday 10
a Dull frosty day with some Showers of snow Charles Crowth^er Went to Hepton Bridge to the Doctor and got some Physic which of use to me through the Blessing of god upon it

Friday 11
a Dull frosty day

Saturday 12 18D
a Cold frosty day William Hirst in the Dean Clough died of a Fever

Sunday 13 19D
a Bright frosty day I being Sick I stayed at home Mr K. Preached in the forenoon from the 1 of Peter Chap 3^d 15 & 16 verses and in the after from Psalm 6 & 2 verse Willam Knight,s wife was buried

Monday 14
a Dull Softie day [l]

Tuesday 15 20D 21D
a Dull Soft day but froze in the night Titus Farrar's Wife of Denham gate and Widdow Farrar from one of the alms Houses in Halifax was both buried at Illingworth

Wednes 16
a Dull frosty day and some Snow fell in the forenoon

Thursday 17
a Bright Windy frosty day and some snow fell in the Evening

Friday 18
a Bright & frosty day in the morning but Snowy in the after

Saturday 19
a Dull frosty day with some Snow in the afternoon

Sunday 20
a Bright frosty day with some Snow in the afternoon I Stay,d at being sick and therefore not fit to go to Halifax Mr K. Preached in in Morning from the 1st Epistle of Peter Chap^r 3 from the (*blank*) to (*blank*) and in the afternoon from Pauls Epistle to the Heb: Chap the 6th and (*blank*) verse

Monday 21
a Dull frosty day day some little Snow fell this day

Tuesday 22
a Dull frosty day with a Little Snow

Wednes 23 22D
a Verry Bright frosty day one of John Savil,s Chi^ldren in Wheatly was buried this day

Thurs 24 23D
a Dull Soft thawing day
(*blank*)Wife of Swillhill was buried this thes day

Friday 25
a Dull Soft day thawed most of the day and a [good deal] little Snow fell in the night

Saturday 26
a Dull frosty day with a good which fell in the Morning

Sunday Feb 27

a verry Windy frosty day I stayd at home [not] being Sick M (*blank*)[3] from Huddersfield Preached in Mr Knight Chapel In the forenoon from the 33 Psalm and 18 verse and in the after from St John,s Gospel Chapter the 10th &16 verse

Monday 28

a Dull frosty day

Tuesday 1 March 24 D M

a Bright frosty day Mrs Horsfield [was buried] of Haworth was buried and Joshua Hepwor^th of Ovenden was married this day

Wednes 2

a Dull frosty day Mr Thomps^on and Brother Rhodes & 3 other Men Came to Our House

Thursday 3

a Dull frosty day

Friday 4

a Dull frosty day

Saturday 5

a Dull frosty day Brother Rhodes Came to see us

Sunday 6

a Dull frosty day I Stay,d at home being sick in Body and therefore not fit to go anywhere - - - Mr Oulton one of Mr Walker,s Pupils of Northouram [and in the] Preached in Mr Knight,s Chapl at Halifax from Johns gospel Chap 6 & 37 verse And in the afternoon Mr Taylor Methodist Preacher[4] Preach,d a Funeral Sermon in the Methodist Chapel near Illingworth[5] for Thos Webs^ter of Wheatly and his wife from the 40 Psalm & 1.2 verses

---

[3] William Moorhouse was Minister at Highfield Independent Chapel, Huddersfield at this time.
[4] Perhaps Rev. Thomas Taylor, a Methodist minister who frequently preached in the Halifax area and published many sermons including 'A Time for All Things' which he preached in Halifax in 1785.
J. Horsfall Turner, *Halifax Books and Authors*, Brighouse, 1906, p.249.
[5] Mount Zion Chapel, Upper Brockholes, which opened in 1773, is less than a mile north of Illingworth church.

Monday 7
a Dull frosty day

Tuesday 8
a Dull frosty day

Wednesday 9
a Dull frosty day
There was a general Lecture in Mr Knights Chappel at Halifax and M^r
Toothilll from Booth in Warely Preach from the Last verse of the general
Epistle by Peter and M^r (*blank*) from Leeds [from] Preached from Pauls
Epistle to the Corinthians Chap the 4 & 17 verse

Thursday 10
a Dull frosty day with Some light Showers of snow

Friday 11
a Bright frosty forenoon but Dull in the afternoon

Saturday 12
a Dull windy frosty day with Some Showers of snow

Sunday 13 25D 26D 27D 28D
a Bright frosty day I stay,d at home being Sick -- M^r K Preached in the
Morning from the 1st of Peter Chap 3 & 7 verse and the Evening from the
112 Psalm & 7 verse

March [14]
Hilbank John Rawson's apprentice ^of Halifax died that day ^[died this day] of a Fever
Timothy Wadsworth in Northrm was buried at Illingworth
Mr Hoyland Painter [of] in Halifax died yesterday Zechara Stancliff died
yesterday of a Few Minutes Sickness

Monday 14
a Dull [frosty] ^mild day for the Season did but freeze little if any

Tuesday 15

a Dull mild day mild for the Season

Wednes 16

a Dull mild day for the Seas^on G Hebblethwait,s wife of Mile Cross was buried who died of Fever

Thursday 17 29D

a Dull mild day for the Season G. Town & my Fath^er thrasht Corn and I Shaked Straw Pooly Daughter of the Mrs Tattersall in wheatly died of a Fever

Friday 18

a Dull Soft day my Father & G town thrasht and I shak'd Straw

Saturday 19

a Dull Soft day my Father & George Town and I winnow,d in the forenoon and work,d in the Barn and field in the after and in 55 Hattocks of freez land Oats[6] had 72 Strikes of Oats

Sunday 20

a Dull Soft day I went To Halifax in the afternoon and heard Mr Knight Preach a Funeral Serm^on for William Hilbank from 23 Psalm and 4 vers my Uncle Benjamin Crap^r was buried this day

Monday 21

a Cold windy day with a good deal of snow in after^noon land froze in the night
I went to Halifax in the (*blank*)
Had G. Town & C. Crowther Spreading Mole hills & dung

Tuesday 22

a Cold frosty day ^we had G. Town & C. Crowther Spreading Mole hills that day

---

[6] 'Freez land oates': Friezeland, Holland or Dutch Oats appear to have been capable of producing higher yields than common oats. Figures from Northumberland suggest yields of between forty and sixty bushels per acre could be expected from Friezeland Oats whereas common oats averaged between twenty and forty bushels per acre. J. Bailey and G. Culley, *General View of the Agriculture of the County of Northumberland,* Newcastle, Hodgson, 1797, p.85.

Wednes 23

a Bright frosty day we had G. Town & C. Crowther ditching in the Holms that day

Thursday 24

a Dull frosty we had G. T and C. Crowther George [Town] Armitage and his Mother,s Horse and Cart leadding Dung and Ashes

Ja^s Charnock,s Daughter Mary aged 7 weeks 3 Days and about 14 hours died died about 5 O clock this morning

Friday 25

I began wearing a wig[7]

a Bright day and began to in the afternoon I went To Halifax with my wife in the afternoon

Saturday 26

a Bright frosty day I went to Halifax and made at the Mill and in 40 Strikes of Oats had 13 Strikes of Shelling 21 ½ Stones of Meal

Sunday 27

a Dull frosty day and a good Deal of Snow fell in the morning I went to Halifax in the after^n and heard Mr Knight Preach from the 4th Chap of Pauls Epistle to the Romans and 25th verse

Monday 28 D M

a dull frosty day a Child of Aron Sutcliff,s in Wheatly was buried who died of a Fev^r Hepworth near Illingworth and [and] Ayrton in Holdsworth was ^Married

Tuesday 29

a Bright frosty day John Town and Jonathan Priestly Finished Graving our wheat field for this year

Wednes 30

a Bright frosty day Charles Crowther went to Gomersal and Came back that day

_____

[7] This note is written in the margin.

Thursd 31

balloted for Militia[8]

I went to Halifax

a Dull frosty day and a good deal of Snow fell in the night Ann Turner Went home who had been a few days with us

Friday 1 of April

a Bright frosty day I went to Halifax

Saturday 2

a Dull frosty day & Some snow fell Brother Rhodes Came to see us the drain from Mr Irvin,s Field to our well Cover in that day

Sunday 3

a Bright frosty day I went to Halifax and heard M[r] K. Prea[ch] in the morning from the 1 of Peter Chap[r] 4th 1 & 2 verse & in the after Romans Chap 6 & 8 verse

Monday 4

a Dull thawing day I wo[rkd] in the Wheat field in the afternoon diging up Briar Close by the wall

Tuesday 5

a Bright warm thawing [we] had 5 Hachers[9] in the afternoon Will[m] Woodhead Came for the Poor Cess[10]

Wednes 6

a Bright warm day but froze hard in the night we had 5 Hachers this day M[r] Parsons was Ordain,d Minister at M[r] Edward,s Chapel in Leeds[11]

---

[8] This phrase is written in the margin.

[9] 'Hachers': Hackers, those involved in hacking. See glossary p.311.

[10] Poor Cess: poor rate.

[11] Edward Parsons was ordained as pastor of White or Whitehall Chapel, Leeds in succession to Rev. John Edwards, the first minister of the chapel, who had died on 17 February 1785. J.G. Miall, *Congregationalism in Yorkshire*, London, Snow, 1868, p.305.

Thursday 7

a Bright warm for the sea^{son} but froze hard in the night

Friday 8

froze hard in the night

a Mild Warm day as it had been most of this week our Red Polled Cow Calved this day and had a verry Painfull Calving & Calved a very large male Calf

I waited on her all night[12]

Saturday 9

a Fine warm droughty day ^{we} had 5 Men this day Water furrowing and break^{ing} Clods till 3 O clock and work,d in the Holms after

Sunday 10

a Cool droughty day I went to Halifax and heard Mr K. Preach in the afternoon from the 1st Epistle of Peter Chapter from the 3 to 6 verse and in the afternoon from Pauls (*blank*) Epistle

(*There are no entries for the period 11 to 15 April inclusive.*)

Saturday 16

a Cold droughty week since 10th ins^t

Sunday 17 D D D

I went to Halifax and heard Mr Knight Preach from the 3 Chapter of the first Epistle of Peter Mrs Lees (Mr Sutcliff, Preacher at St Anns Chapel in the Briar's)[13] died ^{either} this day or yesterday Thos Booth,s wife in Halifax died this day.

(*There are no entries for 18 to 22 April inclusive.*)

Saturday 23

a Verry Warm week with a little rain almost every day My wife came home yester^{day} having been a wcck at Bro^s Rhodes House at Gomers^{al}

---

[12] This phrase is written in the margin.
[13] St Anne's Chapel is in Southowram township and was also known as The Chapel in the Grove.

(There are no entries for 24 to 29 April inclusive.)

Saturday 30
a Warm droughty week

Sunday 1 May
a warm day I went to Halifax and heard Mr K. Preach in the afternoon from the first General Epistle of Peter Chap the 4th

Monday 2
a Droughty warm day Mr. Knight set off for London this day[14]

Tuesday 3
a warm droughty day

Wednes 4
a Drought Windy day

Thursday 5
a Mild warm day I went to Gomersal & Return,d

Friday 6
a Warm droughty

Saturd 7
a Warm droughty day

Sunday 8
a Warm droughty day I went to Bradford and heard Mr Medley ^Baptist from Liverpool[15] Preach in Mr Crabtree Chappel[16] from the 2nd Epis of Peter Chap^r 1 and 1 verse and and in the afternoon from Pauls 1 Epistle to the Cor^n Chap 6 & 17 vers and Mr Moorhouse from Huders^field Preach'd in Mr Knight Chapel in the forenoon from Hebrews Chap the 6th and 20th verse and in the afternoon from the 119 Psalm and 36 verse

---

[14] Titus Knight spent two months every year preaching in the chapels of Whitefield's connexion in London. He was back in his pulpit at Square Chapel on July 10.
[15] Samuel Medley was pastor of the Particular Baptist Chapel, Liverpool from 1771 to his death in 1799.
[16] Westgate Baptist Chapel, Bradford, whose first pastor, William Crabtree, was minister there from 1753 to 1803.

Monday 9

a droughty warm day we had the Carpinters this day Putting ^{Timber} upon the Ashes house

Tuesday 10

a Warm droughty day

Wednes 11 D D D D

a Droughty warm day the Copses of John ^{Dean} in Bradshaw (*blank*) Farnel & Abraham Tetley of Northouram and one of Rufus Sunderland Children in Ovenden Workhouse was all Inter,d in Illingworth Chappel Yard

Thurs 12

a droughty warm day I wen^t to Halifax in the Evening and heard Thos Booth[17] of the Same Place Preach in Mr Knight Chappel from Pauls 2 Epistle to the Corinthians Chap^r 5 & 21 verse

Frid 13

a Droughty warm Day

Saturday 14 D

a Warm droughty I went to Halifax in fore and Painted 3 doors and 1 gate &c in the after

a Child of (*blank*) Wormald in Ovenden Wood died of the small ^{Pox}

Sunday 15 D

a verry Windy droughty day I went to Bradford & heard Mr Medley from Liverpool Preach from Pauls 2 Epistle to the Corin: Chap^r 1 & 4 verse and in the afternoon from Pauls Epistle to Titus Chap^r 1 & 9th ver Mr Lowel of Halifax[18] Preach,d in Mr Knight,s Chappel in afternoon from (*blank*) and in the after from the 46 Psalm and 4th verse Mrs Jones wife of Mr Jones Minister at Mixenden Chap^l died[19]

---

[17] No information has been found about Thomas Booth of Halifax.

[18] Samuel Lowell lived with his family in Halifax and was at this time pastor of North End Chapel, Brighouse although he was not ordained into the Congregational ministry until 1786.

[19] Rev. Daniel Jones, minister of Mixenden Independent Chapel, 1783-1791.

Monday 16
Whi[a]te May'd[20]
a Droughty warm ^{day} with some in the night I and Charles Crowther thatched the Ashes Hous in the after noon

Tuesd 17
a Windy day with frequent Shower of Rain I worked in Fiend and fold

Wednes 18
a Coᵒl wind wind day for the Season with frequent Showers of Rain and Hail I helped Mr Irvin Men to Repair the Road from the Top of our Lane [the] ^{to} Moses Elsworth's

Thursd 19
a windy day with sevrl Showers of Rain I [a]was emply,d in going to John Illingworth,s ☞ and Removing a wall and Charles Crowther assisted me in the afternoon and had John Varely Walling after 11 O clock

Friday 20 D
a Cool windy day I and C. Crowther & G. Town was employ,d in removing an[d] old wall assisting John Varely and walling a little Timothy Smith near Cleck Heaton died this day

Saturd 21
a Droughty warm day I and G. T. & C. C. fetched Stones and wall,d I went to Halx in the Evening Took our Cows out of the Spring gress this day

Sunday 22 D
a warm day with Some Rain in the Morning I went to Halifax and hear'd Mʳ Dawson from Cleck Heaton[21] Preach Preach in Morning from Pauls Epistle to the Colosians Chapter 1ˢᵗ and (*blank*) and in the afternoon from the 39 Psalm & 7 verse John Houldsworth died this day

Monday 23
a Bright warm day I went to Hunsworth to the Burying of Timothy Smith of that Place I went to Gomersal and Came home that night

_____

[20] This phrase is written in the margin.
[21] Rev. James Dawson, minister of Cleckheaton Independent Chapel, 1769-1795.

Tuesday 24
a warm day with Some Showers of Rain I went to the Potters house in Northouram in forenoon & to and to Halifax in the after
John Crowther flitted into the Slippy lane

Wednes 25
a Warm day with frequent Showers of Rain I worked in the Holms fitting up gutters in the lowers & spreading the water in the upper

Thursd 26
a Warm day with [freq] a little Rain in the night I went to Halifax & heard M^r (*blank*) one of Mr Walkers Students Preach from St Johns gospel Chap^r 8th and 36 verse

Friday 27
a Windy day some Showers in the day and in the night also
I worked in the field

Saturd 28
a Windy day with Frequent^& ^heavy Showers of Rain Easpecially in the forenoon

Sunday 29
a Windy day with frequent Showers of Rain I went to Halifax and heard Mr Toothill from Hopton Preach in the morning from St Marks gospel Chapter 14th & 72 vers and in the afternoon from the 3 Epis of John & 2 verse and in the Evening from the Epistle of James Chap^tr 1st & 22 verse

Monday 30
a Windy Rainy day I work'd in Pulling up weed in the lathe Croft in forenoon & in the after gathering Stones in the Gate Field

31
(*no entry for this day*)

Wednsday [Tuesday]²²1 D D D
a Dull Cool day with some Showers of Rain I was this day employ,d in going to the Harwood well and all over Halifax Seeking for Piggs with intent to buy one and weeding the garden a little afterwards
Maʳy Smith in Ovenden near Illingworth and Joseph Crowthᵉʳ and Nathaniel Houls,s wife in Northouram was all buried this day

Thurs 2
a Warm Droughty day I was employ this day in gathering Stones in the gate Field & went to Halifax in the Evening & me & my wife heard Mr Lowell of Halifax Preach from S [J] Lukes gospel 14 & 24

Friday 3 V
a Warm droughty I work'd in the Gate field gathering Stones My Son Edmund Marsden Came to our house on a Visit from London

Saturday 4
a Warm Dull day I went to Halifax & Boᵗ a [a Swine]Hog the Price 1£ [S]&1ˢ

Sunday 5
a Dull day and there fell Plenty of Rain as it began Soon in Morning & Rain frequently in [d] the day I went to Halifax and heard Mʳ Brewer from Sheffield²³ Preach in the forenoon from Exodus Chapter 3ᵈ & 2 verse

Monday 6
a Warm wet day I workd in the [little f] Gate field

Tuesday 7
A Warm wet day I work,d in the Gate field gathering Stones [out of] ⁱⁿ it

Wednes 8
a Dull warm wet day I was employd [in] thes day in Spreding Ashes and dung upon the ground which we had Imclos,d in the Gate field

---

22 Ashworth obviously got his days muddled up at this point, which suggests that he wrote his Diary up retrospectively.
23 Rev. Jehoiada Brewer, minister of Queen Street Independent Chapel, Sheffield, 1783-1795.

Thursd 9
went to Staincliff E ᵈ Marsden²⁴
a Verry warm day I work,d in the Fields and Garden till evening then
Went to Halifax & heard Mʳ (*blank*) one ᵒᶠ Mʳ Walker,s Pupils of
Northouram Preach from the 1ˢᵗ of Peter 3 Chapter & 13 ᵛʳˢ

Friday 10
a Verry hot day I was employ,d in going to Halifax to buy half Load of
wheat for which I gave 12ˢ/9ᵈ in it had 6 St of Flower I went to John
Illingworths ☞

Saturday 11
a Verry hot day I was employd in fulling up [the] Part of the Swilling dam
and other work about the house and went Halifax in the Evening and
Bought
A new hat for my self at 12/s Price had a new wheel Barrow brought home
the Price of the Barrow Exclusive of the wheel was (*blank*)

Sunday 12
a Verry hot day I went to Halifax & heard Mʳ Gallan from Holmforth
Preach from the 1ˢᵗ of Corinthians Chapter 2ⁿᵈ & 12 verse & in the
afternoon from John Gospel Chaptʳ the 5ᵗʰ & 40 verse

Monday 13
a hot droughty day I work in the Holms in the fore and & Went to Halifax
in along with Charles Crowther and undertook to break up some new
enclosed ground of Mʳ Irvins & began of it ᴵᵐᵉᵈⁱᵃᵗˡᵉʸ

Tuesday 14
a verry hot day I & C. Crowther and Moses Elsworth worked at Breaking
up in grey Stones Croft

Wednes 15
a verry hot day I & C. C. and M. E. work,d in the grey stones Croft

---

²⁴ These words are written in the margin.

Thursday 16 D
a Dull hot day with Thunder and verry heavy Showers of Rain in the afternoon work,d as above
Jaˢ Grarrson ᴳʳᵉᵍᵒʳʸ died of the small Pox

Friday 17
a hot day I work,d in the Garden all day ᵐʸ Brother Willᵐ Swaine & [Ed] my Son Edmund Marsden [from]Came from London & Sister Rhodes & her Daughter Sally & Charlotte Came to our house in the Evenⁱⁿᵍ

Saturday 18
a hot day

Sunday 19
a hot day I went to Halifax and heard Mʳ Parsons from Leeds Preach in the Morning from Jeremiah Prophecy Chaptʳ 50 & 4 & 5 verses and in the afternoon from (*blank*) And in the Evening heard Mʳ Cocking Preach at Illingworth from the 119 Psalm and 19 verse

Monday 20
a a Verry hot day

Tuesday 21
a Verry hot day I Pulled up Briers in Sun Door Field Broʳ Willᵐ Swaine &ˢᵒⁿ Edmund Went to Mʳ Thompson Esq of Southouran

Wednes 22
a Verry hot day Broʳ Rhodes Came to our house and Return,d that night and took his Daughter Sally with him

Thurs 23
a hot day I and Brother Swaine went to Fair Wether Green in the Township of Manningham about 1 ½ miles from Bradford Return,d that ⁿⁱᵍʰᵗ

Friday 24
a hot day I Pull,d up Briers and went to hear Mʳ Hindle Preach near Illingʷᵒʳᵗʰ from Deutr Chap 32 & 29 verse

Saturday 25 D
George Ibbotson of Halifax was buried this day
a verry hot day more so that had been this Summer Brother Swai^{ne} and ^{son}
Edmund Marsden Set off for London and ^{my} son Thos Marsden went went
with them to Manchester I went with them [l]a little beyond the King,s
Cross Brother & Sister Rhodes & their daugh^{ter} went home that Day
George Ibbotson was buried this week

Sunday 26
a Verry hot day I went Halifax & heard Mr Cock^{ing} Preach in the forenoon
from Rev ^{ch} 14 ^{Ch} & 3^v after from 1st of Timothy 4^{Chap} 8 ^{ver} in Evening from
Matt^w 13 Chap & 44 verse

Monday 27 D
a verry hot day I was employd in Pulling up Briars thistles and Ketlock[25] in
the little field Thos Mar^sden Return,d from Manchester where he went with
his Uncle and his Brother
John Wilson of Lee Bridge was ^{buried}

Tuesday 28
a hot day but more wind than yesterday I was empl^{oy,d} this day in Pulling
Briars &c in the Gate field ☞

Wednes 29
a verry hot day I worked in the wheat field Pulling up Weeds round about
& in the Corn

Thursd 30
a verry hot day I work,d in the long field Pulling up weeds gathering
Stones ^{&c}

Friday 1 of July
 a hot day & droughty till afternoon then began the Rain,d all night

---

[25] Ketlock: a dialect term for any large umbelliferous plant such as cow parsnip, colewort or common charlock.

Saturday 2
a Warm Rainy day [Iwork,d] I Jobb'd in the house this Day as ^{it} was a wet day

Sunday 3 D
a Warm Day with some rain I went to Halifax & heard M^r (*blank*) from (*blank*) Preach in the forenoon from the 1 Epistle to Timothy the 4 Chapter and 8 verse & in the afternoon M ^{r} (*blank*) from (*blank*) Preach from Pauls 2 Epistl To the Corinthians Chapt^r 4 and 6 verse and the Evening M^r (*blank*) Isaac Holroyd,s Daughter was buried that day

Monday 4
a Warm Day with some rain I work,d the long field Pulling up Weeds

Tuesday 5
a Warm Day with a good Deal of rain in the afternoon I work,d in the gate field that day the water was let into the new mill dam this day
J
Wednesday 6
a Dull warm Day I work,d in the long field & Went to John
 Illingworths ☞

Thursd 7 D D
a Dull hot day I work,d In the long field that day
A Child of Joshua Charnock,s & a Child of John Wilsons was Buried at Illingworth to day

Friday 8
a hot day I went to seek Mowers in the forenoon & Work,s in the long field in the afternoon & went to Halifax in the Evening Widdow Crabtree was buried this day

Saturday 9
a Dull [a]warm day & fair in the fore but several showers of Rain in the afternoon we had Jacob Turner John Wormald & William Craven Came to mow grass but Jacob was Sick but the other Towo mowed

Sunday 10

a Hot droughty day I went to Halifax & heard Mr Knight Preach in the forenoon from the 2 Book of the Kings Chapter 5 & later Part of the 14 vers

Monday 11

a Hot day we had 3 Mower till almost 8 O clock [wheof] 3 hay makers this day   3

Tuesd 12

a Fine hot day had 3 hay Makers this day & had 3 Mowers also from 10 O clock in the forenoon till night & ^{they} Mow,d the grass in the Wood field   3

Wednes 13

a Dull forenoon but verry Bright in the after we had 5 hay Makers that Day & we housed the hay in Lathe Croft   5

Thurs 14

a Dull wet forenoon but droughty in after we had 5 hay makers in the after G. Town & Wm Craven mow,^d in afternoon   3

Friday 15

^{a Dull forenoon but} [a] Bright & droughty in the afternoon We had 5 hay Makers that day & 1 Mower in forenoon & 2 in the after[&] we house,d the ^{hay} in wood field in the afternoon   5

Saturd 16

a Verry Fine droughty day till 2 O clock and some rain after we had 6 hay Makers our grass was mown off at noon that day   6

Sunday 17

a Dull warm day with frequent Showers of Rain I went to Halifax & heard Mr Knight Preach in the forenoon from the 1st Epistle of Peter Chap the 4 & 14 vers and in the after from the 10th Chapt^r & 38 verse of St Marks gospel

Monday 18 M M

a Warm Day & Dull & wet till 2 O clock but verry dry after John Wigglesworth with his horse & Cart C. Crowther and I led Mainer & G Town spread a Part of it

John Garforth was Married to Dolly Chapman Jonas Robert^shaw and Alice Binns was married also Tol

Tuesday 19

a Dull forenoon with some Showers of Rain we had 6 Haymakers in the after from 2 O clock to 6 when it began to Rain heavily   [6] 3

Wednes 20 D D D

a Dull [with s] day till 4 O clock some Showers before but verry droughty Samuel Garforth in Mixenden Buried two Children of the small Pox Willm Smith in Wheatly buried one of the same

Thursday 21

a Dull day Moderate droughty till noon after there was Thunder & some Rain we 6 hay Makers till 2 Oclock (besides 2 or 3 which helped us to get up our hay) and afterwards they spread mainer & hous,d a few Bursdens of ^hay & Clear,d among our hay Cocks   4

Friday 22

a Dull hot day ^fair till 2 O clock we had 7 hay Makers till 3 O clock it began thundering at noon a was not much Rain   6

Saturday 23

a Dull forerenoon but verry hot & droughty in the afternoon we had 7 hay makers from11 till 8 O clock at night we finisht our hay that day   6

Sunday 24

a Dull warm day I went to Halifax and heard Mr K. Preach from the 1st Epistle of ^Peter in the forenoon Chap^r 4th from the 15 verse to the end of the Chapter & in the after from Pauls Epistle to Epihesians Chaptr 5th & 1. 2 verses & in the even^ing Mr Joseph Brooksbank[26] from London Preached from Pauls Epistle in the Colos^ns Chapter 3 & 2 verses

---

[26] No information has been found about Joseph Brooksbank.

Monday 25
a Dull hot day I worked at the hay at Mr Lees mill between our house & whea ^tley

Tuesday 26
a hot day I work,d at the hay at Mr Lees Mill

Wednes 27 D
a hot droughty day I work,d at the hay at ^the Mill
Widdow Crabtree in wheatly was buried

Thursday 28 D
a Dull day & droughty till afternoon some showers of Rain after I went to Halifax in the fore and work,d in the fields in the afternoon Mr Foxhall died in the night or on Friday Morning verry Suddenly going to bed Preetty ^well

Friday 29
a Dull day with a good deal of Thunder & Rain in the afternoon I work,d in the lathe Croft Cleaning the Neces^saries[27]

Saturday 30
a Dull hot day with frequent & heavy showers of Rain I went to Halifax & Jobb'd about the House that day

Sunday 31 D
a Bright droughty day I went to Halifax and heard Mr Knight Preach from the 1st of Peter Chaptr 5th from the 1st to the 5 verse & in the after noon from Pauls Epistle to the Ephisians Chap the 5 & 2 verse Mr Sam,^l Knight[28] Preach,d at Dewsberry and Mr Henry Foster[29] at Huddersfield
Mr Steel in Ovenden died in the night or Monday morning

Monday 1 August
a Bright hot day I work,d in the sumer Pasture Pulling up weeds

---

[27] 'Neces^saries': privies.
[28] Possibly Rev. Samuel Knight, son of Titus Knight. See above footnote on p.141.
[29] Rev. Henry Foster, B.A., Minister of Orange Street, Leicester Square, London. His father was William Foster of Halifax. *Surman Index*, Dr Williams's Library, London.

Tuesday 2
a Dull hot day I was employ that in [d] makeing a drain in our yard

Wednes 3
a Dull day with Rain in the afternoon & most of the nigh I worked in a drain in [of] our yard in the afternoon & went to Halifax in the fore an & heard M^r allinson of Cross Stone[30] Preach in the Church from the 16 Chapter of St Matthews gospel & 26 verse

Thursday 4
a Dull warm day ^Thunder with frequent Showers of Rain I work,d in our fields in the forenoon & in Gray Stones Croft in the afternoon

Friday 5
a [B] warm day I was emp^loy'd in Wheeling & Spreading Dung and earth in the lathe Croft

Saturday 6
a Bright warm I worked in the gray Stones Croft Mrs Houlden of Halifax was Married to ^Mr Benjamin Chambers of D°

Sunday 7
a Dull warm day with some rain in the Evening I Stay,d at home till noon as I discover,d a wound in a young Heifer I thought it work of necessity to get it dres,d Imediately

Monday 8
a Dull fair day till the Evening but was a good deal of Rain after Six O clock [in] I was employ,d that day in our fields

Tuesday 9
a Dull warm day with a little Rain I was empl^oyd in the sun Door field that day

---

[30] No information has been found about Mr Allinson of Cross Stone

Wednesday 10
a Bright warm day & that being the day appoint^{ed} for the Ordination of Mr John Toothill to be Minister of Booth Chapel in Warely I went and heard Mr Jonathan Toothill from Hopton Preach from Pauls 2 Epistle to Timothy (*blank*) Chapter & 2 verse & Mr Cocking Preach,d from Pauls Epistle to the Philipians Chaptr (*blank*)

Thursday 11
a Bright warm day I work,d the Garden that day

Friday 12
a Dull warm day with frequent and heavy showers of & a good deal of Rain in the night I and C. Crowther work,d in the grey Stones Croft

Saturday 13
a Dull warm day with a good Deal of Rain I Jobb,d in the House and garden & went to Halifax in the Evening

Sunday 14
a Dull warm day with Showers of Rain I went to Halifax and heard Mr Knight Preach in the forenoon from the 1st Epistle of Peter Chaptr. 5 & 8 verse in the after from Isiah Chap 43 & 25 verse

Monday 15
a Dull day I went to Bradshaw & work,d in the field

Tuesday 16
a Dull wet forenon but Bright and Clear in the after I went to Halifax in the fore & work,d in the fields in the afternoon

Wednes 17
a Dull day with some Showers of Rain I work,d in the Garden & fields

Thursday 18
a Dull day with some Rain I work in the fields was at mill in afternoon

Friday 19
a Bright droughty day I was at Jumples Mill most of the afternoon Charles Crowther undertook [dig] the Cleaning & inlarging the above Mill [day]Dam and I assisted in ^{the work}

Saturday 20
[a] Bright & droughty [da] most of the day I went to Halifax in fore & went to Jumpls Mill in after

Sunday 21
a Dull day with some Rain I went to Halifax & heard Mr Knight Preach in the forenoon from the 1st of Peter Chapt^r the 5 & 8 verse & in the after from the (*blank*) & the (*blank*) verse
Mr John Ramsden of High field Buried a (*blank*) of (*blank*) old

Monday 22
a Dull soft day I work,d at Jumples Mill along with C. Crowther & Moses Elworth

Tuesday 23
a Dull soft day I work,d at Jumples Mill with the above ² Men

Wednesday 24
a Dull day and verry Rainy in the afternoon & in the night

Thursday 25
a Bright droughty day I work,d at the above Mill Dam with C. Crowther John Crowther Marsden Turner and Moses Elsworth

Friday 26   3
a Bright droughty day I work,d at the above mill Dam with the above 4 Men we had 3 Shearers this day share 25 Hattocks

Saturday 27   6
a Verry Bright droughty day We had 5 shears and myself that day & share 52 Hattocks my son Doughty Thos & Rade to Gomersal that & Thos Came back the ^{next day}

Sunday 28

a Bright droughty day [I worked……………………..] I went to Halifax & heard Mr Knight Preach in the forenoon from the 1st Epis of Peter Chapt^r 5th & 9 vr^s and in the afternoon from the 149 Psalm & Part of the 9 verse

Monday 29

a Bright droughty fore but dull & wet most of the afternoon I work,d at Jumples Mill [and] with the fore mention'd 4 Partners & we had 3 shearers till afternoon

(From 30 August to 14 October inclusive Ashworth made no entries. The Diary resumes on 15 October)

Saturday 15 October

it had been a been a verry wet time since the beginning of sept^r except one week of frost which was in the begining of this month

Sunday 16

a Dull day & Moderate droughty I went to Halifax and Heard Mr Knight Preach in the forenoon from the 2 Epis general of Peter Chapter the 1st 3 & 4 verses & in the afternoon from Heb^r Chaptr 8 & 19 verse

Monday 17

a Bright droughty day I went twice to Whealy [to] and Jumples Mill in the forenoon and assisted in Measuring Stones &c and work,d Husbandry in the afternoon

Tuesday 18

a [Bet] Dull I went to Robt Parkers to Oven^den to James whitworths &c &c and mended Ja^s Charnock a Chest

Wednes 19

a Mild droughty day I was Employd in Walling in gatefield

Thurs 20

a Dull mild day I wove Tamy in Charles Crowther Loom in the day & went to Halifax in the Evening & heard Mr Knight Preach from the 77 Psalm & (*blank*) verse

Friday 21
a Dull day I was employd that day in walling in the Gate field

Saturday 22
a Dull day I wall,d in the forenoon & went to Halifax in the after

Sunday 23
a Dull mild day I went to Halifax & heard Mr K. Preach in the forenoon from 2 Epistle of Peter Chap 1st & 4 verse and in the afternoon from the (*blank*)

Monday 24
a Dull Soft day I went ^to Harwood well to Warely Tow^n to Halifax & to Mr Houls Sale &c

Tuesday 25
a verry Dull ^day with [s] heavy Showers of s[h]now ^& Hail and a good Deal of snow fell in the night I work,d Husbandry I the forenoon and went to the above sale in the afternoon

Wednes 26
a Dull wet Day I Jobb,d in and about the House

Thursday 27
a Cold frosty day I Jobb In the House in the foreno^on and Went to Halifax and to Illingworth in the after

Friday 28
a wind day and Exceeding wind and wet in the Evening Jobb'd about the house in the and Went to [Hal]Halifax, to Ware town and Illingworth in the after

Saturday 29
a Cold day with some show^ers of snow and Rain I went to Halifax & Jobb,d about the House

Sunday 30
a Dull Cold wet day I went to Halifax & heard Mr K. Preach in the forenoon the 2 of Peter Chap 1st & 5 vers and in the afternoon from the 16 Psalm & 11 verse
Sarah Blagbroug was taken verry ill that Morning about 3 O clock

Monday 31
a Dull Soft day I work'd Husbandry that day

Tuesday 1 November D
a Dull mild day and verry Rainy in the afternoon I went to Halifax & work,d Husby Richd Longbottom Buried a Child

Wednes 2
a Dull mi^ld day I was employd that day in Gathering up dirt &c in our lane

Thursday 3 D
a Dull mild day with [a good] some Rain in the Evening I went to Halifax & heard Mr K. Preach from the 125 Psalm & 1 & 2 verses
John Banister was Buried that day

Friday 4 D
a Dull mild day I was employ,d in ditching & scraping up Dirt in our lane
Hannah the wife of Timothy Norminton died verry suddenly

Saturday 5
a Dull day & Rainy in the afternoon and ^in night I work,d Husbandry Willm Blagborough died at nine O clock at night

Sunday 6
a Dull day I went to Halifax & heard Mr K. Preach in the forenoon from from the [1]2st Epistle of Peter Chapter 1 & 6 & 7 verses and in the after from Pauls 2 Epistle to the Corinthians Chap (*blank*) and the 9th verse

Monday 7 M D
a Calm Bright day I went to Hunsworth & Gomersal and Retur^nd home that night Joseph Bancroft an[d] aprentice to a [W]Clock maker in Halifax Hanged himself

Tuesday 8
a mild day I work,d in [the] our fields in fore & at Jumpls mill in the after noon

Wednes 9 D V
a Dull mild day Willm Blagborough was buried that day Sister Rhodes Came to our House

Thurs 10 D
a Dull mild day I was employ,d in Jobbing in and about the House [the] till noon and went to Halifax in the after
Samuel Cockroft in Ovenden Buried a Child that day

Friday 11
a Dull mild day I was employ,d in our fields that day

Saturday 12
a Brigh Cold day I was Employ that Day in Jobbing about the House Sister Rhodes Went home that day

Sunday 13
a Dull mild day I went to Halifax & heard Mr Knight Preach in the forenoon from the 2 of Peter Chapt^r 1st and 8 & 9 verses and in the after from the 78 Psalm & 24 verse

Monday 14
a Bright [mild] day ^{froze hard in the} night I began working in Wheatly edge with James Hains^{worth} who was getting Stones to Build a House with for John Smith

Tuesday 15
a Bright mild day I work,d on Wheatly edge

Wednes 16
a Dull day I work,d on Wheatley edge

Thursday 17
a Bright mild day I worked on Wheatly edge

Friday 18
a Dull mild day I worked on Wheatly edge

Saturday 19
a Dull [w] day & verry Wet in the afternoon & in the night I work,d on Wheatly edge till noon & Jobb,d about the lathe in the afternoon and went to Halifax in the Evening

Sunday 20
a Dull Soft day I went to Halifax & heard Mr Lard[31] one of Mr Walkers Pupils of Northouram Preach from the 1st of Peter 2 Chapter & 7 verse and in the afternoon from Pauls Epistle to the (*blank*) and (*blank*) verse

Monday 21
a Dull wet day I workd on Wheatly edge in fore noon but [ine]

Tuesday 22
a Bright frosty day I work,d on Wheatley edge

Wednes 23
a Dull frosty day I work,d on Wheatly edge

Thursday 24
a Dull Cold day I work,d on Wheatley edge

Friday 25 D
Dull Sof (*blank*) I work,d on Wheatly edge
Jeremiah Ingham,s wife died

Saturday 26
a Wet windy day I work'd on Wheatly edge till 10 O clock and work'd in our fields in the afternoon

Sunday 27
a Dull windy Cold day I went to Halefax & heard Mr Knight Preach in the forenoon from the 2 of Peter 1 & 10 in after from Matt Chap 8 & 2 verse

---

[31] Mr. Lard: Thomas Laird was one of the students who moved with the Heckmondwike Academy to Northowram on the death of Rev. John Scott.

Monday 28
a Cold windy day with my heavy Showers of Rain & Hail I assisted John Sheard & Isaac Sharp in Putting up a vent in [Jo] the house where Jonathan Priestly lived

Tuesday 29   D
a Dull day with many Showers of Snow Hail and Rain I went with Charles Crowther John Sheard & Isaac sharp to the Triangle beyond Sowerby Bridge to to vew a Place whe a Mill was to errected
John Crowther's wife died about 6 O clock in the Morning

Wed 30
a Cold windy day [I] I asisted Isaac Sharp in setting a Range

Thursday 1 December

a verry Cold frosty I asisted Isaac Sharp in settin a Pan
John Crowthers wife was Buried that Day

Friday 2
a Dull Soft day I asisted Isaac Sharp in setting a Bakeing stone [32] in the fore and [an] did other Jobbs went with Madam to Bull in the afternoon

Saturday 3
a Dull wet day I [s]asistid in [Ca] flitting Marsden Turer & John Crowther

Sunday 4
a Dull day I wnt to Halifax and Mr K. Preach in Morning from the 2 of Peter Chapter the 1st & 10 verse and in the afternoon from (*blank*)

Monday 5
a Dull mild day I work,d on Wheatly edge

Tuesday 6
a Dull day and verry Rainy all the afternoon I went to Bingly along with John Smith and James Hainsworth To a Justice Meeting there

---

[32] 'Bakeing stone': backstones were set over a small grate and used to bake oatcakes.

Wednes 7
a Dull Rainy day I was employ,d in Husbandry

Thursday 8
a Dull day and verry Rainy in the night I was employ,d that day in forenoon in Husbandry and in the after in going to Halifax To Salterhebble Wharf To King Cross &c

Friday 9 D
a Dull Soft day I workd Husbandry in the fore noon & Helped John Crow[her] in the after Ely Wigglesworth,s wife was buried that Day

Saturday 10
a Dull wet day I was employ,d in Husbandry

Sunday 11
a Dull day I went to Halifax and heard M[r] Knight Preach [in morning] from the 2 Epistle of Peter Chaptr the 1st & 11 verse and in the afternoon from the 40 Psalm [&] & 17 verse

Monday 12
A Dull Soft day we Killed our Hogg I assisted in Killing it and Cleaning after &c

Tuesday 13
a Dull Soft day I [wen] Help,d to the Hogg in the fore & went [H] Salter Hebble Wharf in the afternoon for a Paket of Hops[33]

Wednes 14
a Dull Soft day I went to Halifax weigh,d hops &c

Thursday 15 B
a Bright mild day and Moderate droughty
I went with young Wibsy to be Cover'd the 1st time & I did sundry Jobbs of Husbandry and went To Halifax in the Even and heard M[r] Knight Preach from (*blank*)

---

[33] This is the first time that Ashworth specifically mentions hops.

Friday 16
a Dull mild day I Jobb,d in & about the house went Twice to Halifax &c

Saturday 17
a Dull mild day I went into Ovenden and workd Husbandry

Sunday 18 1785
a Dull mild day I Went Halifax & heard Mr Knight Preach in the forenoon from 2 of Peter Chaptr 1 & 12 vers & in the after heard Mr Hindle Preach a Funeral Sermon from the 2 Book of Samuel Chapter 23 & 4 verse for the wife of Thos Haulden of Halifax

Monday 19
a Dull day I went Saltor Hebble Wharf & to James Keighley Sale in Halifax

Tuesday 20
a Dull mild day I work,d in the lathe Croft in forenoon and at Jumples mill in the afternoon Mr Hill of Halifax [died] was taken ill in the night and died the ^next morning after

Wednes 21
a Dull mild day I work,d at the Jumples Mill

Thursday 22
a Dull mild day I wor^k,d at the Jumples Mill Benj: Blagbroug^was Bap^ised

Friday 23
a Dull mild day I work,d at the Jumpls Mill

Saturday 24
a frosty Snowy day I was employ that day in Jobbing in the fields and ^in & about our House

Sunday 25
a Frosty Snowy day I went to Halifax and heard Mr Knight Preach in the forenoon from the 1st of Timothy Chap (*blank*) and in the afternoon heard Mr Hindle Preach a funeral Sermon for Thos Fearnly in Ovenden from the 14th Chapter of Proverbs of Solomon & laster Part of 32 verse

Monday 26 V

a Dull frosty ^{on} I was employ,d in and about the House & Lathe 3 nephews Came & stay,d^{all night}

Thos Marsden Went to Gomer^{sal} and Stay'd till Wednesday

Tuesday 27

a Dull frosty day I and Charles Crowther thrasht Corn that Day

Wednes 28

a Dull frosty day I and John Town Thrasht Corn and C. Crowther shak,d Straw. Polly Fletcher. Polly Armitage Alice Acroyd and Betty Buttery Came to our House

Thur 29 B B

a Moderate Bright droug^{hty} day I went to Wheatly to Illingworth & to shakeing & Charles Crowther our apprentice & I winow^d after & in (*blank*) Hattocks had 62 Strikes of Oates

Brother Willm Ashworth[34] had a Son Born that day John Tetly,s 1st Born Doughter also was Born that Day

Friday 30 B

a Moderate Bright frosty day I went to Halifax & Diverse Place therein David Varely had a Doughter Born

a Dull frosty day

(*The rest of this page and the following page are blank and there appears to be some text missing before the next entry.*)

on Sunday Jan 1 1786 from 2 of Peter Chap 1st & 13 verse and in afternoon from Ephesians Chap 5 & 18 verse

2 Monday

A Dull frosty I went to Luddenden & other Jobbs

3

A Dull frosty day & some snow fell I Jobbs [at] in the House

---

[34] One of the three brothers of the Diarist.

4

A Dull frosty and some snow I went to Illingworth &c S

5 Thursday

a Dull frosty Sarah Blagbrough died between 12 & 1 O clock this Morning I went Halifax in the afternoon it was a verry snowy windy night

6 Friday

a Dull thawy Day and Rain,d a good Deal in the night
I Jobbd up Stairs in the great Chamber and Put window Shutters in little Chamr

7 Saturday

a Dull mild Thawing Day I made at the and in 55 Hattocks 24 Strikes of Shilling & 39 Sts of Meal besides moolter

8 Sunday

a Dull Soft day I went to Halifax & heard Mr Knight Preach in the forenoon from the 2 of Peter Chapter 2 & 13 verse and in the afternoon from (*blank*) and (*blank*)

9 Monday

a Dull Soft day I work,d Husbandry at home in the forenoon & at Jumples Mill in the afternoon Methodists Chapell at Halifax was on fire [35]

10 Tuesday D D

a Dull Soft mild day I work at Jumples Mill
Peter Bever in Wheatley and Jonathan Mitchel in Bradshaw Died that Day

11 Wednesday

a Dull soft Mild day I worked at Jumples Mill

---

[35] Fire nearly destroyed the chapel. However a quarry opposite the chapel happened to be full of water and once a fire engine was brought to the scene, Joseph Bramley, a woollen draper, bravely entered the chapel dragging the hoses with him and succeeded in putting the fire out. The gallery and many windows were however destroyed. J.U. Walker, *A History of Wesleyan Methodism in Halifax*, Halifax, Hartley and Walker, 1836, pp.164-165.

12 Thursday

[a Bright frosty] Dull Soft day day I work.d near Hebble Brig^d

13 Friday

a bright Day in the afternoon [Th] a froze hard in the night I work,d near Hebble Bridge

14 Saturday

a Bright frosty day I and some snow fell in the night I work,d at Jumples Mill and it wa Reer,d that Day & the Rearing Feast was at Savil Green that night³⁶

15 Sunday

a Dull Frosty day I went to Halifax & heard Mr Knight Prea^ch in the forenoon from the 2 of Peter Chapter 1st & 1[7]6 verse and in the afternoon from the 119 Psalm & 94 verse Bins wife in the Dean Clough died

16 Monday

a Dull fresh day & [a] Some snow fell in the night I went to Halifax & King Cross in the afternoon

17 Tuesday

a Bright frosty day I work,d in the House

18 Wednesday

a Bright frosty day I work,d in the House that day

19 Thursday

a Dullish frosty day I work in the House in the forenoon & Went into Midgley in the after to Richard Taylors

20 Friday

a Bright a [thawing] frosty day I work,d in the House in the foreno^on and Went to Illingworth [in] to Ovenden Workhouse into Houldsworth &c

21 Saturday

a Soft Bright day I work,d at Jumples Mill

---

³⁶ The rearing feast was held to celebrate the roofing in of the building.

22 Sunday

a Windy wet day I went to Halifax & heard Mr. K. Preach in forenoon from the [1]2 of on Peter Chapter 1st 19.20 & 21 verses in the afternoon from Pauls Epis to the Hebrews Chapter 13 & 5 vers

23 wasMonday

a Mild Soft day I work,d Jumples Mill

24 was Tuesday

a Dull Soft Day I work,d at Jumples mill

25 was Wednesday

a Winday day I work,d near Hebble Bridge

26 was Thursday

a verry windy Rainy day I work,d near above Bridge in the forenoon & was at home in the afternoon

27 was Friday

a wing day with a little Rain I was at home in the forenoon & at th[at]e above Place working in the after

28 was Saturday

a windy day with some Rain I worked at the above Place

29 was Sunday

a Windy with Some Rain I went to Halifax and heard Mr Knight Preach from the 2 of Peter Chapter [1st] 2 last verse of it 1st verse of Second Chapter and the after from (*blank*)

30 was Monday

a Windy day with Some Rain. I work,d near Hebble Bridge

31 was Tuesday

a Windy [R] day with some Drizling Rain I worked near Hebble Bridge

Feby 1 Wednesday
a Verry wet Windy day Especialy in the forenoon I work,d near the Hebble Bridg on 2 day work'd at the above Place

3 was [Th] Friday
a mild Bright frosty day I began working at Jumples Mill along with John Town Richd Longbotton Timothy Wash &c in enlarging a Mill Day 8 Person worked

4 was Saturday
a mild Day I work,d at Jumples Mill along with 7 others

5 was Sunday
a Windy day much more so in the night I went to Halifax and heard Mr K. Preach in the forenoon from the 2 of Peter Chapter the 2 & 3 verses & in the afternoon from Isaiah Chapter 43 and 21 verse

6th Monday
was a wind day with heavy Showers of hail and Rain I worth at the above mill with 8 others

7 was Tuesday
a Windy day with Showers of Hail & Rain I work,d at Jumples Mill with 8 others

Wednesday 8
a Dull ^{frosty} day and a good Deal of Snow fell in the afternoon & in the night I work,d at Jumples Mill with 4 others

Thursday 9th
a Dull frosty day I work.d at Jumpls Mill with 3 others

Friday 10th
a Dull windy day and thaw,d verry Swiftly
I work'd at Jumples Mill with 4 others   (5 [37]

---

[37] On this and subsequent days there are figures like this which all refer to work at Jumples Mill.

Saturday 11

a Windy day I work,d at Jumples Mill in the fore & went to Halifax in the afternoon with Richd Longbottom to Mr Cha^rles Houdson for Money to Pay the Men we their Wages with (10

Sunday 12

a Windy day I went to Halifax and heard Mr K. Preach from the 2 of Peter 5 [C] Chapter 2 & 4 & 5 verses and in the afternoon from Jeremiah,s Prophecy Chapter 8 and 22 vrs and in the Evening heard Mr. Hindle Preach from Pauls Epistle to the Romans Chap 8 & 6 verse

Monday 13

a Dull Mild day I workd at Jumples Mill (10

Tuesday 14

a Dull day With Showers of Rain I work,d at Jumples Mill (9

Wednesday 15

a Mild Brightish day I work,d at the above mill (9)

Thursday 16

a Bright mild day I work'd at Jumples mill with [10]9 others

Friday 17

a Dull mild day I worth at Jumples mill ^that Day
I work at Jumls mill Day with 9 others

Saturday 18th

a Dull wet [d]day I worke at the above mill Dam in the after

Sunday 19

a Dull wet day I went to Halifax and Heard M ^r (*blank*) one of Mr Walkers Pupils of North Northowr ^from acts 9 & 21 verse and in the afternoon heard Mr Crabter from Bradford[38] Preach in Mr Hindles Chappel at Halifax[39] from Revelation Chapter 14th and 4 verse

---

[38] 'Mr Crabter': Rev. William Crabtree, minister of Westgate Baptist Chapel, Bradford, 1753-1803.
[39] 'Mr Hindles Chappel at Halifax': Pellon Lane Baptist Chapel.

Monday 20

A Dull Soft day and was much Rain & a high wind in the nigh I work,d at the above mill with 8 others

on Tuesday 21 D

a Dull day and began to freeze verry hard in the afternoon I work,d at the above mill with 8 others Mary the wife Moses Elsworth died about 3 O clock in the afternoon

Wednesday 22

a verry Cold windy frosty day I worked the above Mill with 9 others

Thursday 23 B

a Cold windy frosty day I work,d at the above mill with 8 others Ja^s Charnock Son was born

Friday 24

a windy frosty day I work,d at the above mill with 8 others

Saturday 25

a Cold windy frosty day I work,d the above Mill with 10 others

(*One leaf of the Diary appears to be missing at this point. The next entry is presumed to be for March.*)

Wednesday 8th *(March)*

a Bright frosty day I workt at Jumples mill with 4 others

Thursday 9

a Brigh frosty day I was at home in the fore but went to Halifax in the afternoon

Friday [9] 10

a Dull soft [day]Thawing day I work,d with Richard Longbotton & John Town in Leebank Shrogs getting Stones Benjamin Blagbrough was Married To Sally Drake in Bradshaw

Saturday 11
a Dull Soft day with some Rain I work,d in Shrogs with 2 Others

Volume 3

1 January 1809
to
31 December 1809

This volume of the Diary is written in 'The Daily Journal or Gentleman's, Merchant's and Tradesman's Complete Annual Accompt-Book.........For The Year of Our Lord 1809', in which the pages have the day and date printed on them. These are reproduced in the printed text. The space for each entry runs across both left and right-hand pages with the right-hand page being headed 'Account of Monies' (see Figure 38). Ashworth sometimes made an entry on the right-hand page, these entries have been represented by beginning them on a new line.

(*Inside front cover*)
John Spencer Book May
Joho………….
John Spencer Book August 11 1842

1 January
a [frosty]Cold day and a little snow fell in the Night Wm Acroyd[1] Preached Morning from 139 Psalm 1. 2. 3. & 4 verses in the afternoon from Job 31 Chapter and 4 verse

Monday 2
a Dull frosty day and a little fell in the day Some fell also in the Night

Tuesday 3
a Dull frosty day and rather Windy and Some Snow fell in the Night

Wednesday 4
a Dull Windy day and Much Snow fell both in the day and the Night

Thursday 5
a Verry Windy day and Much Snow fell both in the day and in the Night Also

Friday 6
a Mild Calm day and thaw.d all the day and in the Night also

Saturday 7
a Dull Soft day I went to Halifax in the Afternoon
froze in the Night

---

[1] William Ackroyd was minister at Pellon Lane Baptist Chapel, Halifax, from 1800 to 1831.

Sunday 8

a dull frosty day William Acroyd Preached in the Morning from Matthew 5
Chapter 6 verse in the afternoon from Jerʰa 31 & 19

Monday 9

a Mild Soft day I went to Meet Hannah Edmund and Susanʰna Marsden[2]
Comeing from a Visit to Hathershelf

Tuesday 10

a Dull Soft Day I went to Halifax in the Afternoon
froze in the Night

Wednesday 11

a Dull Soft day and froze in the Night
Paid Composition Money To John Illingworth Surveyor of the Roads 0 18 0

Thursday 12

a Dull Mild day I went to Elland the Doctor Crowther,s for Phisic froze in
the Night
Samuel Appleyard was Buried this week   D

Friday 13

a Dull frosty day I was Employᵈ in laying up the Dung Hill a Shoveling
snow

Saturday 14

a Bright frosty day I went Halifax after 2 O clock in the afternoon

Sunday 15

a Dull frosty day I heard William Acroyd Preach both Morning and
afternoon from Matthew 7 Chap and 14 verse
John Rothera'ˢ wife died   D
                                                                                0 18 0

---

[2] The step-grandchildren of the Diarist. Hannah and Susannah were the daughters of Thomas and
Susannah Marsden and Edmund was the son of Edmund and Ann Marsden.

Monday 16
a Dull frosty day I went to Houldsworth Illingworth and Moorside in the afternoon

Paid for prorty Tax	3. 18. 0
Bro^t Over	0 18 0
	3 14 0

Tuesday 17
a Dull frosty day I went to Halifax in the Afternoon

Wednesday 18
a Dull frosty a Heavy frost in the Night

Thursday 19
a Dull Morning but rather Brighter part of the afternoon and froze very Hard all day

Friday 20
a Frosty day but rather Brighter than Some Preceding day
John Ashworth[3] Came from Plymouth Dock[4] on J...itor[5]

Saturday 21
a Bright Frosty day I went Halifax after ^{at} 1 O clock in the afternoon

Sunday 22
a Dull frosty day a Some Snow fell in the afternoon & in the Night
I heard Wm Acroyd Comment on the 15 Chapter of John and the afternoon Preached from 63 Chapter of Isiah & 1 verse

---

[3] Probably the Diarist's brother who subsequently worked on the farm at Walt Royd. See Diary, 11 March 1809.
[4] Plymouth Dock owed its origin to the establishment of a naval dockyard there about 1690. By 1725 it was the headquarters of both the military and naval forces based at Plymouth. During the late eighteenth century it was heavily fortified and in 1810 further work of fortification was commenced. The town changed its name to Devonport in 1823. W. White, *History, Gazetteer and Directory of Devonshire*, Sheffield, printed for the author, 1850.
[5] It is difficult to decipher this word especially as Ashworth may have omitted a letter. It could be 'Jupiter'.

Monday 23
a Bright frosty day I went to the Ewood Hall with Edmund in the afternoon
& Jaˢ Went with Hannah Marsden to Gomersall
Broᵗ Over   3 14 0

Tuesday 24
a Dull frosty day and Much Snow fell in the afternoon and Night

Wednesday 25
a Dull frosty day and Some Snow fell in the Night and rain & hail fell in the
Night and froze in the Morning

Thursday 26
a Dull wet day and the Snow Lessen'd Much but froze hard in the Night
William Acroyd Preached at our House in the Evening from Genesis 7
Chapter and 16 verse   A

Friday 27
a Dull day and frequent Shower of Rain

Saturday 28
a Dull Soft day and Drizling Showers of Rain I went to Halifax before Noon
Charles Hudson's Wife at Shaw Hill near Halifax died this day

Sunday 29
a Dull Soft day and Much Rain in the afternoon and in the Night I heard
William Acroyd Preach both Morning & afternoon from 27 of Matt an 35
verse

Monday 30
a Dull day and Much Rain both in the day and in the Night
Broᵗ Over   3 14 0

Tuesday 31
a Bright Mild day froze in In the Evening and Rain the Night I went to
Halifax in the Afternoon

Wednesday February 1
a Dull day [and] and verry Wet in the afternoon and Rain.d in the Night
Also

Thursday 2
a Dull Mild day and Much Rain in the afternoon and in the Night
Paid for little Cow Called Brear Covering   0 1 0
Edward Birdwhisler,s Son in Ovenden wood died this day   0 0 0 D
                                                            3 15

Friday 3
a Dull Soft I went to Illingworth [in th] and Moorside in the the afternoon

Saturday 4
a Dull Soft day with Showers of Drizling Rain I went to Halifax in the
afternoon

Sunday 5
a Dull Rainy day I heard Wᵐ Acroyd Preach in the Morning from Johnˢ
Gospel 19 Chap 41 & 41 verse In the afternoon Isiah 53 Chap & 11 verse

Monday 6
a Dull Cold day and a little Snow fell in the Night and froze a little
I was afflicted this day with Pain in My back Head and Knees
Squire Houlden's wife in Ovenden Wood died this Morning   D

Tuesday 7
a Dull frosty day and a light Showers of Snow My Bodly Pains Much
yesterday

Wednesday 8
a Windy frosty day and Some Snow fell in the Night My Pane Much the
Same as yesterday
Richard Hindson at Haily Hill died this day in Morning   D
Broᵗ Over   3 15 0

Thursday 9
a Cold day frosty in the Morning with Some Snow an a little Rain in the Evening I Slept better this than 4 Nights past

Friday 10
a Dull Soft day my Bodily Pains was Much as Yesterday

Saturday 11
a Dull day with Some Showers of Rain I stay.d Home all day

Sunday 12
a Mild Dull day I Stay.d at Home all day as I was not verry well in health I thought it not Prudent to go out this day

Monday 13
a Dull Mild day and Some Showers of Rain in the Night and Drizling in the day also
Bro^t Over   3 15 0

Tuesday 14
a Dull wet and hight Wind at times and heavy Showers of Rain in the Night

Wednesday 15
a Dull Windy day and verry heavy Showers of Rain both in the day and in the Night

Thursday 16
a Bright Droughty day and Some Rain in the Night

Friday 17
a Dull Soft day with Some Showers of Rain both in the day in the Night [Hannah Marsden died this Evening Near 11 O clock at Gomersall Moravian School]

Saturday 18
a Dull Widy day Rain in the Morning Clar.d a little in the Afternoon Hannah Marsden died this Evening

Sunday 19
a Windy Cold day I heard Wᵐ Acroyd Comment on the 28ᵗʰ Chaptr of Matthew to the 8 verse in the Morning and Preached in the afternoon from the three last verse of Chapter (*blank*)

Monday 20
a Windy frosty day and a Little Snow fell in the Night [Hannah Marsden was Buried at the Baptist Chappel in Halifax]
Mr Prescot of Callco Hall in (*blank*) was Buried this morning   D

Tuesday 21
a Dull frosty Windy day Hannah Marsden was Buried at Baptist Chappel in Halifax to day
Hannah Marsden was Buried this day in the Afternoon at Baptist Chappel in Halifax   D

Wednesday 22
a Dull Mild and a Little rain
Mʳ Cockin Preached at our House from Jude 24 and 25 verses
Mʳ Wharf of Sowerby Bridge was Buried this Moring   D
Broᵗ Over   3 15 0

Thursday 23
a Dull Mild day I went to Doctor Sunderland's at Noon and again in the Evening

Friday 24
a Dull Mild day Mrˢ and Miss Rhodes returned Home in the afternoon

Saturday 25
a Fine Mild day for the Season I went to Halifax in the Afternoon

Sunday 26
Fine Mild day for the Season
I heard Wᵐ Acroyd Coment on the 1ˢᵗ 8 verses of the 1 Chapter ofActs in the Morning and he Preach,d from the 9 verse in the afternoon

Monday 27
a Bright Droughty day

Tuesday 28
a Bright Droughty day Jane Hartley was Delivered of a Son a little after 10
O clock in the morning   B

Wednesday March 1
a Bright Mild day
a Meeting of the Baptist Ministers at Bradford

Thursday 2
a Dull Misty Morning but Clear.d and was Bright and Drough I went
Halifax in the afternoon
James Bancroft of Roper Green had a Child Born   B

Friday 3
a Bright Droughty day and froze in the Night
a Young Woman of the Name of Liley was Buried this day   D

Saturday 4
a Bright Droughty day and froze in the night I went to Halifax in the
Afternoon
Bro^t Over   3 15 0

Sunday 5
a Bright Droughty day and froze in the night I heard Willim Acroyd
Coment on he 15 Chapter of John,ˢ Gospel to the 26 verse a Preached from
the last Clause of 26 verse in the Afternoon

Monday 6
a Bright Droughty day and froze in the Night verry hard
Bro^t Over   3 15. 0
Bro^t Over

Tuesday 7
Bright[y] Droughty day but Cold Wind

Wednesday 8

a Bright Cold Droughty Day I and Brother John began Opening the Ditches in the holms

Thursday 9

a Dull Cold Morning but Clear^d and was Droughty we had 3 Man[d] -- a Cart and 2 Horses Leading Ashes till Noon

I and Brother John was Opening Ditches in our Holms in the Afternoon Leading Ashes   0 8 0

Friday 10

a Fine Droughty Cool day I and Brother John work,d in the Holms opening the Ditches

Saturday 11

a Fine Droughty Cool day I and Brothers John & Abraham^6 work,d in the Holms till Noon and they Continued working in the Holms taking the Water and I went to Halifax in the afternoon

Sunday 12

a Fine Droughty Cool I heard Wm Acroyd Preach in the Morning from Hebrews 7 Chapter and 21 & 22 verses in afternoon from Hebrews 9 Chapter & 15 & 16 verses

7 days work in the Holms and Other field   0 17 6

                                                                  4 12. 6

Monday 13

A Fine Mild day and a Little Drizling rain I and Brothers J and A work in the Holms Most of the day and Some Part of it in the Lathe Croft and Sun door field

Tuesday 14

a Bright Droughty day I and Brothers was Employd in Gardening and Laying up Lime and Ashes

---

6 Abraham and John Ashworth, the Diarist's two brothers.

Wednesday 15

a Fine Cold Droughty day I was Employd in Pulling Over and Brother Jn°
and Abraham in Graveing after 1 O clock

Broᵗ Over   4 12. 6

Thursday 16

a Cold Droughty day I and Brothers Jn° & A was Employd in Graveing and
Pulling Over a James Hacked in the Afternoon

16 Wᵐ Thomas at Illingworth died this Morning   [D]D

Friday 17

a Dull Mild Morning with a Little Rain in the Morning but Cleard and
Droughty after 10 O clock

I and Brothers Graved and Pulled Over all day and Jaˢ Midgley Hackd

Saturday 18

a Verry Mild Droughty day I and Brothers John & Abraham Graved and
Pulled Over all day

To 6 days [days] work in the Holms & other fields   0 15 0
To 12 days Graveing and Pulling over   1 10 0
To 1 ½ [H] Days Hacking   0 3 0
                                                                                               7 0 6

Sunday 19

a Fine Cool Droughty day I heard William [Preach] Acroyd Preach from
Lukes Gospel 24 Chapter and 26 verse both Morning & afternoon.

Monday 20

a Fine Droughty day I and Brothers John & Abram Graved and Pulled
Over all day Misty in the Morning

Paid 8 Bushels of Oats Called Poland Oats⁷ to Sow in Wheat field 2 8 0
Paid Window Money ¼ Year   0 10 6
Broᵗ Over   7 0 6

---

⁷ Poland oats: A variety of oat which had many of the characteristics of the Friezland oat, including its
high yield, but it produced short stiff straw. J.C. Loudon, *An Encyclopaedia of Agriculture*, London,
Longman, Hurst, Rees, Orme, Brown and Green, 1826, p.761.

Tuesday 21

Misty Morning but Clear.d and Droughty I and 2 Brother Graved till noon
& Hack,t in the Afternoon and J. Midgley Hack't most of the day

Wednesday 22

a Fine Droughty day I and Brothers and Ja^s [and] Midgley Hacked and
Spread Lime and Ashes
Wm Acroyd Preached at our house in the Evening from the 7 chapter of
Micah and 9 verse

Thursday 23

a Fine Mild day for the Season I and Brothers Jno & Abraham & Jas Midgley
Sowed and [H] Harrow,d all day

Friday 24

a Dull day and Some Drizling Rain and More heavy Rain in the Evening
I and Brothers Jno and Abraham & Ja^s Midgley Harrowing & F urrow.d all
day

Saturday 25

a Mild Warm day I went Halifax after 3 O clock in the Afternoon Some
Rain in the Night

4 ½ Days Graveing	0. 11. 3
4 Days Hacking	0. 10. 0
8 Days Spreading Ashes Harrowing	1. 0. 0
9 Months poor Cess[8]	3 8 4
	15[8]9 7

Sunday 26

a Dull day and Heavy Showers of Rain in the Afternoon & in the Night I
heard Wm Acroyd Preach both Morning and afternoon from 2 ^{Ep} of
Thesalonians 3 Chapter and 5 verse

Monday 27

a Dull Mild day and some Rain in the Night I was Employd in laying up
the Dung Hill and other jobbs In Cleaning in the lathe [and] and Yard

Bro^t Over	15. 8. 7

---

[8] Poor Cess: the poor rate.

Tuesday 28
a Dull Cold Droughty I was Empoyd in Spreading Mole Hills and Dung in the lathe Croft and Went Illingworth in the Evening

Wednesday 29
a Verry Cold day and light Showers of Snow and Hail in the Afternoon and in the Night
29 I and Brother John was working in the Garden and Meadows
2 Day labour in the fields   0 5 0
                                                               15 18 7

Thursday 30
a Verry Windy Coly and Some Showers of Snow and Rain I went to Hipperholm Coly and Northowram in the afternoon
Edmund Marsden Came from Ewood Hall to Stop a few days with with us

Friday 31
a Droughty Cold day I was Emplyd in Breaking Clod and Whicking[9] in the Afternoon

Saturday April 1
a Verry Cold Day and Some light Showers of Hail I and Brothers Jno & Abraham and Hiram Spencer and self was breaking Clods all day

Sunday 2
a Dull Cold day and Showers of Snow I heard William Acroyd Preach both Morning and afternoon from Hebrews 7 Chapter and 25 verse Last Clause
Sarah Crowther Came from Manchester to See us   V

Monday 3
a Dull Cold and heavy Showers of Snow I and Brothers John & Abraham Hiram Spencers was Employd in breaking Clods till 5 O clock in the afternoon

---

[9] Probably a variant of whacking, which in this case would mean striking the clods to break them up. See Diary entry for Tuesday 4 April 1809, below, where Ashworth writes 'Whecking'.

Tuesday 4
a Dull Cold day and Showers of Snow I and Brothers John and was Employ
in the afternoon in Breaking Clod in Sundoor field

Bro^t Over	15.13. 7
4 days Whecking and Breaking Clods	1 7 6
	17 1 1

Wednesday 5
a Dull Cold day I was Employd in lathe Croft and Sundoor Field

Thursday 6
a Dull Soft day and Rather Milder Air In the afternoon I went into foreside
Swill Hill and Bradshaw

Friday 7
a Dull Cold and light Showers of Rain in the Night

Jane Hartley,^s Child died this morning	D
Wm Wadsworth at Haily Hill was Buried	D
Thos Bwititt was Buried on the 6 of the Month	

Saturday 8
a Dull Mild day and a little Rain in the Night I went to Halifax the
afternoon
Little Cow Cover,d 2 time

Sunday 9
a Dull day and a Little Rain in the Morning I heard William Acroyd Preach
both Morning and afternoon from the 2 Epistle to the Corninthians 5
Chapter and 10 verse

Widdow Mitchell died	D
John Varely at Brockholes was Buried this day	D
Mariah Midgley died	D
Miss Priestley in King Cross lane died this Week	D

Monday 10

a Dull Windy day and Showers of in Rain both in the day and in the Night
I work.d in the Sun door field Most of the day
1 Days work in the Sun door field   0 2 6
Mr Thos Ramsden died   D

Tuesday 11

a Dull Cold day and heavy Showers of Snow and Hail and Some Rain and
froze hard in the Night I went Halifax in the Evening
Sarah Crowther Sett off for home to Manchester   V
Brot Over   17 1 1

Wednesday 12

A Cold Droughty day and Showers of Rain in the Night I was Employd in
Picking Pottatoes for Setting

Thursday 13

a Dull day and Showers

Friday 14

a Dull Cold day with Heavy Showers of Rain and Snow I went to the
Funeral of Thomas Ramsden in the afternoon

Saturday 15

a Mild Droughty day I went to Halifax in the afternoon
Paid for Moles Catching   0 1 6
                                                                 17. 5. 1

Sunday 16

A verry Cold day a High Wind and Much Snow and Rain almost without
Intermision from Morning till Night and in the Night also
I heard Wm Acroyd Preach both Morning & afternoon from Isiah 19
Chapter from the 18 verse to the end of the Chapter

Monday 17

a Cold frosty day with frequent Showers of Snow and Hail I was Mostley
Employd in the House
froze hard in the Night

Tuesday 18
a Dull frosty day and Showers of Snow and Hail and froze hard in the
Night
Richard
Bro^t Over   17 5 1.

Wednesday 19
a Dull Cold day with Showers of Snow and Rain and froze hard in the
Night Mr Cockin Preach.d with us in the Evening from 1 of Peter's Chapter
& 9 verse

Thursday 20
a Dull Cold day and froze hard in the Night I went to our Church Meeting
in the Evening

Friday 21
a Dull Cold day and Rain and Snow in the Evening In the Afternoon I went
into Warely Skircoat & Halifax

Saturday 22
[a Bright Cold day I heard Wm Acroyd Preach from John,^s Gospel 3 Chapter
and 3 verse both Morning and afternoon]
a Cold Droughty day I went to Halifax in the afternoon Joseph Firth Came
to see us in the Evening   V

Sunday 23
a Bright Cold Droughty day I heard Wm Acroyd Preach both Morning and
Evening from John,^s Gospel 3 Chapter and 3 verse and in the Evening
at Thos Priestly in Wheatley,^s in Wheatley from the 42 Psal and 11 verse

Monday 24
a Droughty day and Rather Milder James Howarth Came to see us this
Evening

Tuesday 25
a Fine Droughty day till 4 O clock in the Evening James Howarth Set off
For Home this Evft[enin]

Wednesday 26

a Dull day and Frequent Showers of Rain Brothers John and Abr^m and Self was Employd in Setting Pottatoes

Thursday 27

a Dull day and some Drizling Rain in the day and Some in the Night

Friday 28

a Cold Droughty Windy day I and Brothers John and Abraham was Employd in Setting Potatoes all day and Finished Setting for this Year

28 Bro^t Over	17 5 1
6 Days labour in Setting Pottatoes	0 15 0
	18 0 1

Saturday 29

a Fine Cold Droughty day I went to Moor Side and Halifax in the afternoon

Sunday 30

a Cool Droughty and Some Rain in the Evening I heard Wm Acroyd Preach both Morning and Afternoon from Epistles to the Ephesians Chap 4 and 18 verse

Monday May 1

a Fine Droughty Cool day and a Little Rain in the afternoon

Tuesday 2

a Fine Droughty Cool day I went to Farsley with William Acroyd Minister at Halifax

Wednesday 3

a Fine Droughty Cool day I heard Mr William Acroyd of Halifax Preach in the Morning from the Epistle to the Romans 8 Chapter and 1 verse
and Mr Banister[10] from Genesis 49 Chapter & 10 verse and Mr Steadman[11] Preached in the afternoon from Exodus 3 Chapter and 14 verse

---

[10] Mr Banister has not been traced.
[11] William Steadman was visiting the north of England at this time preparatory to accepting the pastorate of Westgate Church, Bradford, which he combined with the presidency of the nascent Baptist Academy there.

Thursday 4
a Dull Wet Morning but Clear.d and was Droughty in the afternoon Ja^s
Midgley Set off to Leeds to take the Coach for London
Bro^t Over   18 0 1

Friday 5
a Dull Cool day day

Saturday 6
a Bright Droughty I went to Halifax in the afternoon and the Weather
changed to be a Little warmer in the Evening

Sunday 7
a Bright warm day I heard Wm Acroyd Preach from the 1st Epistle 1 of Peter
5 Chapter and 6 & 7 verses both Morning and afternoon

Monday 8
a Fine Warm day I went to Halifax in the Afternoon with 3 Chars to mend

Tuesday 9
a Fine Hot day I went to Halifax in the Morning with 3 Chars to Mend

Wednesday 10
a Fine Hot Droughty day

Thursday 11
a Hot Droughty day

Friday 12
a Hot Droughty day
Bro^t Over   18 0 1
To 3 days labour in Sowing Hay Seeds and Rolling our Oats   0 7 6
                                                                18 7 7
                                                                    V

Saturday 13
a Hot Droughty day [M]Thos Marsden and his wife Came to our House this
Night

Sunday 14
a Fine Warm Droughty I heard William Acroyd Preach

Monday 15
a Fine Hot day and Droughty

Tuesday 16
a Fine Hot day and Droughty
Mrs Rhodes came on a Visit   V

Wednesday 17
A Fine Hot Droughty

Thursday 18
a verry hot [and]day with Thunder Hail and Rain in the Evening
Bro^t Over   18 7 7

Friday 19
a Hot day with Tunder and Heavy Shower of Rain
Mrs Rhodes returned home and 2 of her Daughters Came on a Visit to our
house   V

Saturday 20
a Hot day and Heavy Showers of Rain the Evening and in the Night

Sunday 21
a Hot day and Much Rain I heard William Acroyd Preach in the Morning
From (*blank*) and the afternoon he Preach^d a Funeral Sermon from Hannah
Marsden

Monday 22
a Hot droughty Thos Marsden & his wife and his Son Edmund and Daughter
Susanah and 2 Miss Rhodes^s went to Hathershelf

Tuesday 23
a Hot doughty day I went to Halifax to See to Grave Stone laid upon
Hannah Marsden and a Monument set up at the Head of her Grave.

Wednesday 24

a Hot Sultery day I and Brother John was Employd in filling up Ditched in the Holms till 4 O clock and Pulling Hemlock up after[noon] till Night

Thursday 25

a Dull [h]Misty day verry hot and Much Rain in the Night Brother Jnᵒ and I Pull,d Hemlock all day

Friday 26

a Dull hot day and a Bundance of Rain in the Night I and Broʳ John Pulled Hemlock & Thistles

Broᵗ Over   18 7 7
6 Days labour in Holms filling up the Ditches and Weeding
in the Meadow and Summer Pastures   15 0
                                                                               19 2 7

Saturday 27

a Dull hot day I went to Halifax in the afternoon Jas, Thoˢ and Miss,ˢ Rhoda and Theo Rhodes return,d from Hathershelf to our house Mʳ Sheaniah Rhodes Junʳ Came for his sister Theo¹²

Sunday 28

a Dull hot day and Heavy Showers of Rain at Noon & in the Evening
I heard Wᵐ Acroyd Preach both Morning and afternoon from 51 Psalm and 11 verse
Mʳ Sheaniah and his Sister returned home
Mary Chambers of Halifax died this day   D

Monday 29

a Dull hot day and Rain,d Heavily Most of the day till 6 O clock in the Evening & in the Night
Son Thoˢ Marsden went to Hathershelf in the Evening

Tuesday 30

a Dull hot day and Some rain in the Night I went to Halifax in the Evening
Thoˢ & Edmund Came back this Morning   V

---

12 Sheaniah or Shechaniah and Theodora Rhodes were children of Shechaniah and Susannah Rhodes and niece and nephew of the Diarist.

Wednesday 31
a Dull warm and Much in the afternoon and in the Night Also
Paid to John Hauldsworth Overseer for Poor Cess   2 19 9 ½
Broᵗ Over   19 2 7
         22 2 4½

Thursday June 1
a Dull day and heavy Showers of a Heavy Showers of Rain Son and
Daughter and their Children Came from Hathershelf

Friday 2
a Dull Warm day and Much Rain both Morning and Afternoon
Son and Daughter ᴹᵃʳˢᵈᵉⁿ went to Howarth
a verry High Wind this day Especialley in the Evening

Saturday 3
a Warm day and Rain in the Evening I went to Halifax Son & Daughter
Marsden return.d from Howarth

Sunday 4
a Warm day and frequent and Heavy Showers of Rain I heard Wᵐ Acroyd
Preach both Morning and afternoon from Galatians 3 Capter and 29 verse

Monday 5
a Dull day and heavy Showers of Rain in the Afternoon My Son Thoˢ and
his wife and 2 Children Edmund and Susannah and William Norminton
and his wife Set off from Halifax for London this Morning
Michael Midgley was hurt this day

Tuesday 6
a verry Windy day and frequent and heavy Showers of Rain in the day and
Much Rain in the Night

Wednesday 7
a Dull day and light of Rain in the day and Some Rain in the Night
Son Thoˢ Marsden and his Daughter Susannah and Mrˢ Norminton his
Sister in Law Got to London at Noon

Thursday 8
a Bright Droughty day I worked in the Garden all the day
Bro^t Over   22 2 4 ½

Friday 9
a Dull day with Some light Showers of Rain I worked in Hoeing the
Pottatoes till 4 O clock and Went to Halifax in the Evening

Saturday 10
a Dull warm day and verry Heavy Show^{rs} of Rain in the afternoon I went to
Halifax after 3 O clock in the afternoon

Sunday 11
a Bright Droughty day I heard William Acroyd Comment on 17 verses in
the 2 Chapter of the General Epistle of James and Preach.d in the afternoon
from the 18 verse
Widdow Priestley was buried   D

Monday 12
a Dull day with Light Showers of Rain
Paid for [O]Cow called old Brear Covering   0 1 0

Tuesday 13
a Dull Morning and light Showers of Rain but Clear.d in the Afternoon
Bought a Black Cow Price   7 15 0
Bro^t Over   22. 2 4 ½
                                                                            29 18 4 ½

Wednesday 14
a Dull day and Showers of Rain in the Afternoon Mr Sugden from Skipton[13]
Preached at our House in the Eveng. from the 70 Psalm and 24 verse[14]

Thursday 15
a Dull day and Moderate Droughty I went to our Church Meeting In the
Evening

---

[13] Rev. Benjamin Sugden, minister of the Independent Chapel, Skipton, 1799-1809.
[14] Ashworth must have recorded this incorrectly because Psalm 70 has only five verses.

Friday 16
a Dull day and Showers of Rain in the Afternoon I work.d In the Hooing of Pottatoes

Saturday 17
a Dull Cool Windy day with I went Halifax in the Afternoo^n

Sunday 18
a Bright Cool Droughty day I heard Willliam Acroyd Preach both Morning and afternoon from Proverbs [3]12 Chapter and 3 verse

Monday 19
a Windy Droughty day I work.d in our Gate field in Walling and Weeding (*blank*) Wainhouse near King[15] Hanged himself till he was Dead this Morning

Tuesday 20
a Warm Droughty day I work.d in Gate Field and long Field Most of the day
Bro^t Over   29. 18. 4 ½

Wednesday 21
a Hot Droughty day I worked in Gate Field long Field and Little Field Most of the day

Thursday 22
a Hot Droughty day I went Halifax in the Morning & came back at Noon

Friday 23
a Droughty Hot day I work.d in the Fields till till 5 O clock and went Halifax after 6 O clock

Saturday 24
a Hot Droughty day I work.d the Field Most of day

---

[15] Ashworth probably intended to write King Cross here.

Sunday 25
a Hot Droughty day I heard Wm Acroyd Preach in the Morning from the 119 Psalm 3 & 4 verse and in the afternoon from 37 Chapter of Ezekiel 37 Chapter and 10 verse

Monday 26
a Hot Bright Droughty I went to Halifax in the Morning and Pulled up Weeds in the [f]Corn in the afternoon
Bro^t Over   29 18 4 ½

Tuesday 27
a Dull hot day a Heavy Showers Showers Rain in the Afternoon I was Employd in the Evening in Pulling up Weeds in the field

Wednesday 28
a Dull hot day with Some light Showers of Rain I was Employed in Pulling Weed in field

Thursday 29
a Dull hot day I was Employ.d in the Morning weeding and Went to Ewood Hall in the Afternoon

Friday 30
a Dull hot day I and Brother John [and Abra^m Longbottom in] Weeding the Corn [and afternoon I went to]

Saturday July 1
a Dull hot day I and Brother John and br^m Longbottom was weeding Corn in the Morning and I went To Halifax in the (*blank*)

Sunday 2
a Bright Droughty day day I went to Halifax and heard William Acroyd Preach both Morning and afternoon and in the Evening at Thos Priestley^s near Illingworth from Hoshea 14 Chap in an and 1st verse Much Rain in the Night

Monday 3
a Dull day and Heavy Rain in the Morning and After 2 Oclock in the
Afternon I and Brother John Ashworth and Abraham Longbottom Weeded
Corn from 10 O clock in the Morning till 2 in the Afternoon

Tuesday 4
a Dull day and Showers of Rain in the afternoon I went to Halifax in the
Afternoon
Bro^t Over   29 18 4 ½

Wednesday 5
a Dull day and Heavy Showers of Rain the after I weeded in Patures

Thursday 6
a Dull day an Light Showers in the afternoon I went to Warely and
Sowerby Bridge

Friday 7
a Dull day and Droughty till till 4 O clock and Some Rain in the Evening
12 days weeding our Oats a Hoeing Pottatoes   1 10 0
Weeding the Pastures 4 Days by Self   0   8 0

Saturday 8
a Bright Hot day and a High Wind
I went to Hipperholm and Halifax after 10 clock in the Morning
Paid for 2 Dozen of Lime   2   2 0
                                                                  33 18 4½

Sunday 9
a Bright Cool day I heard Wm Acroyd in the Morning from 23 Psalm and 3
verse and the Afternoon from Isiah 40 chapter 6.7 & 8 verses

Monday 10
a Bright Droughty day I was Employd in Weeding in our Summer Pastures

Tuesday 11
a Bright Droughty day I was Weeding till 4 O clock and went to Halifax in
the Evening

Wednesday 12

a Bright Droughty day till 5 O clock and Wet in the Evening Wᵐ Acroyd Preach.d at our In the Evening from 4 Chapter of Matthew and 31 verse

Thursday 13

a Dull Soft[16] Morning and Clear.ᵈ about 10 ᴼ clock we began Mowing our Grass this Morning

Had 6 hay Makers after 10 Oclock

Broᵗ Over   33 18 4½

Friday 14

a Dull Morning and a little about 11 O clock we had 5 hay Makers all the day

Saturday 15

a Dull Morning and Drizling Rain till Noon we had 6 hay Makers till 8 O clock in the Evening

Sunday 16

a Bright Droughty day Mʳ Aston from Lockwood[17] Preach at our Chappel in the Morning from the 4 Chapter of Markˢ Gospel 37. 38 & 39 verses in the Afternoon from Zechariah 3 Chapter

Monday 17

a Dull Morning but Clear.d before noon we had [6]7 Hay Makers all day

Mrs Charnock wife of Mʳ James Charnock Minister at Howorth Church[18] was buried this day

Tuesday 18

a Bright Droughty day till afternoon we had 7 Hay Maker all the day

Wednesday 19

a Droughty ᵈᵃʸ but Dull at times in the afternoon we had 7 Hay Makers all day

Broᵗ Over   33 18 4½

_____

[16] Soft: mild.

[17] Rev. James Aston, minister of Lockwood Baptist Chapel near Huddersfield, 1805-1830.

[18] Rev. James Charnock was incumbent at Haworth from 1791 to 1819.

Thursday 20
a Dull hot day We had 6 Hay Makers all day

Friday 21
a Dull hot day we had 7 Hay Makers

Saturday 22
a Bright hot day we had 6 Hay Makers and finish,ᵗ our hay Makeing this day
Broᵗ
54 Days labour in Hay Makeing at 2/6 Per Day Per Man   6. 15. 0
Money & Boarding for Mowers   2   1   9
                                                              42 15 1½

Sunday 23
a Bright Hot day I heard Thoˢ Meller ᶠʳᵒᵐ ᴸᵒᶜᵏʷᵒᵒᵈ Preach at our Chappel both Morning and afternoon Philipeans 3 Chapter and 27 verse [19]

Monday 24
a Dullish day but verry hot I went Halifax in the Evening

Tuesday 25
a Hot Droughty day I went to Warely [and]in the afternoon and Came back by Way of Halifax

Wednesday 26
a Hot Droughty day I went to Halifax in the Afternoon

Thursday 27
a Hot Droughty day My Son Mʳ E. Marsden Came to our House this Night
I went to our Church Meeting this Evening   V
Broᵗ Over   42. 15. 1½

Friday 28
a Dull warm day and Severᵃˡ Showers of Rain both in the day and in the Night

---

[19] No information on Mr Meller from Lockwood has been found.

Saturday 29
a Dull warm and heavy in the Afternoon and in the Night I went to Halifax after 4 O clock

Sunday 30
a Dull Hot day I went to Halifax & Heard Wm Acroyd Preach both both Morning & afternoon from the 12th of Matthew and 35 verse

Monday 31
a Dull warm day I went to Halifax with my Son Edmund In the afternoon

Tuesday August 1
a Dull Hot day My Son Edmund went to Wakefield & Huddersfield and Returned in the Evening

Wednesday 2
a Dull hot day and heavy Showers of Rain in the day time and Much Rain in the Night
Bro^t Over   42 15. ½

Thursday 3
a Hot day with Some Showers

Friday 4
a Warm day I and my wife and Son Ja^s Midgley and his wife and Son Edmund Marsden Went to Hathershelf and Returned home in the Evening

Saturday 5
A warm day and Droughty till noon and verry wet in the afternoon I and Son Edmund went to Halifax and Return.d home to Dinner

Sunday 6
a Dull hot day and frequent Showers of Rain I heard William Acroyd Preach in the Morning from John ^Lukes Gospel 18 Chapter and 7 verse and in the afternoon from Isiah 6 Chapter 4 of the first verses

Monday 7

a Fine warm Droughty day I went to Halifax in the Morning my Sons Ja^s
Midgley and Edmund Marsden Set of for Liverpool this Morning

Tuesday 8

a Fine Warm day I was Employd this day in Sundry Jobbs in Husbandry

Wednesday 9

a Dull hot day I [was]and Brother John and James Wadsworth was
Employd in Leading our Dung till 2 O clock
I and Brother John was Employd in Spreading Dung after 2 O clock Mr
Cockin Preach at our house in the Evening from Ephesians 5 Chapter and 1
& 2 verse

Thursday 10

a Dull gloomy hot Morning and Much Thunder and verry heavy Rain in
the afternoon
Brother John and I Spread Dung till noon and Thos Priestley assisted us in
triming up the Hay Mow[20] in the afternoon there was a flood in the
Evening

Friday 11

a Dull hot day and frequent Showers of Rain I and Brother Spread Dung
Most of the day My Son Edmund Returned from Liverpool in the Eveng

Saturday 12

A Dull Hot day I and Brother John Spread Dung till noon there was
Thunder and heavy Rain in the afternoon

Bro^t Over	42.	15	1½
Dung Leading	0	7	6
D^o Spreading other work in the fields 6 Days labour	0	15	0
	43	17	7½

Sunday 13

a Dull hot day I heard Wm Acroyd Preach in the Morning from 6 Chapter of
Matthews Gospel from the 9 to the 14 vers in afternoon Deuteronom^ie 30
Chapter & 19 verse

---

[20] Hay mow: a haystack.

Monday 14
a Dull hot day with frequent Showers of Rain I went to Halifax after 5 O clock in the Evening

Tuesday 15
a Dull hot day and frequent Showers of Rain My Son E Marsden Son and Daughter Midgley and Sister Rhodes Sett off in the afternoon for Gomersall

Wednesday 16
a Dull hot day with frequent Showers of Rain I work,d in the fields a Little

Thursday 17
a Dull hot day I went to Halifax in the afternoon

Friday 18
a Dull hot day and Some Light Showers of in the afternoon
Brot Over   43 17 7 ½

Saturday 19
a Dull hot day and Thunder & heavy Showers of Rain in the afternoon I went to Halifax in the afternoon

Sunday 20
a Dull hot and Some Showers of Rain I heard William Acroyd Preach both Morning and Afternoon from the 16 Chapter of Mark & 16 verse

Monday 21
a Bright Droughty day Mr Harrison of Berry[21] came to our house in the afternoon

Tuesday 22
a Dull Warm day and Showers of Rain in the Afternoon Mr Harrison Preached at our house in the Evening from 14 Chapter of Matthew and 28 verse

_____

[21] Joseph Harrison from Bury, Lancashire, preached frequently in the Halifax/Bradford area and was instrumental in building AllertonIndependent Chapel at Bradford in 1814..

Wednesday 23
a Bright day with Some Showers of Rain
the above Harrison went from our house to Halifax

Thursday 24
a Dull warm day with Showers of Rain
I went to our Church Meeting
Brot Over   43 17 7 ½

Friday 25
a Dull warm day and Showers of Rain

Saturday 26
a Dull warm day and heavy Showers of Rain in the Afternoon
I went to Halifax in the afternoon

Sunday 27
a Dull warm Morning and Some Showers of Rain I heard Wm Acroyd
Preached both Morning from (*blank*)

Monday 28
a Bright Droughty Morning but Dull and Wet in the Afternoon

Tuesday 29
a Dull warm day and Some Light Showers of Rain in the Evening

Wednesday 30
a Bright warm Morning and and heavy Showers of Rain in the afternoon
we put our cows to Grass this Morning

Thursday 31
[a Dull day and Some Showers of Rain in the Afternoon] a Bright Droughty
Hot day

Friday September 1
a Bright Hot Droughty day
I was Employd Weeding & Digging in Our Garden

Saturday 2
a Dull Misty Morning and Rainy in the afternoon I went to Halifax after 3
O clock Much Rain in the Night

Sunday 3
a Dull hot day and Showers of Rain in the afternoon I heard Wᵐ Acroyd
Comment on the 14 Chapter of Exodus and in the afternoon
Preached from the 15 of the Chapter
Sarah Crowther Came to See us

Monday 4
a Dull hot day and a little in the Afternoon and Some Rain in the Night
Son & Daughter Jaˢ and Sarah Midgley went up to their House

Tuesday 5
a Dull hot day and some little Rain I went to Halifax in the Afternoon

Wednesday 6
a Dull hot day and frequent and heavy Showers of Rain and Thunder and
Lightening and Heavy Rain in the Evening
William Acroyd Preached at our house in the Evening from Hebrews 13
Chapter and the 8 verse

Thursday 7
a Dull hot day and Some thunder and Lightening and heavy Showers of
Rain

Paid for the Cow called Red Brear Covering		0 1 0
Broᵗ Over	0 ~ ~	43 17 7½
		43 18 7½

Friday 8
a Dull Morning but Clear and Droughty in the afternoon we had 4 Reapers
in the afternoon

Saturday 9
a Fine Droughty day we had 4 Reapers all day

Sunday 10
a Dull hot day and Heavy Show^{rs} of Rain in the Afternoon I heard William
Acroyd Preach in the in the afternoon from the 2 Epistle to the Corinthians
4 Chapter and 16 verse and Commented on the 15 Preceding verses

*(At this point Ashworth must have turned over two pages in his Diary; so the week
commencing Monday 11th September is written in the pages printed for 18 to 24
September. Ashworth realised his mistake, corrected the dates in the margin and
then wrote the next week up on the pages printed for 11 to 17 September. The
transcript follows the amended and correct order.)*

Monday [18] 11
a Dull Morning and a Little Rain in the Morning but Droug^{hty} in the
Afternoon we had 4 Reapers and finish,d Reaping our Oats at 2 O clock in
the Afternoon

8 days labour Reaping	1 0 0
2 Days labour in other Husbandry	0 5 0

Tuesday [19] 12
a Fine Droughty day I was Employd Repairing Yard in the Afternoon

Bro^t Over	44 19 7½

Wednesday [20] 13
a Dull hot day and Some Rain in the daytime and Much Rain in the Night

Thursday [21] 14
a Dull Rainy day till the Evening and not Much Rain in the Night

Friday [22] 15
a Dull day and Some Showers of Rain in the Morning I work,d in Repairing
our Yard

Paid for the Cow Called Prichet covering	0 1 0
	45 5 7½

Saturday [23] 16
a Dull Morning and Rain in the Morning and a Little in the Afternoon I
went to Halifax afternoon after 4 O clock

Sunday [24] 17
a Dull day & Rather Cooler and Some Rain at Noon I heard Wᵐ Acroyd
Preach both Morning & afternoon from Isiah 52 Chapter and 7 verse

by Mistake turned Over 2 leaves

Monday [11] 19
A very Wet Droughty ᵈᵃʸ I went to Halifax To attend the Funerals of James
Sutcliff and his Son John Sutcliff

John died on Sunday at 10 O clock in the night and his Father at		D
4 O clock on Monday Morning		D
& James Hirst died this Morning		D

Tuesday [12] 18
a verry Wet day Indeed

Wednesday [13] 20
a Wet day and Rain the Night

Thursday [14] 21
a Fine Drough day I went to our Church Meeting Jaˢ Hirst was Buried this
day

Friday [15] 22
a Wet Dull Morning but Droughty in the Afternoon [and Much Rain in the
Night]

Broᵗ Over	43	18	7½
Paid 8 Months window Money to George Child on the 18 Instant 1	1	0	
	44	19	17½
Mr Henry Swaine Calld to se us			V
Abram Vickers died			D

Saturday [16] 23
a Dull Wet Morning but Clear.d a little but Heavy Showers in the
Afternoon I went Halifax in the afternoon

Sunday [17] 24
a Dull day and Frequent Showers of Rain I heard Wm Acroyd Preach in the Morning from the 46 Psalm and Part of the 10 verse and in the afternoon from Philipians 1 Chapter and 3. 4 & 5 verses

Monday 25
a Dull day and frequent Showers of Rain I went to Shaw Lane and Houldsworth in afternoon
Bro^t Over   45 5 7½

Tuesday 26
a Dull Rainy day and Rain in the Night

Wednesday 27
a Dull wet Morning and Showers of Rain in the afternoon
I carried Hops to Moorside Shaw lane and Into Houldsworth

Thursday 28
a Dull Soft Morning and Wet but Clear.d and Droughty in the afternoon I and Brother John took the Hood off our Hattocks in the afternoon
verry Droughty in the afternoon and a frosty Night

Friday 29
a verry Droughty day we had 4 Men who Open.d all our Sheaves and Spread them and Got them all Housed that Night

Saturday 30
a Dull Soft Morning Clear.d in the afternoon Brother John and I laid up our Corn in the lathe and began Thrashing in the afternoon
the Cow Call.d Red Brear was Cover.d 2 time

Sunday October 1
a Dull Mild warm I heard William Acroyd Preach in the Morning from Hebrews 9 Chapter and 28 verse and the afternoon from Jeremiah 3 Chapter and 19 verse
Mary Butterworth in Halifax Buried this Evening   D

Monday 2

a Dull Soft Morning but Clear.d a Little in the afternoon Brother John and
Son James Midgley and Self thrash,ᵈ Oats to Day

Paid for a Hand Staff for a Thrashing Instrument	0 0 6
Broᵗ Over	45 5 7½

Tuesday 3

a Dull hot Morning but Clear.d a Little in the afternoon we had the above 2
Thrashers all day And I Shaked Straw

Paid Composition for the Roads to John Illingworth	0 18 0

Wednesday 4

I Dull hot Morning we had the above 2 Thrashers and I Shaked Straw And
there a little Drought in the Afternoon

Mʳ Cockin Preached at our house in the Evening from Isiah 63 Chapter and
9 verse

Thursday 5

a Dull hot Morning but Clear.d a Little in the Afternoon we finishd
thrashing and Winnow.d the Oats and got them to the Mill and in 68
Hattocks we had 118 Strikes of Oats & 6 Strikes Light Corn

Friday 6

a Dull hot Morning but Cleard a Little in the afternoon

To 8 day Housing and driying and laying our Oats	1 0 0
To 12 days labour Thrashing and Winnowing	1 10 0
	48. 14. 1½

Saturday 7

a Fine Mild day I went to Halifax in the Afternoon there was a Little Frost
in the Night

Sunday 8

a Mill Droughty day I heard Wᵐ Acroyd Preach from Malachiah Chapter 7
and 9 verse and in the afternoon from Romans 7 Chapter and 19 verse

Monday 9
a Cool Droughty day and a Little frost in the Night
Bro^t Over   48. 14. 1½

Tuesday 10
a Cool Droughty day Excepting a Little Rain at Noon I Made at the Mill
and in 7 quarters and 5 Strikes of Oats had 3 Loads of Shilling
Paid for Oats Drying   0 2 5
                                                                            48. 16. 6½

I heard Mr Gadsby Preach in Evening[22]

Wednesday 11
a Cool Droughty day I went to Halifax in the Evening to Fetch the Doctor
to Brother John

Thursday 12
a Dull Cold Droughty day I had Pain in my Back and head to day but
Walked a bout Most of the day
Froze hard in the Night

Friday 13
a Bright Cold Droughty and froze hard in the Night I laid in Bed till Noon
of Pain my head & Back

Saturday 14
a Fine Droughty Cold ^day I Stayd at all day Indisposed in health not fit to go
out froze in the ^Night

Sunday 15
a Bright Cold but Dull and Wet in the Evening I Stay.d home all day
John Crossley at Mr Pollard Mill died this Morning
                                                                                   D

Monday 16
a Dull Soft day and the ^wind Blew from the West today
Bro^t Over   48. 16 6½

---

22 William Gadsby was pastor of the Strict Particular Baptist Church, Back Lane, Rochdale Road,
Manchester from 1805 until 1844.

Tuesday 17
a Dull Soft Morning but Clear.d at Noon Charles Widdop Thos Priestley and Self Got Pottatoes in the afternoon

Wednesday 18
a Dull Morning but at 10 O clock it Clear.d and 4 Of us Got Pottatoes in afternoon

Thursday 19
a Dull Morning and Rain.d a little at Noon 4 of us Got Pottatoes till 11 O clock
5 days labour in Getting Pottatoes   0 12. 6
                                                            49   9   ½

Friday 20
a Dull Mild day I went to Illingworth in the Evening

Saturday 21
a Dull Mild day I went to Hipperholm, Coly, Northouram, and Halifax

Sunday 22
a Dull Mild day I heard Wm Acroyd Preach in the Morning from the 1 Epistle of John 4 Chapter & 11 verse in the afternoon from Leviticus 25 Chapter and 9 and 10 verses

 Monday 23
a Dull Misty Morning but Clear.d a little in the afternoon

Tuesday 24
a Dull Misty Morning but Cleard a little before noon I went Halifax in Aftrnoon
a little Rain in the Night

Wednesday 25
a Dull Morning but Clear.d in the afternoon was hot I went to a Prayer Meeting at our Chappel
Some Rain in the Night
Brot Over   49 9 ½

Thursday 26
a Dull Rainy Morning but Clear.d before noon and was hot
Susannah Firth set off this Morning for home / Laid our Cattle in Cattle

Friday 27
a Dull hot day I assisted Richard Gar^forth in Opening a Ditch in our field called Pomfret

Saturday 28
a Dull hot day I went to Hipperholm in the afternoon

Sunday 29
a Bright Cool day I heard Wm Acroy Preach both Morning and afternoon from the 1 Epistle to the Corinthians 14 Chapter and 8 verse

Monday 30
a Bright Cool day

Tuesday 31
a Bright Cool day I went to Halifax to Assist Brother John in Carrying a Box we sent to London
I Assisted Richard Garforth in Opening the Ditch in the Bottom of Pomfret

Wednesday November 1
a Bright Cool day Nancy Pristly Came home from London
Bro^t Over   49 9 ½

Thursday 2
a Dull Cool day Calm day I Made or Rather Open,d a Ditch in our Field Called Pontefract

Friday 3
a Dull Cool day and a Little Rain in the Evening

Saturday 4
a Dull day and a Little in the [the Night]day and Much Rain in the night I went to Halifax in the afternoon

Sunday 5
a Dull day and a Little Rain in the day and Much in the Night I heard W^m
Acroyd Preach in Morning from 9 Chapter of the 1 Epistle to the
Corinthians from the 16 verse to the end of the Chapter & in the afternoon
from the 2 Epistle To Timothy 2 Chapter and 3 verse

Monday 6
a Dull day and frequent Showers of Rain I and Thos Priestley Prepared to
Build a Coal House for Nancy Priestley opposite to our Kitchin door

Tuesday 7
a Dull Mild day I Assisted in Leading Stones to build a Coal House of in
the Morning and went Halifax in the afternoon
Bro^t Over   49 9 ½

Wednesday 8
a Dull Mild day I assisted in building a Coal House till 4 O clock -- W^m
Acroyd Preached at our house in the Evening from Romans 7 Chapter and
(*blank*) verse

Thursday 9
a Dull Mild day I Assisted Thos Priestley in building a Coal House

Friday 10
a Dull day & some Drizling Rain I and Thos Priestley was Emply.^d in
Preparing a Cottage for Joseph Bl^agbrough to Dwell in at Top of our lane

Saturday 11
a Dull Mild day I and T. Priestley was Eployd in the above Named House
till 4 O clock in the Afternoon

Sunday 12
a Dull day and a little Rain in the Morning I heard William Acroyd
Comment upon the first 11 vers of the 1 Chapter of the 2 Epistle to Timothy
^& Preach from the 12 verse in the afternoon a Funeral Sermon for James
Sutcliff of Halifax.

Monday 13
A Dull ^{day} and Some Rain in the afternoon Joseph Blagborough Came to live in a House at the Top of our lane this day

Tuesday 14
a Dull day but Clear.d and froze Verry hard in the Night I and T Priestley was Cleaning and Mending our lane

Wednesday 15
a Bright Wind frosty day I was Emplyd in laying Dung and other Jobbs of Husbandry
Bro^t Over   49 9 ½

Thursday 16
a Bright frosty Windy day and a Little Snow fell in the Night I went Halifax in the afternoon

Friday 17
a Dull windy Soft day Clear.d and froze in the Night and a Some Snow fell in the Night

Saturday 18
a Dull frosty day and Much Snow fell before 4 O clock in the afternoon
our Black Cow Calved Half Past 4 O clock in the afternoon   C

Sunday 19
a Bright frosty day I heard William Acroyd Preach both Morning and afternoon from the 2 Epistle to Timothy 1 Chapter and the [Middle] last Clause of the 12 verse

Monday 20
a Dull day and Soft in the afternoon but froze hard in the Night

Tuesday 21
a Dull day and Mild in the the Wind South West I assisted Thos Priestley in Makeing 2 Coal House doors
Bro^t Over   49. 9 ½

Wednesday 22
a Dull Winday day and Some Showers of Rain

Thursday 23
a Cold Windy day and frequent Showers of Rain I went to our Church
Meeting in the Evening

16 Days labour in Repairing our Cottages	2	0	0
Wood for Coal House doors	0	3	0
Nails used to repairing Houses	0	1	0

Friday 24
a Cold Windy and Some light Showers of Rain

Poor Cess to J Houldsworth	2	11	3
	53	4	3½

Saturday 25
a Dull Soft day and Some Rain in the Night I went to Halifax about 2 O
clock in the afternoon

Sunday 26
a Dull Cold and Showers of Rain in the day and and in the Night also I
heard Wm Acroyd Comment on the 22 Psalm in the Morning and he
Preched from the 1 verse of the above Psalm

Monday 27
a Dull Mild day

Brot Over	53	4	3 ½

Tuesday 28
a Dull Mild day and froze a little in the Night I was Employd in Swilling in
the lathe Croft

Wednesday 29
a Dull Mild day we Kill,d our Hogg in the Morning and Brother John
Swilled in the afternoon

3 Days labour in Swilling in our lathe Croft	0	7	6
	53	11	9½

Thursday 30
a Dull Cold day and Wet in the afternoon and Some Rain in the Night

Friday December 1
a Dull Cold day and Rain in the afternoon and Much Rain and Snow in the Eveng and froze hard in the Night
I went to Ovenden Work house to Assist the Overseer in pay the poor their Allowance

Saturday 2
a Dull frosty day & Some Showers of Some and Rain I went to Halifax after 2 O clock

Sunday 3
a Dull day and Much Rain the afternoon and in the Night
I heard Wm Acroyd in the Morning on the 1 Chapter of the (*words crossed out and illegible*) from the 1 verse the 9 and in afternoon from the 1 Book of Samuel Chapter 6 and verse the 20

Monday 4
a Dull day and frequent Showers of Rain before Sun Sett but froze hard in the Night
Paid for Mossing William Charnocks House [23]   0 2 [3]0

Tuesday 5
a Dull and frequent Showers of Rain in the day and in the Night I went to Salter Hebble in After^noon
Bro^t Over   53 11 9½ [24]

Wednesday 6
a Dull day and Showers of Rain and Much Rain the Night

---

[23] Mossing was a process in which moss was stuffed between the stone flags of a roof from the underside. It had the same purpose as back pointing a roof, namely to make it more weather-proof. It seems to have died out in the early nineteenth century being unsuitable for roofs made of slate and perhaps also being replaced by back pointing which was the usual treatment given to slate roofs.
[24] In making this calculation Ashworth did not include the cost of mossing William Charnock's house. However in the reckoning given below on Saturday 9 December it is apparently included.

Thursday 7
a Dull windy Cold and Rain in the Night

Friday 8
a Dull windy Cold day and frequent Showers of Rain and Rain the Night
Bought a young Heifer Price   12.. 7. 0
Mr H Swain Called upon us   V

Saturday 9
a Dull Cold day I went Halifax after 2 O clock and Much Rain in the Night
Paid for a Lock for Nancy Priestleys House   0 1 3
                                                                  66 2 0½

Sunday 10
a Cold droughty day I heard Willm Acroyd Comment on the 1 Chapter of
the Revelation from the 8 verse to the End of the Chapter In the afternoon
he Preached from the 3 Chapter of Johns Gospel and 16 verse 1 Part of it

Monday 11
a Cold day with frequent Showers of Snow Hal and Rain Mr Swaine Set off
for London by way of Liverpool
Brot Over   66. 2 ½

Tuesday 12
a Dull day and heavy Showers of Snow and Rain and Some Rain in the
Night

Wednesday 13
a Dull day and frequent Showers of Snow and Rain both in the day and in
the Night froze in the Night
Mr Cockin Preached at our house Night in the Evening from Galations 3
Chapter and 2 verse

Thursday 14
a Dull day and froze hard till 8 O clock in the Evening and verry high wind
and Much Rain in the Night

Friday 15
a Cold Windy day and Rather Soft I went to Salter Hebble Wharf in the afternoon

Saturday 16
a Fine Mild day for the Season I walked to Farsley in the afternoon

Sunday 17
a Dull Cold and Much Snow fell in the Night after 4 O clock I heard John Sharp[25] Preach in the Morning from Ephesians 4 Chapter & 30 verse In the afternoon from 2 Epistle to the Thesalonians 2 Chapter & 14 verse and the Evening at Calverly Mill from Judges 3 Chapter & 20 verse

Monday 18
a Mild day but verry wet as there fell Much Drizling Rain
Bro^t Over   66 2 ½

Tuesday 19
a Mild dull day I walk from Farsley to Home before 5 O clock in the Evening

Wednesday 20
a Dull day and a little Rain at Different times in the Course of the day

Thursday 21
a Dull Mild day I assisted Job Hasleden in Setting Our Oven and Boiler
[Thos] Michael Lonsdale died   D

Friday 22
a Dull day and Much Rain in the afternoon

Saturday 23
a Dull day and froze hard in in the Night I went to Halifax after 2 O clock

---

[25] Rev. J. Sharpe was pastor of the Baptist congregation at Farsley from 1807 to 1824.

Sunday 24

a Dull frosty day I heard William Acroyd Comment on the 8.9.10 & 11 verses of the 2 Chapter of the Revelations and in the afternoon heard John Walton from Sutton Preach from Solomon,s Song 5 Chapter & 16 verse T. Priesley died[26]

Monday 25

a Dull and Drizling Rain in the day and Much Rain in the Night I went to our Church Meeting in afternoon

Tuesday 26

a Dull day and Some Drizling Rain in the day and froze in the Night

Wednesday 27

a Fine Mild day and froze hard in the Night

Bro^t Over   66 2 ½

Thursday 28

a Dull Morning but Clear and Droughty the afternoon and Much Rain in the Night

Friday 29

a Dull wet Morning but but fair and verry Cold and Windy in the afternoon

Paid ½ years Property Tax to John Fearly   <u>1. 18. 0</u>

                                                                              68   0 ½

Waiting on the Cow all the past year   10. 2 ½

Self Working in the fields 3 days   <u>0. 6. 0</u>

Paid Lords Rent   <u>80 6 ½</u>

                                                                              80 10 1

Saturday 30

a Dull windy day and Much Rain in the afternoon and in the night I was Employd all day at home

Sunday 31

a Dull Mild day I heard Wm Acroyd Comment on the 2 Chap of Revelations from the 12 to the 18 verse in afternoon from Ezekiel 24 & 16.

---

[26] This comment is written in the margin.

Volume 4

1 January 1815
to
1 April 1816

This volume of the Journal is written in a small pocket book in which Cornelius Ashworth divided up each double page spread to accommodate entries for one week beginning with the Sunday. Ashworth wrote the day of the week and the date in the margin on the left-hand page. In the printed text these have been reproduced as the heading for each entry. Because the pagination of the manuscript and the printed text differ the printed text does not reproduce the year and month which Ashworth wrote at the right-hand on the top of each page as they would make no sense in the middle of a page. Where Ashworth has begun a new line the printed text also begins a new line.

[Hariot Priestley][1]

1 January Sunday[2]
a Dull frosty Some Showers of Snow in the Night I went Halifax and heard William[3] Preach both Moring and afternoon from the 1 General Epistle of John 4 Chapter and 9 verse

Monday 2
a Dull frosty foggy day I went to a Meeting at Illingworth to Consult about Entering into a Bond to Prosecute Felony[4]
Got 9 Packet of Hops Home from Salter[Hebble]

Tuesday 3
a Dull foggy frosty day

Wednesday 4
a Dull frosty and Something Clearer than yesterday I went to Deliver 6 Packets of Hops to Hannah Crossley Samuel Green and Charles Vickerman

Thursday 5
a Dull frosty Day and Some Snow fell in the Night

---

[1] This name is written many times on the verso of the cover and the first page. It is clearly not in Cornelius Ashworth's handwriting.
[2] The days of the week have been almost entirely worn away for this first week.
[3] William Ackroyd, minister of Pellon Lane Baptist Church, Halifax from 1800 to 1831.
[4] Prosecution societies were common at this period both nationally and in the West Riding. Subscribers paid into a fund which was then used to pay for prosecution of those suspected of committing crimes against members of the society.

Friday 6
a Dull frosty day I went to Shaw Lane Houldsworth and [Kipping] Jane Green near Cause way foot to look at a Cow which was upon Sale

Saturday 7
a Dull Cold frosty day I went to Salter Hebble there fell….. Snow and rain and thawed a Little in the afternoon but froze hard Hard in the Night

Sunday 8
January a verry keen frosty day I went Halifax and heard William Ackroyd Preach both morning and afternoon from the prophecy of Isiah 25 Chapter and 9 verse

Monday 9
a verry Cold [f]wet day but froze hard in the Night

Tuesday 10
a verry keen frosty day and Some Snow fell in the day and verry High wind in the Night and Some Thunder and lightening

Wednesday 11
a verry Dull frosty day a High Wind and Some Snow fell I the day and a Little in the Night Also

Thursday 12
a Dull frosty day I went into Warley Sowerby and Skircoat in the afternoon

Friday 13
a Dull frosty day I went to Shaw lane Illingworth and Ovenden Moor Side

Saturday 14
a Dull frosty day I went to Halifax in the afternoon

Sunday 15
a Dull frosty day I went [and] ^{to Halifax heard} Wm Ackroyd Preach both
Morn and afternoon from John,ˢ Gospel 16 Chapter and 8 verse
Samuel Sutcliff John Shaw and Mary Dillot was buried and all   D
Resided in Ovenden   D
                                                                       D

Monday 16
a[C] Dull frosty day I went to Halifax to a Meeting Concerning the
Inclosing the Waste lands in the Township of Ovenden
Paid for our dark Branded Cow Covering   0 1 0

Tuesday 17
a Dull frosty day there was a Sale of a Number of Lotts of Waste lands in
Ovenden at the White Lion Inn in Halifax
I went to Hipperholm & Coly in after^{noon}

Wednesday 18
a frosty day and rather Brighter than yesterday William Ackroyd Preached
at our house in the Evening from (*blank*)
Robert Snowden was buried this day   D

Thursday 19
a Dull frosty day and Some Snow fell in the Course of the day and in the
Night Also I went to our Church Meeting in the Evening

Friday 20
a Dull frosty day and Windy with a great fall of Snow

Saturday 21
a Dull frosty day and Some Snow fell in the Night I went Halifax in the
afternoon

Sunday 22
a verry frosty Dull Dull day I went to Halifax and heard William Ackroyd
Preach both Morning and afternoon from Colosians 1 Chapter & 18 and 19
verse

Monday 23
a Bright frosty day   Hariot Hariot[5]

Tuesday 24
a Bright frosty day and foggy in the Evening I went with John & William Marsden,[s] to Ewood Hall School[6]

Wednesday 25
a Dull frosty Windy day   Hariot Priestley[7]

Thursday 26
a Dull frosty Winday I was verry poorly of a Diszyness in my head and pain in My head and Back in the afternoon and in the Night

Friday 27
a Dull frosty day and a verry High Wind in the afternoon   Hariot Priestley[8]

Saturday 28
a Dull frosty day and and Windy and Snowy verry Stormy in the forenoon but Calm in the afternoon I did not go to Halifax that day

29 Sunday
a mild Soft day I Stopped at home this day as I was Pained in My head and back

Monday 30
a Milder day but rather frosty and froze hard in the Night
My head was less paind this day

Tuesday 31
a Dull Foggy rather Softer in the day time but froze hard in the Night

---

[5] This name is not in the Diarist's hand.
[6] Ewood Hall School was conducted by the Baptist minister John Fawcett at his home at Ewood Hall in Midgley. John and William Marsden were the children of Thomas and Susannah Marsden who lived in London.
[7] This name is not in the Diarist's hand.
[8] This name is not in the Diarist's hand.

Wednesday February 1
a Dull Foggy & Milder in the day but Froze hard in the Night

Thursday 2
a Dull Foggy and rather Softer in the day but froze hard in the night

Friday 3
a Dull Foggy day and froze in the Part of Night S

Saturday 4
a Mild day and thawed in the day and in the Night Also
John Savil in Wheatley died this day
our dark coloured cow was Covered 3 time

Sunday 5
February a verry Mild Bright I Staid at Home being Indisposed in body
James Hoyle in Bradshaw was Bradshaw was buried this day D

Monday 6
a Dull and Some rain in the day and Dull and Some in the Night Also
I was Much better in my head and Throat this day

Tuesday 7
a Dull Soft day and foggy in the Morning we had Son James Brother John Swilling Most of the day Brother John was Deliver.d of a Doughter B
G. Child,s sister was buried this *(blank)* D
Paid Mr Ramsbottom for the roads 0 18 0

Wednesday 8
a Dull Soft day and Showers of rain in the afternoon Brothers little Child died this day We the above 2 Men Thrashing Most of this day
Joseph Drake in Wheatley died this day D

Thursday 9
a Mild pleasant day for the Season Son James thrashed this day
Charles Hudson of Shaw Hill died this day Widdow Illingworth at Moorside died this day D D

Friday 10
a Dull Soft day Soft day but froze a Little in the Night
Brother ^{John} and Son James thrash,d this day

Saturday 11
a Dull day but froze a Little in the Night the above Men thrashed this day

Sunday 12
February a Dull day and Some Showers of rain in the afternoon I was Much better in health but not fitt to go out as I had Only been out once for 10 Days past

Monday 13
a Dull Soft Morning but Clear.d and was a little drought in the in the afternoon our thrashed our the last our Corn for this Season

Tuesday 14
a Dull Morning but Clear,d a Little in the afternoon we had Brother John and Son Ja^s was Employd 12 Days work Thrashing & Other ^{work} in Opening the Ditch in Pomfret and Other Jobbs   1 10 0

Wednesday 15
a Dull Soft day and showers of rain in the afternoon and in the Night
William Ackroyd Preached at our house in the Evening from Hebrews 12 Chapter and 1 verse

Thursday 16
a Dull day and Some rain in the Night also Alce Clayton on Illingworth Moor was buried this day   D
Expenses of Making at the Mill   0 8 0

Friday 17
a Dull day Cold and some rain in the Night   Mary butterworth[9]

Saturday 18
a Dull Mild day for the Season I went into our Barn and Some little work in Barn and Clean.d the Stable the yard and Other Jobbs

---

[9] This name is not in the Diarist's hand.

Sunday 19
a Dull day and rain in the the Night I Stopped at home I thought it was not
Safe to go out as farr as Halifax

Monday 20
a Dull day and Some rain the day and Some in the Night Also
Ann Turner Came to our house on a Visit   V

Tuesday 21
a Dull Soft with Showers of rain and rain in the Night
Paid to T Hirst for Window Mone and House duty   1 4 9

Wednesday 22
a Dull day and Some Drizling in the day but Clear.d at Night

Thursday 23
a Dull Mild day and Some in the day and Some rain in the Night Also

Friday 24
a Dull day and a Little rain
Doughter Sarah Midgley and my Grand Doughter Arrived at our house
from London this Evening near 9 O clock   V

Saturday 25
a Dull day Mild day for the Season I went to Halifax this [Evening]
Afternoon Where I had not been for near 5 weeks Kept at home through
Indisposition of body

Sunday 26
a Dull Morning but Clear.d and was Droughty in the afternoon I went to
Halifax at Noon and heard John Chambers from Warley[10] Preach from
(*blank*) froze hard in the Night
Shechaniah & Jeremiah Rhodes Came to us [11]   V V

---

[10] No information has been found about John Chambers of Warley.
[11] Shechaniah and Jeremiah Rhodes were the children of Shechaniah and Susannah Rhodes and thus
nephews of the Diarist.

Monday 27

a Bright Drought day and froze hard in the Night we had 4 Men in the afternoon

I Paid to Jaˢ Brear for a Heifer   13 12 0

Tuesday 28

a Bright Droughty day and froze hard in the Night we had 4 Men Graving [in] this day all day [and 3 Men 1 Cart and 2 Horses] and 2 Men Cutting Hay and Working in the fields this day

Wednesday 1 March

a verry fine Mild Day for and froze in the Night we had 4 Men Graving & 3 Men and 1 Cart and 2 Horses Leading Ashes in the Morning and 1 Horse in the afternoon

Expense of Ashes Leading   0 15 0

Thursday 2

a verry Mild day for the Season we had 4 Men Graving all day

Friday 3

a verry Mild day we had a Little rain in the Night had 4 Men Graveing till 11 O clock in the Morning when they finish,d the Graveing with us for this Season

Paid wages for the Graveing   1 19 0
victuals and Drink for Dᵒ   0 15 00

Saturday 4

a Dull Mild day and a Little rain I went to Halifax in the afternoon

Sunday 5

a Dull Mild day and a Little rain I went to Halifax and heard William Ackroyd Preach in the Morning from Job the 9 Chapter and 12 verse in the afternoon (*blank*)

Monday 6

a Bright warm day for the Season I and Sarah Marsden went Thomas Charnock's in Swill Hill Top

Tuesday 7
a Dull day and High Wind and Much rain both in the day and in the Night
I signed a Pettition to our Parliament against a Tax on Corn[12]
Thomas at Halifax died this day   D

Wednesday 8
a Dull day and Some Showers of rain in the day and Some Snow in the
Night Sarah wife of John Hebblethwat in Halifax was buried this day
[Next after this Rhoda Rhodes Came on a visit]   D V

Thursday 9
a verry Cold day and frost and Snow in the Night
I went Halifax in the afternoo^n Miss Rhodes

Friday 10
a Dull Cold day and a Little rain I went to Warley Skircoat [and] Sowerby
and Halifax in the afternoon

Saturday 11
a Dull Cold day and a [Little] Heavy Showers of rain in the day and a Little in
the Night Rhoda Rhodes returned home this day

Sunday 12
a Dull Cold day and Showers of Snow in the day and and Much Snow &
rain in the Night
I went Halifax and heard William Ackroyd Preach in the Morning from 5^C
& 20^v in afternoon from Acts 2 & 33

Monday 13
a Dull Cold day and rain & Snow I went to Thos Charnock,^{s} on Swill Hill
Top in the afternoon

---

[12] In the wake of an abundant harvest in 1813 and the conclusion of war with France in 1815 the price of grain had fallen rapidly. In order to secure a stable price and thus protect British farmers, Lord Liverpool's government passed an Act usually known as the Corn Law that prohibited the import of foreign grain until the price of English wheat had reached 80s. a quarter. This had the effect of keeping English grain prices artificially high and thus keeping bread prices high, which was, no doubt, the reason for Ashworth's objection.

Tuesday 14
a Dull Cold day and Showers Snow and rain in the day and rain in the
Night Thoˢ Wade at Spring Hall died this day   D

Wednesday 15
a Windy Cold day and Heavy Showers of rain both in the day and in the
Night Also
William Ackroyd Preached at our house in the Evening from Epheasians 2
Chapter and 10 verse

Thursday 16
a Bright Windy Cold Drought day and Droughty in the Night Also
Joseph Gaukroger near Mount Pellon died this week   D

Friday 17
a Dull Foggy Morning but Cleared in the afternoon was Cold and Windy
and Some in the Evening

Saturday 18
a Cold Drought day I went to Halifax in the afternoon News Came to
Halifax this week repeatedly that Bonaparte had Arrived in Paris in
France [13]

Sunday 19
a Dull Morning but Clear.d in the afternoon I went to Halifax and heard
William Ackroyd Preach in the Morning from the (*blank*)

Monday 20
a Bright Cold Drought day I was was Employ in Laying up our Dung on
the Dung Hill and Other Work in Husbandry
Hodgson in Halifax died this ᵈᵃʸ   D

---

[13] Napoleon had escaped from his imprisonment on the Isle of Elba on 28 February and arrived in Paris
on 20 March.

Tuesday 21

a Dull Windy day and Heavy Showers of rain both in the afternoon and in

14 Bushes of Seed Oats   2 12 6

Joseph[14]

Wednesday 22

a Windy wet Morning a Droughty afternoon and Heavy Showers of rain and Hail in the Evening

Doughty Sarah Midgley and Grand Daughter Sarah Marsden went to Hathershelf   V

Thursday 23

a Dull Windy day and heavy and Frequent of rain we had 4 Men Hacking till 4 O clock in the afternoon

Friday 24

a Windy Cold day and Showers of rain we had 4 Men Hacking in the forenoon and 5 in the afternoon

Saturday 25

a Windy Cold day Some Showers of rain in the Morning and froze in the Night I went to Halifax at 3 O clock in the afternoon we had 6 Men Hacking all day

Sunday 26

a Windy Cold day and frequent Showers of [rain] in the day and in the Night Also I went to to Halifax and heard William Ackroy[d] Preach in the Morning from (*blank*)

Monday 27

a Dull Windy day and verry wet in the Morning and after 4 O clock and in the Night we had 4 Men Hacking and 2 Men Spreading Ashes in the afternoon

	£ S D
16 Days Labour in Hacking	2 0 0

---

[14] Although this name is written in the section for this date it appears to belong to the entry for the following day, ie Joseph Doughty, Sarah Midgley and Grand Daughter Sarah Marsden went to Hathershelf.

Tuesday 28
a Dull day and frequent Shower^s of rain the day and Some rain Night Also our Red Cow Calved this day in the Morning

Wednesday 29
a Dull Windy day verry wet till 11 O clock in the Morning Clear.d and was Droughty in the afternoon we ad 6 Men Spreading Ashes and Harrowing

Thursday 30
a Dull warm day we had 6 Men Harrowing all day I finish,d Sowing our Oats for this Season
16 Day Harrowing & Spreading Ashes   2 0 0

Friday 31
a verry hot day for the Season I went with John and William to[School] Marsd^{en} to Ewood Hall School in the afternoon we ^{nearly} finished Harrowing our Oats in for the Season we had 6 Men Harrowing & Furrowing

Saturday 1 April
a Mild Warm day and froze a Little in the Night I went Halifax in the afternoon we had [2]4 Men Gardening this day from 10 O clock till 6 in ^{the} Evening
2 Days labour in Gardening 7/6   0 7 6

Sunday 2
a Dull Mild day for the Season I went to Halifax and heard William Ackroyd Preach in the Morning from Habakkuk 26 Chapter and 20 verse in the [f]afternoon from (*blank*)

Monday 3
a Dull Cold day we had Brother John & Son James opening Ditches in our holms preparing for takeing the Water into them
Shechainah Rhodes Came and took Sarah Marsden with him $^{to\ Gomersall}$

Tuesday 4
a Dull Cool day we had the above 2 Men Opening Ditches in holms
George Pearson,s wife died yesterd^{ay} D

Wednesday 5
a Dull Cool day and a Little Rain the day and rain and Wind in the Night
we had the above 2 Men and Self Opening Ditches and takeing Water into
our holms 6 Days labour in holms   0 15 0
Ja^s Midgley^s Daughter was buried this day   D

Thursday 6
a Dull wet windy Morning but Cleard and was Droughty in the afternoon I
went to Ovenden Moor Side and Halifax in the Evening

Friday 7
a Fine Mild Droughty day we had 3 Men regulating the Water in our holms
and Making us Gaps in our Walls 3 Days labour in the Meadows   0 7 6

Saturday 8
a Bright Drought day I went to Halifax in the afternoon by way of Warely
Town

Sunday 9
April a Droughty day and Mild for the Season I went to Halifax [in] and
heard William Ackroyd Preach in the Morning from the 19 Psalm

Monday 10
a Dull Foggy Morning but Cleard and was Droughty in the afternoon I
went Halifax in the Evening

Tuesday 11
a Dull wett Morning but Clear.d and was Droughty in the afternoon and
rain in the Night
Jonathan Shaw at Grey Stones was Married this day to Sarah Gledhill M

Wednesday 12
a verry Mild warm day WilliamAckroyd Preached at our house in the
Evening from St John,^s Gospel 13 Chapter and 15 verse
Doughter Sarah Midgley went Gomersall this day

Thursday 13
a Dull Cold Windy day and Some rain in the night I went to Halifax after 6
Oclock in the Evening
froze hard in the Night   *V*

Friday 14
a Dull Windy day [a] verry Cold and froze hard in the Night I went Halifax
after 6 Oclock in Evening

Saturday 15
a Dull cold day I went Halifax in the afternoon Doughter Midgley returned
from Gomersall this Evening and froze in the Night

Sunday 16
a Cool Dull day and froze in Night I went to Halifax and heard William
Ackroyd Preach both Morning and afternoon from 5 Chapter of Matthews
Gospel and 8 verse

Monday 17
a Bright Cold Drought day and froze hard in the Night
My wife had 5 leeches Set upon her Legg Carpmeal in Halifax died this day D

Tuesday 18
a Bright Drought Cold day and froze in the Night

Wednesday 19
a Bright Cold Droughty day and froze in the Night Sarah Marsden return,d
from from Gomersall we put our cow to Spring Grass this day

Thursday 20
a Dull Cold day and a Little rain in the night I went our Church Meeting in
Evening   ᴇᴪ[15]
Paid the Vickers Easter Dues   0 1 7½
Son Jas Midgley went to Sabden   V

---

[15] An unidentified symbol in the right-hand margin

Friday 21

a Dull day Cool day and frequent Showers of rain both in the day and in the Night Also

I went Halifax after 5 O clock in the Evening

Saturday 22

a Dull Cold Wet Windy day and Some rain in the Night Also I went to Halifax in the afternoon

Sunday 23

a Dull day and frequent Showers of rain both in the day and in the Night I went to Halifax and heard William Ackroyd Preach in the Morning from Cor^s 2 Epis 5 Cha & 1 verse in afternoon from Solomons song 1C & 4 v

John Bates Methodist Preacher in Halifax this day[16]   D

Monday 24

a Dull Cold day and Some Showers of rain in the day and Some rain in the Night also

Tuesday 25

a Dull day and verry Cold and Some light showers of rain in the day

I went Halifax in the Evening

we had 2 Men Cutting Pottatoes & Other in Husbandry   0 4 0

Wednesday 26

a Cold Droughty day and froze in the Night

---

[16] Rev. John Bates died as Ashworth records on 23 April. He had been a Wesleyan local preacher earlier in his life but by the time of his death he had twice been minister of Mixenden Chapel from 1792-1796 and from 1802 until his death. Ashworth probably disapproved of the doctrines preached in this chapel (where he had been baptised) as they had tended towards Unitarianism during the later years of the eighteenth century. Bates seems to have had no settled theological opinions and allowed Methodists to preach from the pulpit at Mixenden. Their Arminian views would have been unwelcome to Ashworth and he would also have disapproved of Bates' preoccupation with teaching at a school he conducted in Halifax, which caused him to neglect his pastoral duties. J.G. Miall, *Congregationalism in Yorkshire*, London, Snow, 1868, p.319. J.U. Walker, *A History of Wesleyan Methodism in Halifax*, Halifax, Hartley and Walker, 1836, p.261.

Thursday 27
a Mild warm day we had 4 Men Setting Pottatoes and Other Jobbs in Husbandry all day
4 Days Labour as before Mentioned   0. 10. 0

Friday 28
a Cold Droughty day and a Little rain
Theodora Rhodes Came to our house on a Visit her brother Jeremiah Came with her and he returned home the Same Night

Saturday 29
a Dull Cold Droughty day I went to Ovenden Moor side in the Morning and to Halifax in the afternoon
John Whitehead in Warley Town died this ^day   D

Sunday 30
a Dull Cool day and Showers of rain I went to Halifax and heard William Ackroyd Preach in the Morning from Matthew,^s Gospel 5 Chapter & 6 verse in afternoon from (*blank*)

Monday 1 May
a Dull Cold day and Some Light [Light] Showers of rain I was Emply.d in Cutting Hay and repairing Fen^ces
1 Day,^s Labour in Husbandry   0 2 0
William Walsh in Wheatley died this day   D

Tuesday 2
a Dull Foggy Morning but Cleard and was Droughty in afternoon I went to Warely Town Luddenden Foot &c and Came back by way of Halifax
Muncaster near Ludden^den had his Furniture Sold yesterday & ^To ^day Sl

Wednesday 3
a Bright Cool Droughty day
Paid for Light Cour.d Cow Covering   0 1 0

Thursday 4
a Bright Drought day and warmer than yesterday I went Halifax in the Evening
Paid for light Colour,d Cow Covering   0 1 00

Friday 5
a Bright Drought day and Warm Also I went to Halifax in the Afternoon

Saturday 6
a Dull day rather Foggy in the Morning I went to Halifax in the afternoon
a Number of Thieves Broke into Mr Greenwoods Counting House in Wheatly yesterday Night or Soon this Morning

Sunday 7
a dull Warm day and in the afternoon an in the Night I went to Halifax and heard William Ackroyd Preach in the Morning from the Book (*blank*)10 Chapter and 24 & 25 verse in the afternoon from (*blank*)

Monday 8
a verry warm day and Much rain in the afternoon and in the Night I went in afternoon to Warely and Skircoat
Paid for Red Cow Covering   0 1 0

Tuesday 9
a Dull Warm day Some in the day and Some in the Night Also I went to Halifax after 5 O clock in the Evening
George Bairstow[17]

Wednesday 10
a Dull warm day and frequent Showers of rain in the day and Some in the Night
William Ackroyd Preached at Our house in the Evening from Isiah

Thursday 11
a Dull warm day and Some Showers of rain

---

[17] This name is not in the Diarist's hand.

Friday 12

a Dull warm day and Some Drought in the afternoon but verry wet and and Windy in the Morning

Theodoea Rhodes went home and her Sister Came on a visit to Our house I went Halifax in the Evening   V

Saturday 13

a Dull warm day and Some Showers of rain in the day and heavy Showers in the Night

Widdow Mitchell at Pellon died this ^week Mary Walton at Luddend Foot died yesterday ^this day   DD

Sunday 14

a Dull ^day and Some ^Showers of rain in the in the day & and rain in the night also I went to Halifax in the Morning heard Abraham Webster from Slaithwait pole[18] Preach in the Morning [Preach] from The 77 Psalm and (*blank*) verse in afternoon from 9th Chapter Matthew,^s Gospell

Monday 15

a Dull day and frequent Showers of rain in the day and Some rain in the Night Also

This is Whisun Tide So Called

Tuesday 16

a Dull Cool day we had 3 Men Gathering Dull of the Meadows after Our Cows been in the Grass

I went in the afternoon to hear Mr Harrison[19] Preach [f] at Mixenden Chappel from Hebrew,s 13 Chapter and 18 ver 1 ½ days Labour in the Meadows   0 3 0

---

[18] Rev. Abraham Webster was minister at Pole Moor Chapel which served Slaithwaite although, due to the opposition of the Earl of Dartmouth, it was actually built just across the boundary in Scammonden Township. Webster was pastor from 1808 to 1818 and again from 1824 to his death in 1828. C.E. Shipley (ed.), *The Baptists of Yorkshire*, Bradford, Byles, 1912, p.233.

[19] Rev. Joseph Harrison, minister of Allerton Independent Chapel near Bradford, 1815-1821. He had frequently administered communion at Mixenden around the turn of the century.

Wednesday 17
a Dull wet day I was Employd in the afternoon in Cutting up Briers and thorns in the Woodfield
Richard Nuttall
½ days Labour in the Meadows 0 1 0

Thursday 18
a Dull day and Some Drizling Showers of rain in the day daytime
I went to our Church Meeting in the Evening

Friday 19
a Bright Droughty day I went to Southowram Coly Shelf and Northowram
In the [A] afternoon

Saturday 20
a Cold Droughty day and Showers of rain in the Evening I went to Halifax
In the afternoon

Sunday 21
a Dull Cool day and heavy Showers of rain I went to Halifax and heard william Ackroyd Preach in the Morning from the 12 Psalm and 1 verse and the afternoon from the 52 Psalm and (*blank*) verse

Monday 22
a Cool Droughty day and rather warm in the Evening I went to Halifax after 6 O clock in the Evening

Tuesday 23
a Dull Cool day and verry wet in the forenoon Some Drought in the afternoon and rain in the Night

Wednesday 24
a Bright Cool Droughty day I went to Halifax in the afternoon

Thursday 25
a Dull Cool day

Friday 26 Summer

a Dull hot day I went to Halifax in the afternoon

Saturday 27

a Dull hot day I went to Halifax after 3 O clock in the afternoon

Sunday 28

a Dull warm day and heavy Showers of rain in the Evening and Some rain in the Night also

I went to Halifax and heard Willm Ackroyd Preach both Morning and Afternoon from Romans 10 Chap and 9 verse

Monday 29

a Dull hot day and Much heavy rain in the day and Some in the Night also

Tuesday 30

a Dull hot day and Showers of rain in the day

Wednesday 31

a Dull hot day I went to Halifax of 3 O clock in the afternoon

Paid for poor and Other Rates to Wm Sutcliff   3 8 4

Joseph Dillott of Illingworth was Convey.d to York on Supision of Breaking into Thos Scott^s House in Illingworth

Thursday 1 June

a Dull hot day I went Halifax after 6 O clock in the Evening

Friday 2

a Dull warm day I was Emply.d Most of the day in Weeding our Garden after 6 O clock in the Evening I went
to Halifax

Saturday 3

a Dull hot day and Much rain Epecially before noon and Some
rain in the afternoon I went to Halifax after 3 O clock in the afternoon

Sunday 4

a Dull warm day ^{a heavy Showers of rain} I went Halifax and heard William Ackroy Preach in the Morning from 24 Chapter of Acts of ^{apostles} & 25 verse and in the afternoon heard Mr Street from London[20] Preach from 22 Chapter of Genesis and 2 verse and he Preached at our house in Evening from Ezekiel 37 Chapter and 3 verse

Monday 5

a Dull warm day and frequent Showers of rain in the Morning I went to halifax in the afternoon

Tuesday 6

a Dull hot day and verry rain in the Morning I went Halifax after 6 O clock in the Evening

Wednesday 7

a Bright hot day William Ackroyd Preached at our house in the Evening from the 1 Chapter of Pauls Epistle to the Ephesians the 7 verse
Matthew Hiley in Mixenden Stones was Buryed this day   D

Thursday 8

a Bright Droughty hot day I worked in our Garden in afternoon
Aron Sutcliff in Wheatley was Buried this day   D

Friday 9

a [Dull] ^{Bright} hot day I went to Halifax Southowram and Hipperholm in the afternoon
Paid for our young Cow Covering   0 1 0

Saturday 10

a Bright hot day I went Halifax in the afternoon

Sunday 11

a Dull Hot day and Showers of rain in the Evening I went to Halifax and William Ackroyd Preached to us in the Morning from (*blank*) and in the Evening from the Acts of the apostles 24 Chapter & 25 verse

---

20 No information on Mr Street of London has been found.

Monday 12
a Dull warm day and frequent Showers of rain in the Course of the day

Tuesday 13
a Dull hot day Some Thunder in the forenoon I did a Little work in [the] Our holms and weeded our Turnips Beans &c

Wednesday 14
a Dull hot day and raiᶦned Most of the day Son Jame Midgley Went to Gomersall and return,d

Thursday 15
a Dull hot day and Showers rain in the Morning I went our Church Meeting in the Evening

Friday 16
a Dull hot day and rained a little in the day I was Employ.d Most of the day in Weeding our Pottatoes and Thoˢ Priestly Assisted in the afternoon 1 dayˢ Labour in Weeding our Pottatoes   0 2 0

Saturday 17
a Dull hot day and rained Most of the day I went to Warely Town, Sowerby Street Salter Hebble and Halifax in the afternoon

Sunday 18
a Dull hot Soft day Some Drizling rain I went to Halifax and heard William Akroy Preach both Morning and afternoon from Pauls Epistle to the Romans 14 Chapter and 1 verse

Monday 19
a Dull hot day and some Drizling Showers of rain Mrˢ Rhodes Senʳ Came to our house on a visit her son Shechainah Came with her on Horse back

Tuesday 20
a Dull hot day and a Little rain William and John Marsden Came to our house from Ewood Hall to spend their [Christmas] Hallidays for Midsummer Vacation

Wednesday 21
a Dull hot day and a verry little rain in the afternoon I went to Halifax after 3 O clock

Thursday 22
a Bright Hot day I went to Hal˟ to Meet my Doughter Marsden Thoˢ Marsdens wifeˢ who had Traveled from London to Leeds in a Stge Coach in 23 hours[21]

Friday 23
a Bright hot day I was Employd in the afternoon in Hoeing our Pottatoes

Saturday 24
a Dull hot day and verry heavy Showers of rain in the Evening I went to Halifax in the afternoon

Sunday 25
a Bright hot day I went to Hal˟ heard William Ackroyd Preach in the Morning from 40ᵗʰ Psalm and 3 verse and in the afternoon from Lukes Gospel 11 Chapter & 28 verse and Joseph Cockinˢ Chappel being Shut up for repairs he Preached in the Baptistˢ at ½ past 6 O clock

Monday 26
a Bright Droughty Mʳ Josep Rhodes and his Son[22] Came on a Visit to ur house on a Visit and returned the Same Evening   V

Tuesday 27
a Bright hot day Foggy in the Morning but Cleared and Was Droughty in the afternoon I went to Halifax after 8 O clock
Paid for our young cow covering   0 1 0

Wednesday 28
a Bright hot Droughty day Mrs Marsden Returned to Our house from Hathershelf

---

[21] In the 1790s this journey took thirty hours ten minutes according to a *G.P.O. Leeds to London Time – Bill*, sold by Cavendish Philatelic Auctions in May 2010.
[22] Joseph Rhodes was a son of Shechaniah and Susannah Rhodes and a nephew of the Diarist.

Thursday 29

a Bright hot Droughty Jeremiah Rhodes Came to our house on a Visit and returned home the Same day

Friday 30

a Bright hot Droughty day I went to Halifax in the Evening

Saturday 1 July

a Bright hot Droughty day I went Halifax in the Morning and returned home at 11 O clock in the Morning and went to Luddenden foot in the afternoon and return.d home by way of (*blank*)

Sunday 2

a Bright hot day I went to Halifax and heard Mr Cockin Preach in our Chappel in the Morning from Jonah^s prophesy 4 Chapter and 2 verse in the afternoon from (*blank*)

Monday 3

a Dull hot Morning but Clear.d a Little in the afternoon we had 4 Mowers all day and James Midgley & John & William Marsden Spread a Little Grass this day Left it abroad all Night

Tuesday 4

a Dull hot Morning but rather brighter in the afternoon we had 5 Hay Makers all this day who was Jno Ashworth Joseph Blagbrough Jas Midgley and Harry Charnock and Self

Wednesday 5

a Bright Droughty day we had 5 Hay Makers J.A. J.M. J.B. H.C. and Self

Thursday 6

a Bright Hot Morning but Dull in the afternoon and Some rain in the[23] Evening and a Little in the Night we had 5 Hay Makers J.A. J.B. J.P. H.C. and Self till 6 O clock in Evening

---

[23] The rest of this entry is carried on under the heading '6 Day of July' on the right-hand page in the space intended for 5 July.

Friday 7

a Dull Morning and a Little rain but Clear.d and was Droughty in afternoon we had 7 Hay Makers in afternoon we had 6 Mowers from 2 O clock in afternoon till 10 O clock in the Evening

[S] Doughter Sr Marsden and Grandaughter Sarah Marsden return,d from Hathershelf

Saturday 8

a Droughty Morning but Dull and Drizling rain in the afternoon we had 7 Hay Makers this day and 5 Mowers and they finished Mowing our Grass for this Season

Sunday 9

a Bright hot day I went Halifax and heard William Ackroy Preach in the in the Morning from Isiah 2 Chap & 3 verse I heard Joseph Cockin Preach in the afternoon from the 46 Psalm and 5 verse and William Preached Immediately after him from Ishiah ^{c} 4 & ^{verses} 6. 7. 8

Monday 10

a [Dull] Bright hot we had 7 Hay Makers

Mr Sheckainah Rhodes Came for Sarah Marsden to Gomersall on a visit

My Doughter Susannah Marsden d her Son William Went to Hathershelf

Tuesday 11

a Bright hot day we had 7 Hay Makers all day   8 2 0

Wednesday 12

a Bright hot day we had 9 Hay Makers all day finished hay Makeing
for this Season

54 Days hay Makeing at 3^s Per day	8	2	0
Mowing Victuling and Wages	2	12	6
Leading and Spreading Dung	1	11	0

Thursday 13

a Dull hot day with Thunder and abundance of Rain in the afternoon and in the Night I went to Halifax in the afternoon & heard Joseph Cockin Preach in our Chappel from Cor 11 Chap & 32 vers

Friday 14
a Dull hot day and Much Rain in the afternoon and in the Night

Saturday 15
a Dull Hot day and Some in the Morning but Clear.d and Some Drought in the afternoon I went to Halifax in the afternoon

Sunday 16
a Droughty hot day I went Halifax & heard William Ackroyd Preach in the Morning from Luke 18 Chapter & 1 verse
And Joseph Cockin at ½ past 1 O clock from from the Book of Job 36 Chapter and 22 verse and William Ackroyd from the 2 Epistle to the Corinthians 4 Chapter & 5 began at 3 O clock

Monday 17
a Dull day and Some showers of rain in the Morning but Some Drought in the afternoon a high wind in the afternoon Mr Shechainah Rhodes Came with Sarah Marsden to our house and he Stopped with us all Night

Tuesday 18
a Dull day and Drizling rain in Most of the forenoon and a High but Droughty in the afternoon S. Rhodes returned home in the (*blank*)
we had 3 Men Dressing up the hay Mow in the forenoon and weeding our Summer Pastures in the afternoon

Wednesday 19
a Dull day and rather Cooler and frequent Showers of rain in the day
we had 4 Men 1 Horse & 1 Cart Leading ^{Dung} and Rubbish till 4 Oclock

Thursday 20
a Dull hot day we had 3 Men Spreading Dung all day

Friday 21
a Bright hot day we had 3 Men Spreading Dung all day

Saturday 22
a Bright hot day I went to Farsley in the afternoon

{1832 Sep[r] 2nd Geo & Harriet Spencer was at Tea at Jonas Spencr at Greystones on this Day and Han[h] Spencer Jonas' Daughter in Law}[24]

Sunday 23
a Dull hot day and frequent Showers of rain both in the day Some in the Night Also
I heard John Sharp Preach both Morning and [Evening] Afternoon from 10 Chapter of Romans and 10 verse

Monday 24
a Bright hot day [I] and a Little rain in the Morning I Came home after 5 O clock in the afternoon

Tuesday 25
a Bright hot day

Wednesday 26
a Bright hot day I went to Halx in the afternoon to see Doughter Susannah Marsden and her 2 Sons John and William Marsden and [Sar] Grand Daughter Sarah Marsden Sett off for London   *V V V V*

Thursday 27
a Bright hot day I went to Halifax and heard Alexander Fletcher[25] Preach at M[r] Cockin Chappel from St Luke,s Gospel 2 Chapter and (*blank*)

Friday 28
a Bright hot day I went to Moor Side Illingworth Houldsworth and Shaw Lane Ovenden & Wheatley In the afternoon

Saturday 29
a Bright hot day I went to Halifax in the afternoon

---

[24] On the right-hand page, opposite the entries for 21 and 22 of July, this entry is written in pencil.
[25] No information on Alexander Fletcher has been found.

Sunday 30
a Bright hot day I went Halifax and heard WilliamAckroyd Preach in the Morning from the 17 Chapter and (*blank*) verse and ⁱⁿ the afternoon from John Gospel 19 Chapter and 30 verse

Monday 31
a Bright hot day I went to Halifax in the afternoon
we received a Letter from London this A^dvising us of the Safe Arrival of our Relatives Safe Arrival in London

Tuesday 1 August
a Bright hot day I went to Illingworth in the Evening to the half yearly Meeting of a Society formed the purpose of Punishing of Evil doers

Wednesday 2
Hot Bright droughty day William Ackroy Preached at our house from Pauls ² Epistle to the Corinthians 5 Chapter and 8 verse

Thursday 3
a Bright hot day I went to Halifax in the Evening this afternoon I saw 9 Or 10 Young Persons about Batheing in our holms 5 of them young Men whose names Names was John Hargreaves Joseph Hargreaves Joseph Crossley Isaac Alderson and William Balmforth

Friday 4
a Bright hot Droughty day I went Halifax in the Evening

Saturday 5
a Dull Morning and light Showers of rain but Clear.d and was Droughty in the afternoon
I went to Halifax in the afternoon

Sunday 6
a Dull Morning and a little rain in the Morning and a heavy Showers of Hail and in in the afternoon
I heard William Ackroyd Preach in the Morning from 5 Chap of Pauls 1 Epistle to thesalonians & 23 verse in afternoon from Galations 5 Chapter and 7 verse

Monday 7
a hot Droughty this was the day that was Appointed for the Cow Club⁵
yearly Meeting in Illingworth at David Walter⁵

Paid Thoˢ Hirst for Window Money & house ᵈᵘᵗʸ	1 4 9
Paid for Thatching Jo⁵ Blagbrough⁵ [Coal] Necessary	0 2 0

Should have been Enterd the day below

Tuesday 8
a hot Droughty day I went to Swillhill Top Causeway foot and Mixenden
Ings &c &c in the afternoon

Wednesday 9
a Dull hot day and verry Droughty

Thursday 10
a Bright hot day and a Little rain in the Night I was Employ^d in Weeding
our Garden in the afternoon

Friday 11
a Dull hot day with Thunder and Lighting and Much rain in the Evening I
went our Church Meeting in the Evening

Saturday 12
a Dull day and in the afternoon and in the Night I went Halifax in the
afternoon

Sunday 13
a warm droughty day I went to Halifax and heard William Ackroyd Preach
both Morning and afternoon from the Revelations 11 Chapter and 15 verse

Monday 14
a Dull warm day and heavy Showers of rain in the Course of the day

Tuesday 15

a Dull warm day and rain,d verry [heavily till noon and] little in the day but rained a Little in the Night

I went to Moor Side in the Morning and to Halifax in afternoon John John Wilkinson of Halifax was buried ^{this day}   D

Wednesday 16

a Dull hot day and rained verry heavily in the Morning but Clear^d at noon I was Employ.d the afternoon in Weeding our beans pease and Turnips in afternoon

Walton^s wife ⁱⁿ Norland was Killed near King Cross   0 1 3 D

Thursday 17

a Dull day and Some drought and Some Showers of rain I was Employ.d in the Weeding as above Mention,d   *D*

James Moor,s wife at Long house in Mixenden died this day   D

½ Days work in the fields   0 1 3

Friday 18

a Dull ^{day} with Some Drought but Heavy rain in the Evening for Several hours I heard Joseph Cockin Preach at William Illingworth,^s in the Evening from Isiah 11 Chapter and 10 verse ½ a Days labour   0 1 3

Saturday 19

a Bright Droughty day I went Halifax in the afternoon

Sunday 20

a Drighty day Cool in the Morning but ^{hot} and Clear in the afternoon I went ^{to} Halifax and heard William Ackroyd Preach bothe Morning and afternoon from 1 Epistle to Timothy 4 Chapter & 8 verse

Joseph Smith in washer Lane died this day   D

Monday 21

a Bright droughty day Cool in the Morning but Hot in the afternoon I was Employ.d in the afternoon in pruneing the thorns on which our neighbours hang their Linen to dry ½ Days labour in the above   0. 1. 3

Tuesday 22
a verry Dull hot wet and Some Lightening and a Little rain in the Evening
and heavy Showers before 7 O clock in the Morning follow^{ing}
I went Skircoat Warely Town and beyond Luddenden Foot in ^{afternoon}

Wednesday 23
a verry Dull hot wet day till 3 O clock and a little Drought after 4 O clock
I was Employd in afternoon in Pulling up weeds in our Paster   00 1 0
one Man was Kill,d and Another Much hurt in a Coal pitt near Swill hill   D

Thursday 24
a Dull hot [hot] day and Some light Showers of rain I was Employ^d ⁱⁿ
Pulling up weeds in our Pastures in the afternoon

Friday 25
a Dull hot windy Morning but the wind Lower.d in afternoon and Much
rain in the Evening
I went Hipperholm and Coly and Halifax in the afternoon

Saturday 26
a Dull warm day Some Showers of rain I went Halifax in the afternoon

Sunday 27
a Dull hot day I went to Halifax and heard William Ackroy^d Preach in the
Morning from St John^s Gospel 13 Chapter & 35 vers and Joseph Cockin at
½ past 1 O clock from (*blank*)

Monday 28
a Dull hot day and wet in the Morning but Clear.d in the afternoon
I went to Halifax in the Evening

Tuesday 29
a Dull day and Some Showers of Rain in the afternoon

Wednesday 30
a Dull hot day and Showers of Drizling rain in the afternoon
William Ackroyd Preached at our house in the Evening from the 89 Psalm
& 2 verse

Thursday 31
a Dull hot day and Many Showers of rain in the Course of the day Joseph Shaw from Keighley Called upon us Soliciting a little Money towards paying Some Debt they had upon a Baptist Chappel[26]

Friday 1 September
a Dull hot day I went to Halifax in the Evening

Saturday 2
(*no entry*)

3 Sunday
a Dull warm day I went to Halifax and heard William Ackroyd Preach in the Morning from Judges 8 Chapter and 4 verse and at ½ Past 1 O clock Mr Cockin Preached from Matthew,s Gospel 13 Chapter and 33 verse John Lees in Halifax died this day   D

Monday 4
a Dull day and rathe Cooler and verry wet for several hours in the Middle of the day but Clear.d in the Evening
being what is Called Illingworth Rush bearing[27] we had 5 of Joshua Stancliffs Children on a visit

Tuesday 5
a Bright Droughty [F] day Francis Midgley and his wife Came to our house on a visit

Wednesday 6
a Bright Droughty day and Cooler in Morning and Evenings
I was Employd in Clearing our Garden of weeds and Digging

Thursday 7
a Bright Droughty day I worked in our Garden in the afternoon

---

[26] Rev. Joseph Shaw was the first pastor at Keighley Baptist Chapel, which had been opened in 1815 at a cost of £990. C.E. Shipley (ed.), *The Baptists of Yorkshire*, Bradford, Byles, 1912, pp.187–188.
[27] 'Illingworth Rush bearing': the festivities associated with the ancient annual festival of bringing new rushes to church to strew on the floor.

Friday 8
a Bright hot Droughty

Saturday 9
a Bright Droughty day I went to Halifax in the afternoon

Sunday 10
a hot Droughty day I went to Halifax and heard Will Ackroyd Preach in the Morning from 49 Psalm and 9 verse and [in the Evening] at 3 O clock from the Same Text and Joseph Cockin at ½ past 1 from 2 Thes 2 Chap & 14 verse

Monday 11
a Bright hot day

Tuesday 12
a Bright hot day I went to Warely and Shorest in the afternoon

Wednesday 13
a Bright hot day [S] Nancy Howarth wife of James ^{Howarth} of Sabden Came to our house on a Visit   V

Thursday 14
a Bright day and verry hot we had We had C Widdop H. Charnock Joseph Blagbrough and John Ashworth Ja^{s Midgely} & Self reaping our Oats

Friday 15
a verry hot day we had the above 6 reapers all this day
a Man of Name of James Garlick in Halifax died this day his Death occation,d by throwing up Blood   D

Saturday 16
a Dull hot day we had ^{the above} 6 reapers 2 hours before breakfast and 5 of them reaping and [fr]Getting up Weeds in our Long field the the day out
I went to Halifax in the Evening
12 days [S]Reaping   1 16 0
4 days weeding in our Pastures   0 12 0

Sunday 17
a Bright hot day and Some rain in the Night
I went Halifax and heard William Ackroyd Preach both Morning and afternoon from Rev 6 Chap 1 & 2v Josep Cockin,ˢ people took posesion of Barraclogh,ˢ Chappel[28]

Monday 18
a Dull hot day and Drizling rain Most of the day Son Jaˢ & Self Spread Dung and pulled up weeds in Our fields this day
2 Days labour   0 5 0

Tuesday 19
a Dull hot day and Drizling rain frequently in the Course of the I was Employ in the afternoon Pulling up Weeds in our Pastures
½ Days labour in the Pastures   0 1 0

Wednesday 20
a Bright Droughty day we had [6] the before named 6 person reaping our Oats all the day
Will Ackroyd Preached at Our house in the Evening from the (*blank*)
6 Days reaping Oats & finisht   0 18 0

Thursday 21
a Bright Droughty day
Mary Horsfall Jonathan Horsfalls wife and 3 Children Came to our house on a Visit and return,d the Same day

Friday 22
a Dull day and Some Showers of rain in the day and a Little in the Night
I went to Halifax in the Evening
3 Days labour in Husbandry   0 9 0

---

[28] 'Barraclogh,ˢ Chappel' is most probably that at Stainland where Rev. Samuel Barraclough was minister from 1793 to 1804 when he joined the United Methodist Church. The chapel had always had a very mixed congregation comprising Anglicans, Congregationalists, and Wesleyans. In 1813 the Congregationalists separated and it was presumably this congregation that took possession of the chapel. J.G. Miall, *Congregationalism in Yorkshire*, London, Snow, 1868, p.367.

Saturday 23
a Dull Morning and wet but Clear.d and was verry Droughty in the afternoon Brother John Son James and Self House Some of our Oats I went Halifax after 6 O clock

Sunday 24
a Dull wet Morning but Clear,d and was Droughty I went Halifax and heard William Ackroyd Preach in the Morning from John,s Gospel 1 Chap and 16 vers in afternoon from Colosians 1 Chapter & 12 verse
Jeremiah Rhodes Came on a Visit   V

Monday 25
a Dull Soft Morning and Droughty in the afternoon I went to Halifax in the Morning we had Brother John & son James Thrashing and housing Oats all day I Assisted in the afternoon

Tuesday 26
a Dull Windy day and heavy rain in the Evening we had the above Brother and Son and Self houseng Oats and Thrashing all day and Got 3 Men to help us a little

Wednesday 27
Some Showers of rain but Droughty Most of the day had Brother & Son Thrashing all day and I Shak,d Straw all day

Thursday 28
a Bright Droughty day we had Brother John & Son James Thrashing all day and Shaked Straw my Self
Paid to Rabort Ramsbottom Composition Money for Roads   1 7 0

Friday 29
a Dull day and rained Most of the day Brother John and Son James Thrashed till noon & I shaked the Straw and we winowed In the afternoon
14 Days labour in Thrashin and Houseing Our Oats and work   2 0 0

Saturday 30

a Dull warm droughty day and Some rain in the Night I went Ludenden foot with Nancy Howarth who was returning to Sabden the place of her abode and I Came back by way of Halifax.

Sunday 1 October

a Dull Soft Morning but Clear.d & was droughty I went Halifax and heard William Ackroyd Preach in the Morning from Rev 3 Chapter & 11 verse in the afternoon from 119 Psalm and 60 verse

Monday 2

a Dull wet Morning but Clear.d and was droughty I went to the Mill to see our Oats Ground into Meal

Expense Attending the above   0 6 0

in 4 quarters of Oats had 3 Packs Meal

Tuesday 3

a Fine Drought day but Some rain in the Night

Wednesday 4

a Mild Droughty day and a Little rain in the Night I went to Carry Hops & Collect Money to Ovenden Moor Side in afternoon Paid to A. Hodgson for poor Church & Constable Rates   4 5 5

Thursday 5

a Bright Mild day and Some rain in the Night

Friday 6

a Mill Droughty Droughty day

Saturday 7

a verry Mill warm day I went to Warely Town with half a Pocket of Hops and Brother John assisted me in Carrying them and I Came back by way of Halifax

Sunday 8
I went Halifax and heard William Preach in the Morning from St John Gospel 8 Chapter and 58 verse in afternoon from the 42 verse of the Same Chapter
a Cool Droughty day

Monday 9
a Cool Droughty day

Tuesday 10
a Cool Droughty day
I got up a few Pottatoes in the afternoon

Wednesday 11
a Dull windy Cool Droughty day Son James and Self got Pottatoes up all day

Thursday 12
a Dull Cool Droughty day and a Little rain in the Night Son James and Self was Employ.d in getting (*blank*)
I went our Church Meeting

Friday 13
a Dull Mild day and light Showers of rain in the day and Much rain in the Night Son Ja^s and Self were Employ.d getting up Pottatoes all day
6 Day Labour in getting Pottatoes   0 15 0
Lay,d our Cattle in this Night[29]

Saturday 14
a Dull day and frequent Showers of rain both in the day and in the Night I went to Halifax in the afternoon
John Sutcliff near Jumples in Ovenden was Buried this week   D

---

[29] Ashworth brought his cattle in for the winter.

Sunday 15
a dull day and Showers of rain both in the day and in the Night I went to Halifax and heard Wm Ackroyd Preach in the Morning from 92 Psalm & 24 vers^e and the afternoon from the Book of [Proverbs] ^Solomons ^Song 2 Chap & 4 verse

Monday 16
a Dull day and ^heavy Showers of rain both in the day and in the Night

Tuesday 17
a Dull day and heavy Showers of rain both in the day and in the Night

Wednesday 18
a dull day and heavy Showers of rain in the day and Some in the Night William Ackroyd Preach^d at our house in the Evening from Proverbs 18 Chapter & 24 verse ^Last clause
Ann Halliday near Booth Town was buried this day   D

Thursday 19
a Dull windy day and a bundance of rain in the day and Some rain in the Night that Made a flood with us

Friday 20
a Dull day Some drought but ^some Showers of rain in the Course of the day
I went to Halifax in the Evening

Saturday 21
a Dull day and heavy Showers of Hail and rain in the day Clear in the Evening
James Smith at Shaw Hill was found Drowned in the river near home ^this day there was an[d] Orotoria in Halifax Old Church this week which lasted 3 days

Sunday 22
a Bright Cool day I went to Halx and heard William Ackroyd Preach in the Morning from 22 Chapter of Revelations and 5 verses in the beginning of the Chapter in afternoon from the 35 Psalm and 3 verse

Monday 23

a dull day and verry rainy but Cleard in the Evening and
[I went Halifax for Southouram and Hipperholm in the afternoon]

Tuesday 24

a Bright ^{day} and Some Drought a Light Shower of rain in the Evening I went
to Halifax Southouram and Hipperholm in the afternoon

Wednesday 25

a Dull day and Some Showers of rain in the day and Some in the Night
Also
I was Employ this in Cleaning repairing of Lane towards the Top

Thursday 26

a Dull Mild day and Some Showers of rain I was Employd this in Packing
Some Goods for London and Going with the Box to Halifax   D
Sarah wife of T Priestley in our yard died this ^{day}   D
Jonas Jowett was Buried this day   D

Friday 27

a Dull day and Much rain this day Mr^s Wainhouse in North Gate in Halifax
died yesterday
Kennith Patterson,^s wife was Buried this week   D

Saturday 28

a Dull day and Some rain I went to Halifax in the afternoon
Robert Ramsden in Halifax was buried this day   D

Sunday 29

a Dull Mild day and and a Little rain in the Night I went to Halifax & heard
William Preach both Moring and afternoon from (blank) Gospel 22 Chapter
61 & 62 verses

Monday 30

a Dull day and frequent Showers of rain in the day
I was Employd this day Gathering up Tillage[30] in our lane

---

[30] Tillage: manure.

Tuesday 31
a Dull Mild day I was Employd in ditching and Gathering up Tillage in our Lane

Wednesday 1 November
a verry Mild day I was Employd in Makeing up a Gap in our Sun[o] door Field

Thursday 2
a Fine Mild Droughty day I went to Halifax Hipperholm &c in the afternoon frozen the Night

Friday 3
a Mild Droughty day I was Employ in the afternoon in our Meddow and went Moor side and Ovenden in the Evening
2 Days labour my Self in Husbandry this week   0 4 0

Saturday 4
a Dull Mild day and a Little rain I went to Halifax & Warely in the afternoon

Sunday 5
a Dull Mild day I went to Halifax and William Ackroyd Preach both Morning and and afternoon from the 5 Chapter of Matthew.ˢ Gospel and 13 verse

Monday 6
a Dull Mild day and frequent Showers of rain Joshua Stancliffˢ
wife and Mrs Worstenholm Came to our house on a Visit

Tuesday 7
a Bright Droughty day and ^Some rain in the Night Some light Showers of rain
I was Employ in the afternoon in laying up our Dunghill

Wednesday 8
a Dull day Cold day and froze a Little in the Night a verry high Wind both in the day and in the Night

Thursday 9

a Dull day and verry Cold & High Wind and Some rain I went to our Church Meeting in the Evening

Friday 10

a Cold Windy day and Some rain Ja^s Priestley returned from London in the Evening and my Son Thos Marsden Came down with him   V

Saturday 11

a Dull Cold ^day I went Halifax in the afternoon

Sunday 12

a Dull Cold day I went to Halifax ^& in the Morning heard William Ackroyd Preach from the Epis^t of Jude and 6 verse and in the afternoon from Hebrews 12 Chapter 4 verse

Monday 13

a Dull day and Some rain and a little Snow in the Night
I and Son Thos Went to Halifax to a Meeting of the Commissioners for our Inclosure of our Wa^ste lands[31]

Tuesday 14

a verry Dull day and heavy Showers of Snow and froze verry hard in the night I went to Halifax in the afternoon

Wednesday 15

a Dull day and Showers of rain but froze hard in the Night William Ackroyd Preached at our house in the Evening from the Book of Job 5 Chapter (*blank*) verse

Thursday 16

a Dull Cold day and froze hard in the Night I went to Warely Skircoat Salter Hebble & Halifax in the afternoon Son Thos Went to Hathershelf V

Jas Wormald at Luddinden died this day   D

---

[31] The Ovenden Enclosure Act had received the Royal Assent on 27 May 1814 and the Commissioners had held their first meeting on 1 August 1814. This is the first time that Ashworth mentions the process of Parliamentary Enclosure in the Diary.

Friday 17
a Bright frosty day
I went to Wheatley and Ovenden In the Evening

Saturday 18
a Bright frosty day I went to Halifax in the afternoon Son Tho.ˢ Marsden
returned from Hathershelf to our house this afternoon

Sunday 19
a Dull frosty day I went to Halifax and heard William Ackroyᵈ Preach both
Morning and afternᵒᵒⁿ from the 1 Epistle to the Coriⁿˢ 9 Chapter and 24 & 25
verses
Mrˢ Holm near Lee Bridge was buried ^this day   D

Monday 20
a Dull frosty day and Some Showers of Snow

Tuesday 21
a Dull frosty and Some [heavy] Showers of Showers of Snow
my Son Thomas went to Howorth in the afternoon

Wednesday 22
a Dull frosty day I went to Broad Tree in Ovenden in the Morning
Nanny Bairstow was Deliver.d of a Doughter this Mornⁱⁿᵍ

Thursday 23
a Bright frosty day Abraham Mitchell of Esps near Mount Pellon was
buried this day   D

Friday 24
a Bright frosty day I went to Halifax in the afternoon

Hear lieth the body of a Ass
 as big a roague as ever Was
he robed the rich and stoned the poor
he's gone to hell to Come no more[32]

---

[32] This rhyme has been written on the right-hand page opposite the entries for 23 and 24 November. It is quite clearly not in Ashworth's hand.

Saturday 25
a Dull frosty day I was[t] at Home this day and we Killed our Hogg this day in th[is]e Evening

Sunday 26
a Dull day and froze a Little a Little rain in the Evening I went to Halifax and heard William Ackroyd Preach both Morning & afternoon from John Gospel 5 Chapter and 69 verse[33]

(Ashworth's entries for the period 27 November to 11 December are missing. The lower part of this page has been filled in a different hand with the following remedy.)

Piles[34]

Take of the rots ceandie And bruise them then Press out the Juse take Take half a tabe Spoonful of the above Fuse in tea Cupfuf of yarrair decoction Three times a day

(These remedies have been inserted upside down on the next double page.)

epsom Salts	1 ounce
Saxefrage	2 ounce
guaicum	1
Sarsaprilla	1 dram

2 quarts of warter and reduced to 3 gills strain and bottle it and strain and half a cup full to be taken twice a day – every other day
half and ounce of spirits of wine quarter of an ounce of spirits of salt put together in a bottle
the dose is one teaspoon full to be taken twice a day in 3 teasponfu of warter every other day this to be taken 1 day and the doction the

---

[33] This reference is wrong. John's Gospel Chapter 5 has only 47 verses. In John's Gospel only Chapter 6 has a verse 69; which is probably the text intended:'And we believe, and are sure that Thou art Christ, the Son of the living God'.

[34] This remedy is written in the space that Ashworth had already ruled out and inserted the dates for 27 to 30 November and 1 and 2 December. Ashworth had made no entries for these dates and the remedy is not written in his hand.

(The remainder of this page has been cut away and the remedies continue on the opposite page.)

	Oun ds gr
Compound Colycynth pill	1
Calomel	15

The above pill is to be taken two in the morning fasting and worked of with gruill

Tinckture of Sack for the bleeding of the gums it hardens them and takes away all Scorbutie humes that are in the gums the way to use is take a little in 3 teaspoonfuls of water every morning and wash with it

	ounc
Iceland Liverworth	2
Balsam of Life	½
Peruvian Bark	¼

For strengthening of the inside

	grs
Besilic powder for worms	
For a child in sugar of 2 years old	12
For an adult	20

(The diary continues in the original orientation.)

Mrs Butterfield of Halifax was buried this^day [35]   D

Tuesday December 12
a Fine Cold day and I went Halifax and Salter Hebble in the afternoon Son
Thos Went to Gomersall   V

Wednesday 13
a Dull Soft day Son Thos returned from Gomersall at Noon
William Gath in Halifax died this day   D

Thursday 14
a Dull day and a little rain in the Morning Son Thos
Sett out from Halifax for London by way of Leeds [36]

---

[35] The top part of the left-hand page has been cut away. This entry is written on the right-hand page and was presumably part of Ashworth's entry for 10 December.

Friday 15

a Dull day and heavy Showers of rain in the day and in the Night and froze in the later Part of the Night Son Tho ˢ Arrived in London at 5 O clock this Evening

Saturday 16

a Dull frosty day and Some Snow fell in the Night
I went to Halifax in afternoon

Sunday 17

a Dull frosty day and Some Snow fell in the Night I went to Halifax and heard William Ackroyd Preach in the Moring from the 73 Psalm (*blank*) verse in afternoon from the (blank) of Samuel

Monday 18

a Dull frosty day and Some Snre Snow fell in the day and Some in the Night also
Luke Shaw in Halifax died this day   D

Tuesday 19

a Dull frosty day and heavy Showers of Snow fell in the day and Much Snow fell in the Night

Wednesday 20

a Dull frosty day and Some Snow fell in the day and Softenᵈ a Little in the Evening but froze hard in the Night

Thursday 21

a Bright frosty day
I was Employ.d in Shoveling Snow and Layin up the Dung Hill

Friday 22

a Dull frosty day and heavy Showers of Snow in the Evening I went to Warely Town Luddenden foot and Halifax in the afternoon

---

[36] This part of the entry has been written under the date Wednesday 13 December but by reference to the entry for 15 December appears to refer to Thomas' departure and thus belongs to Thursday 14 December.

Saturday 23
a Dull frosty day and heavy Showers of rain and Snow in the Night and thawed a Little in the former part of the Night but froze hard before Morning I went to Halifax in the afternoon

Sunday 24
a Dull frosty day & [a] Heavy Showers of Snow in the Evening and in the Night
I went Halifax and heard William Ackroyd Preach both Morning and Evening from Isiah 9 Chapter and 6 verse

Monday 25
a Bright frosty day I went to Luddenden foot and Halifax in the afternoon
Nacy Bairston and George Laistercliff was Married this day   M

Tuesday 26
a Dull day and rained thawed Most of the day Brother John and Son James thrashed Oats this day and I Shaked Straw this day

Wednesday 27
a Bright frosty day
Brother John and Son Jame Thrashed Oats and I Shaked Straw this day

Thursday 28
a Dull day and frequent Showers of rain and thawed Swiftly both in the day and in the Night we had the above named thrashers all day and I Shaked Straw

Friday 29
a Dull day and Rained Most [Most] of the day and a verry high wind and a great flood in the Night we had the Thrashers and I Shaked Straw
John Walton of Highroad well was buried this day   D

Saturday 30

a Dull day and froze a little in the day we had the above thrashers all day and I Shaked Straw till noon and went to Halifax in the afternoon Tho⁵ Binns at Stanry died this week   D

Sunday 31

Jas Harpers wife was buried this day   D
a Dull day and froze in the Morning and thawed a little in the afternoon
I went to Halifax & heard William Ackroyd Preach in the Morning from Romans 13 Chapter 11 & 12 verses in the afternoon Corⁿˢ 1 Ep 7 Chap and 29 ver

Monday 1 January

a Mild day for the Season and froze hard in the Night
I was Employ.d in the afternoon with Spreading Dung and Swilling in the Our Meadows

Tuesday 2

a Mild day and froze a little we had Brother John and Son James thrashing in forenoon and Winnowing in the afternoon and I Assisted them all that day

Wednesday 3

a verry Cold dull day and froze hard in the Night Brother John Son James and Self was Employd in Swilling Spreading Dung all day Tho⁵ Binns of Stanry was buried this day

Thursday 4

a Dull Cold day and thawed in the afternoon I went Halifax
in the Morning [Th] James Boulton in Ovenden died this day

Friday 5

a Dull Soft day I went to Causeway foot and Tops of Swill Hill in the afternoon

Saturday 6
a Dull day and windy and heavy Showers of Hail and Snow.d in the Evening a froze hard in the Night I went to Halifax in the afternoon

Sunday 7
a Dull day and light Showers of Rain in the Night and High Wind in the Night
I went to Halifax and heard William Ackroyd Preach both Morning and afternoon from (*blank*)

Monday 8
a Dull Windy day and rained Most of the day and in the Night
I went to the Corn Mill to see Oats Ground into Meal

Tuesday 9
a Dull day and Some Drought I went Illingworth Some Hops -- a High Wind in the Night

Wednesday 10
a Dull day and Wett Most of the day and a High wind and Much rain in the Night froze in the Night William Ackroyd Preached at our House in the Evening from Romas 8 Chapter & 3 of last verses

Thursday 11
a dull day a verry High Wind and Drizling rain Most of the day and verry heavy Showers of rain in the Evening I went to our Church Meeting in the Evening

Friday 12
a Dull day and some Shower in the day and some in the Night Also

Saturday 13
a Dull Soft day I went to Halifax in the afternoon

Sunday 14
a Dull Soft day and froze in the Night I went to Halifax and hear William Ackroyd Preach in the Morning from the Book of Genesis (*blank*) Chapter & (*blank*) verse and in the afternoon from John,ˢ Gospel (*blank*) Chapter & (*blank*) verse

Monday 15
a Dull wet day and Some rain in the Night I went Illingworth in the afternoon to pay the Rent to the Lord of the Monor

Tuesday 16
a Dull day and frequent Showᵉʳˢ of Snow and rain in the day and rain and Snow frost and thaw in the Night

Wednesday 17
a verry Cold frosty and a verry High wind I was Employd in the afternoon in laying up our Dunghill and Swilling in our Meadows

Thursday 18
a Dull frosty day I went to Halifax in the afternoon

Friday 19
a Dull frosty [day] Morning but Brighter in the afternoon

Saturday 20
a Bright frosty day I went to Halifax and Hipperholm in the afternoon

(*The right-hand page for the week 21 January to 27 January is missing. The entries for this period are therefore incomplete.*)

Sunday 21
a Dull day and thawed a Little and some Showers of Snow I went to Halifax

Monday 22
a Dull day and frequent Showers of Snow Hail & rain I went Lee Bridge in afternoon

Tuesday 23
a Dull day and thawed a little and heavy Showers of Snow I went Hipperholme in afternoon

Wednesday 24
a Dull Mild day for the Season I was Employd in Swilling a Little and layin up

Thursday 25
a Dull Mild day and light Showers of Snow in the day and a Little in the Night also and thawed

Friday 26
a Dull frosty day

Saturday 27
(*no entry*)

(*The following entries are from the right-hand page, which is now opposite the entries for the week 21 to 27 January 1816. At least one page has been removed and these entries have no dates. They do not correspond with the entries for 21 January to 27 and could be either Sunday 28 January to Saturday 3 February or Sunday 4 February to Saturday 10 February.*)

Sunday
......10 Chapter part of the 9 verse in afternoon from the (*blank*) verse of the same Chap Dolly Iles was buried   D

Monday
......the afternoon in Spreading Mole Hill and Cow Dung in our Medows

Tuesday
(*no entry*)

Wednesday
......Ackroyd Preached at our house in the Evening from Matthew,[s] Gospel 4 Chapter and 15 & 16 verse

Thursday
…… for the Inclosure of the waste land in Ovenden

Friday
(*blank*)

Saturday
…. Joseph Swaine and Shechaniah Rhodes Came to our house on a visit in the Evening

Sunday 11
a verry Dull frosty I went [H] to Halifax and heard William Ackroyd Preach both Morning and afternoon from (*blank*)

Monday 12
a verry Cold Bright frosty Morning but thawed a Little in the afternoon I went to Warely in the afternoon

Tuesday 13
a Dull Soft day and thawed in the afternoon I went went to Warely in the afternoon

Wednesday 14
a Dull Soft day I was Employd the afternoon in our Meadow Spreading Mole Hills &c

Thursday 15
a Dull Soft day I went to our Church Meeting in the Evening

Friday 16
a verry Cold Windy day I was Employd a little in the afternoon in Spreading Dung & Mole Hills it froze verry hard in the Night

Saturday 17
a Dull frosty day I went to Halifax in the afternoon

(*The text for the week Sunday 18 February to Saturday 25 February is missing.*)

Sunday 26
a Dull Cold day I went to Halifax in the Morning heard William Ackroyd
Preach both Morning and afternoon

Monday 27
a Dull Cold day   Hariot[37]

Tuesday 28
a Dull ^{Cold} day and verry wet in the Morning I Sett off
for London by way of Leeds

Wednesday 29
Warrensr °ver
Leadbetter[38]

Thursday 30
(*blank*)

Friday 31
Hariot Priestley[39]

Saturday 1 April[40]
Mary Fearnely[41]

---

[37] This name has been written on the left-hand page at this point. It is not in the Diarist's hand.

[38] These names have been written on the left-hand page at this point. They are not in the Diarist's hand.

[39] This name has been written on the left-hand page at this point. It is not in the Diarist's hand.

[40] It appears Ashworth made no entries for March and wrote April here, perhaps with the intention of taking up his pen again.

[41] This name has been written on the left-hand page at this point. It is not in the Diarist's hand.

Appendix

Nonconformist Ministers

The object of this appendix is to provide brief details of the nonconformist ministers who preached at services attended by Cornelius Ashworth. Where possible, details of their education and beliefs have been included so that a picture of the kind of doctrine Ashworth was familiar with can be built up. It has not proved possible to identify all the ministers whom Ashworth heard but information has been gathered on a sufficiently large number to provide a representative picture.

Research on the Independent or Congregational ministers has been greatly facilitated by the *Surman Index* held at Dr Williams's Library, London. For the Yorkshire churches the denomination is also fortunate in having J.G. Miall's *Congregationalism in Yorkshire* with its substantial appendix comprising the Synoptical History of the Yorkshire Churches. The Baptists are slightly less well served but the Centenary Memorial Volume of the Yorkshire Baptist Association, *The Baptists of Yorkshire,* edited by C.E. Shipley, has proved indispensable. The sources for the brief biographies that follow are cited at the end of the entry. The three sources mentioned above have been abbreviated as follows:

> Miall: J.G. Miall, *Congregationalism in Yorkshire*, London, Snow, 1868.
> Shipley: C.E. Shipley, *The Baptists of Yorkshire,* Bradford, Byles and London, Kingsgate Press, 1912.
> Surman Index: *The Surman Index of Congregational Ministers* held at Dr Williams's Library and also available on-line at: surman.English.qmul.ac.uk

William Ackroyd, Baptist minister at Pellon Lane Chapel, Halifax from 1800 to 1825. He came to Pellon Lane from Hebden Bridge, and died in 1826. T. Michael, *A Brief Historical Account of the First Baptist Church, Halifax,* Halifax, Whitaker, 1890, p.19. Shipley, p.216.

Thomas Ashworth, Baptist Minister of Gildersome from 1754 to c.1800. Shipley, p.92.

James Aston, 1756-1830, Baptist minister. Pastor at Lockwood Baptist Chapel near Huddersfield, 1805-1830. He had a remarkably successful ministry at Lockwood, adding 120 new members to the congregation in six years. Shipley, pp.235-236.

Jehoiada Brewer, Independent minister. A popular preacher and pastor of Queen Street Chapel, Sheffield from its inception in 1783 to 1795 when he went to Carr's Lane Chapel, Birmingham. Miall, p.356.

David Bruce, 1752-1808, Independent minister. Born at Heckmondwike 1752. Educated at Heckmondwike Academy 1772-6. Minister of Newington Independent Chapel, Liverpool, 1787-1808. Surman Index.

John Burnett, Independent minister. Probably born in Reading where he was minister of the chapel in Broad Street. He had pastorates in Suffolk and Essex before moving to be minister of Dagger Lane Independent Chapel, Hull, in 1761. He was still minister when he died c.1782. His suspected Arianism led to schism in the congregation and many left to build a new chapel in Blanket Row. Miall, p.290. Surman Index.

Joseph Cockin, 1755-1828. Independent minister. Born at Honley the son of a clothier, he worked in the textile trade until he was twenty. He was converted as a young man through the preaching of Henry Venn and, although his mother encouraged him, his father expelled him from home for going to hear Venn's sermons. He lodged for a year in the house of a clothier of Evangelical views at Lockwood and received some religious instruction from Venn's curate, Henry Ryland. Moving in search of work to Huddersfield he was balloted for the militia and sent to Leeds. Here he attended meetings at the Whitehall Chapel and was noticed by the pastor, John Edwards who was instrumental in his being admitted to the Academy at Heckmondwike in 1774. He became minister of Kipping Chapel, Thornton, near Bradford in 1777 and remained there until 1792. Under Cockin's ministry the congregation at Kipping increased and he also began an itinerant ministry in villages and hamlets of the surrounding district. Titus Knight resigned as minister of Square Chapel, Halifax in

1791 and Cockin succeeded him in the following year. This was a difficult period for Dissenters as they held liberal views in politics and were identified in the popular mind with the French Revolutionaries. The result was a good deal of popular hostility and Cockin had his share of that at Halifax. During his time in Halifax, Cockin continued his itinerant ministry in the surrounding countryside, often working alongside ministers of other denominations. He remained minister at Square Chapel until his death in 1828. He was one of the ministers associated with *The Evangelical Magazine* and, like his predecessor Titus Knight, was in demand as a preacher in London. J. Cockin, *Memoirs of the Rev. Joseph Cockin*, Idle, printed for the author, 1829.

William Crabtree, minister of Westgate Particular Baptist Chapel, Bradford, 1753-1803. He had been a founder member and Deacon of the Church at Wainsgate. In 1753 he was invited to preach to a small congregation gathering in Manningham and was called to be their pastor when the church was formed in December. There were just twenty-three members at the foundation of the church but their numbers soon grew so that they were able to build their chapel on Westgate in Bradford in 1755. Shipley, p.99 and p.117.

James Dawson, c.1737-1795. Independent minister. Born at Silkstone and educated at Heckmondwike Academy. His first and only pastorate was at Cleckheaton where he was minister from 1769 to his death in 1795. He was a successful minister and the chapel was rebuilt and enlarged during his ministry. Miall p.249. Surman Index.

John Edwards, c.1714–1785. Independent minister. Born at Shrewsbury. He became a Wesleyan minister in Ireland. A secession from the Independent chapel in Call Lane, Leeds established the White or Whitehall Chapel and the congregation invited Edwards to become their minister in 1755. He remained pastor there until his death in 1785. During 1784 Edward Parsons became assistant pastor to this congregation. Miall, p.305. Surman Index.

John Fawcett, 1740–1817. Baptist minister. Born at Lidget Green, Bradford. He received an education in the classics although he was apprenticed to a trade for six years. Influenced by George Whitefield and William Grimshaw he attended Methodist meetings before becoming a Baptist under the ministry of William Crabtree at Westgate, Bradford in 1758. He became minister of the Baptist chapel at Wainsgate in 1763 and was ordained in 1765. He first visited London in 1772 and preached extensively in the capital but refused an offer of a metropolitan pulpit. He opened a school and began to train men for the Baptist ministry. In order to further this work he went to live at Brearley Hall in the Calder valley in 1776. In the following year he opened Ebenezer Chapel in Hebden Bridge and remained pastor there until his death. Fawcett wrote a considerable number of devotional and educational works and in 1795 set up a printing press at Brearley Hall. In the following year Fawcett moved his school and printing press to Ewood Hall less than half a mile to the west of his former home. He continued to write prolifically and an American college awarded him the degrees of MA and DD. His most influential works were *An Essay on Anger*, published in 1787 and his *Devotional Family Bible*, which was finished in 1811. J.A. Hargreaves, 'Fawcett, John (1740-1817)', *Oxford Dictionary of National Biography*, Oxford, Oxford University Press, 2004. J. Horsfall Turner, *Halifax Books and Authors*, Idle, published by the author, 1906, pp.65-71. *An Account of the Life, Ministry and Writings of the late Rev.John Fawcett, D.D.*, Halifax, Holden, 1818. Shipley, p.219.

William Gadsby, 1773–1844. Baptist minister. Born at Attleborough, Nuneaton, Leicestershire, the son of a road mender. He was converted when he was seventeen. He was a stocking weaver who set up his own business in Hinckley in 1796. He began preaching locally while remaining in business. Gradually he preached further afield and eventually became pastor of the Strict and Particular Baptist chapel in Back Lane, Rochdale Road, Manchester in 1805. He remained pastor of this chapel until his death in 1844 and had a considerable reputation as a preacher. His theology tended towards 'High Calvinism', his politics towards radicalism. I.D. Sellers, 'Gadsby, William (1773-1844)', *Oxford Dictionary of National Biography*, Oxford, Oxford University Press, 2004.

Robert Galland, 1739-1801. Independent minister. Born at Swanland, East Riding of Yorkshire. Educated at Heckmondwike Academy, 1764-8. Minister at Horton in Craven, 1768, Warwick, 1769-70, Ilkeston, Derbyshire, 1770-79. First minister of Lane Independent Church, Holmfirth, 1779-1800. This church was formed by a number of Holmfirth people who had been influenced by the preaching of Henry Venn. After participating in a joint chapel with the Methodists at Netherthong they withdrew and built their own chapel at Lane in 1777. Galland died in 1801, shortly after resigning his pastorate. H.J. Morehouse, *The History and Topography of the Parish of Kirkburton and the Graveship of Holme, including Holmfirth,* Huddersfield, for the author H. Roebuck, 1861, pp.219–221. Surman Index.

Thomas Grove, c.1748-1817. Independent minister. Born at Wooburn, Buckinghamshire. Educated, St Edmund Hall, Oxford, 1767-8, sent down in 1768 for 'praying, reading and expounding the Scriptures', in other words for being a Methodist. Immediately he began preaching. Minister at Cores End, Wooburn, Buckinghamshire, 1768-77. Minister at Masbro' or Masborough, Rotherham, 1777-93. Shortly after his arrival at Masbro' the congregation built a new chapel. Minister at Walsall, 1794-1817. He died at Walsall in 1817. C.J. Chislett (ed.) *Masbro' Independent Chapel Bicentenary, 1760-1960,* Rotherham, Henry Garnett, n.d. Surman Index.

Joseph Harrison, 1749-1821, Independent minister. The son of Edward Harrison, minister of Greenacres Chapel, near Oldham. He was a pastor in Essex and Cambridgeshire before moving to Skipton in 1789. After serving briefly to congregations in Bingley and Wilsden he became minister at Bethel Chapel, Bury, in 1805 remaining there for ten years. He did much to promote the building of Allerton Independent Chapel in 1815 remaining there until his death. Miall and Surman Index.

William Hartley, a pupil of Dr Fawcett was ordained Pastor of Pellon Lane Baptist Church in 1772 and remained until 1779. He then became Pastor of the Baptist Chapel at Bingley returning to Pellon Lane in 1792 and remaining until 1794. Shipley, p.216. T. Michael, *A Brief Historical Account of The First Baptist Church, Halifax,* Halifax, Whitaker, 1890, pp.11-12, 14 and 18.

John Hindle, a pupil of Dr Fawcett, was the minister of Pellon Lane Baptist Chapel 1779-1789. Hindle was an able preacher but of 'unamiable disposition' and left because some 'trifling matter discomposed him'. He went to Blackley Chapel but only stayed two years 'owing to his irascible temper'. T. Michael, *A Brief Historical Account of the First Baptist Church, Halifax,* Halifax, Whitaker, 1890, pp.12-13. Shipley, pp.94, 216.

Joseph Houlton, ? –1813. Independent minister. He is also recorded as Joseph Houlson and, by Ashworth, as Oulton. He was one of the students transferred from Heckmondwike Academy on the death of John Scott to Northowram where the academy was conducted by Samuel Walker pastor of Heywood Chapel. Houlton was subsequently pastor at Kendal, Saffron Walden, Essex (1787-1797) and Finchingfield, Essex (1797-1813) where he died. M. Pearson, *Northowram: Its History and Antiquities*, Halifax, King, 1898, p. 192. Surman Index.

Daniel Jones, Independent minister. Pastor of Mixenden Chapel from 1783 to 1791. He read his sermons and seems to have had a poor reputation. Miall, p.319.

Titus Knight, 1719-1793. Independent minister. Watson, the Halifax historian who is unlikely to have sympathised with Knight's Calvinism, describes him as, 'a Collier in this parish, who turned preacher'. This is to underestimate a triumph of self-improvement and a remarkable career. Born of Anglican parents at Shibden, near Halifax. He taught himself to read at the age of six. He went to work with his father at a coal pit at Shibden aged seven. Converted in 1747 by hearing John Wesley preaching in Halifax, Knight became a Methodist lay preacher in 1749. He taught himself Latin, Greek and Hebrew in order to read the Scriptures in the original. In 1762, convinced by Lady Huntingdon's arguments in favour of Calvin's doctrine of predestination, Knight separated from the Wesleyans but continued to preach. He continued to command a considerable following and with the help of William Grimshaw, Evangelical incumbent of Haworth, financial assistance was obtained from Lady Huntingdon which enabled his supporters to convert two cottages in Gaol Lane, Halifax, into a chapel for him. The place became known as Chapel Fold. Lady Huntingdon offered to use her influence to obtain Episcopal ordination for Knight, an offer he eventually refused and he was ordained as Independent minister of the Chapel Fold congregation in 1763. Knight's preaching attracted large numbers to Chapel Fold and a larger chapel was soon required. James Kershaw, a former Unitarian, converted by Knight and Henry Venn, took the lead in raising a subscription for a larger chapel. Henry Venn, Vicar of Huddersfield collected £170 towards the project and in May 1772 Square Chapel was opened at a cost of about £2,000. Knight preached twice every Sunday, thrice in summer, gave a lecture on Thursdays and celebrated Communion once a month, preaching on the Friday preceding. He was responsible for establishing numerous small religious societies in the Halifax area. In 1764 Knight first preached for George Whitefield in London and thereafter spent two months every year preaching for him there. Knight suffered strokes in 1790 and 91 which, as he said, reduced him from 'a working to a waiting servant' and he resigned his pastorate in September 1791, dying in March 1793. He published several sermons, *An Elegy on the Death of George Whitefield*, and the intriguing *Amyntas and Philetus*. The Evangelical Magazine, 1793, pp.89-97. J. Horsfall Turner, *Halifax Books and Authors*, Idle, printed for the author, 1906, pp.83-4. J. Sutcliffe, *Square Chapel, Halifax; The History and Architecture*, Heptonstall, J. Sutcliffe, 1996, pp.15-24.

Thomas Laird, 1761-1831. Independent minister. Born in Bolton, Lancashire. Entered Heckmondwike Academy in 1782 and transferred to Northowram when the Academy moved there to be taught by Samuel Walker, minister of Heywood Chapel. Laird subsequently supplied Skipton and was minister at Keighley (1788-1792) and Pudsey (1792-1831) where he died. He married the only daughter of Rev. John Toothill of Hopton. M. Pearson, *Northowram: its History and Antiquities with a Life of Oliver Heywood*, Halifax, King, 1898, pp.160, 192. Surman Index.

Thomas Langdon, Baptist minister. He was the first minister of the newly built Baptist chapel in St. Peter's Square, Leeds that had been opened in July 1781. Langdon was born in Uffcalm, Devon, into a family of the Independent persuasion, his father being a deacon of Uffcalm Independent Church. He was converted to Baptist doctrines and educated at the Theological College, Bristol. Requested to supply the pulpit of the new Baptist chapel at Leeds as a student in the summer of 1781, Langdon was appointed pastor in the same year but had leave of absence for a year to complete his training at Bristol. In the meantime his pulpit was supplied by Rev. William Price, another Bristol student, who was so popular that a number of the congregation followed him to form Ebenezer Chapel when Langdon commenced his regular duties. In spite of this inauspicious start Langdon remained as pastor for forty-two years, until his death on 12[t] October 1824. From 1794 to 1796 Langdon supplemented his meagre stipend of £30 by running a bookshop. He replaced this activity by teaching a school, which lasted until his death. Not long after Langdon's death the chapel moved to new premises in South Parade, Leeds, where it remained until 1909. J.W. Ashworth, *The Jubilee of South Parade Baptist Chapel, Leeds*, Leeds, Spark, 1877, pp.7-8. J.J. Scottorn, *A Short History of South Parade Baptist Church, 1779-1979*, Leeds, (no publisher), 1979.

Samuel Lowell, 1759-1823, Independent minister. Born in Birmingham Lowell became a Wesleyan itinerant. He came to Halifax and supplied the pulpit at the non–denominational chapel at Stainland and after 1782 at Bridge End Chapel, Brighouse where, in 1786, he was ordained pastor on the departure of John Meldrum. His ministry in Brighouse was very successful and he was able to liquidate the debt on the chapel. In 1789 he moved to the pastorate of Woodbridge, Suffolk, whence he migrated to be minister of Bridge Street Chapel, Bristol in 1799. He died in Bristol in 1823. Miall, p.245 and p.367. Surman Index.

Samuel Medley, 1738-1799. Baptist minister. Born in comfortable circumstances in Enfield, Essex. His father was deacon of Eagle Street Particular Baptist Church and his grandfather had been a diplomat. Medley was apprenticed to a city oilman but soon followed his brothers into the navy. A serious wound occasioned Medley's religious awakening which was furthered by hearing his grandfather reading a sermon by Isaac Watts and his conversion was completed under the preaching of George Whitefield and Andrew Gifford in 1760. Medley became a schoolmaster and educated himself especially in theology using his grandfather's library. Meanwhile during his time at Eagle Street under Andrew Gifford his faith deepened and after ministries at Harlington and Watford he was ordained into the Baptist ministry in 1768. Medley was invited to be pastor of the Particular Baptist Church in Liverpool in 1771 when it was facing difficulties occasioned by the behaviour of its pastor. Medley rapidly built up the congregation and the church had to be enlarged in 1773 and replaced by a larger chapel in 1789. Together with John Fawcett of Wainsgate Church, Hebden Bridge, Medley was one of the principal promoters of the Lancashire and Yorkshire Baptist Association that deprecated high- or hyper-Calvinism as an obstacle to evangelicalism. Medley was well known in his own day for his hymns and for supplying Whitefield's pulpits in London. He died in July 1799, still minister of the Particular Baptist Church in Liverpool. J.Y.H. Briggs, 'Medley, Samuel (1738–1799)', *The Oxford Dictionary of National Biography*, Oxford, Oxford University Press, 2004. Shipley, pp.270-276. C. Stell, *An Inventory of Nonconformist Chapels and Meeting-Houses in the North of England*, London, HMSO, 1994, p.104. A.H. Stockwell, *The Baptists of Lancashire*, London, Stockdale, n.d., p.120.

John Meldrum, ? – 1814. Minister of Bridge End Independent Chapel, Brighouse, 1785-1786 (Ashworth's Diary entry of 20 July 1783 suggests that perhaps Meldrum had settled at Brighouse as early as 1783). He came to Brighouse from Malton. Bridge End Chapel had been founded as a result of the preaching of Henry Venn and George Burnett of Elland, which had inspired a number of people at Bridge End to start cottage meetings. James Cockin, who had nominal charge over the Brighouse district was one of the preachers who supplied the meetings. Cockin, Moorhouse, Toothill, Dawson were all named on the trust deed. The chapel was opened in 1779 and Meldrum was said to have made the plan for the chapel house, Brighouse, which had a date of 1783. Meldrum was a Scot and farmed land at Bridge End that became known as Scotty Croft. He left Brighouse to become minister of Hatherlow Chapel, Cheshire in 1786 dying there in 1814. J. Horsfall Turner, *Independency At Brighouse or Bridge End Chapel, Pastors and People,* Brighouse, J.S. Jowett, 1878, pp.26 – 7.

William Moorhouse, 1742-1823. Independent minister. Born near Penistone, the son of a clothier. He was taught to read and write by his father who was a devout Anglican; before he was six he had read The Bible completely through. Moorhouse became a clothmaker and lived as a workman with a Wesleyan Methodist family. He was converted by the combined action of Wesleyan Methodist preaching and the ministry of Henry Venn at Huddersfield. In due course Moorhouse became a clothier on his own account. He became a Methodist lay preacher but, espousing Calvinism, he split local Methodism by continuing to preach. Henry Venn recommended him as the first minister of the newly-built Highfield Chapel, Huddersfield, in 1772. The chapel owed its origin to some of Henry Venn's congregation who were dissatisfied with the less evangelical ministry of his successor Horcar Brook. Venn supported the building of the chapel and contributed to its funds. Encouraged by Venn, Moorhouse resigned his business interests to be ordained as pastor of Highfield. His only formal preparation for the ministry was some instruction from his friend Titus Knight of Square Chapel, Halifax. In the first year of his ministry Moorhouse increased church membership from eighteen to seventy-four; by 1820 membership had reached 177. Throughout his ministry Moorhouse had a high reputation as a preacher. Moorhouse died, still pastor at Highfield, in 1823. At his burial the address was given by Joseph Cockin of Halifax and on the following Sunday a funeral sermon was preached by Jonathan Toothill of Hopton. R. Bruce, *Centenary Memorial of Highfield Chapel, Huddersfield,* Huddersfield, W.H. Woodcock, 1872, pp.20-68. W. Moorhouse, *A Brief Memoir of the Life and Character of the Rev. William Moorhouse….,*

Huddersfield, William Moore, 1823, reprinted in *The Evangelical Magazine,* January and February 1824.

Edward Parsons, 1762-1833. Independent minister. Born at Stepney, Middlesex in 1760. One of the first students at Lady Huntingdon's college at Trevecca he became a minister in her Connexion, taking charge of chapels at Tunbridge Wells and then at Norwich. Parsons gradually moved away from Lady Huntingdon's Connexion and into Independency. After applying unsuccessfully for the pulpit of Cannon Street Chapel, Manchester in 1784, he was appointed assistant pastor to the congregation at White Chapel, Leeds to help the ageing John Edwards. In 1785 he was ordained as minister of this congregation, which he served until the majority of the congregation moved with him, in 1791, to the more commodious and newly built Salem Chapel where Parsons remained pastor almost until his death in 1833. Parsons regularly supplied the pulpits of The Tabernacle and Tottenham Court Road Chapels in London. B. Porter revised by J.M.V. Quinn, 'Parsons, Edward (1762–1833)', *Oxford Dictionary of National Biography*, Oxford, Oxford University Press, 2004. Surman Index.

John Sharpe, Baptist minister. A former Inghamite preacher and latterly a member of the Baptist cause at Halifax, Sharpe was pastor at Farsley from 1807 to 1824. He accepted this call when the congregation had almost ceased to exist and for the first two years of his ministry at Farsley he had to maintain himself by working as a carpenter in a workshop he established adjoining the chapel. Shipley, p.157.

Joseph Sowden, c.1746-1822. Independent minister. He was born at St. Columb, Cornwall. He was minister at Rehoboth, Morley, 1782-1787; Booth, 1787-1794 and Sowerby 1794-1800, where he was very successful. He then held pastorates in Lancashire, ending his ministry at Mount Street Chapel, Blackburn. Miall, p.232, p.323 and p.366. Surman Index.

William Steadman, Baptist minister. Originally pastor of the church at Plymouth Dock. He was invited to take charge of the projected Baptist Academy at Bradford and came north on a preliminary visit in 1805. Later in the year he accepted the pastorate of Westgate Chapel, Bradford, a post which he combined with the presidency of the Academy. He died, still in office, in 1837. Shipley, p.118, pp.280-287

Benjamin Sugden, Independent minister. He was born at Northowram and probably educated at Northowram Academy. He is recorded as holding pastorates at Ilkeston, Derbyshire, 1795-99; Skipton, 1799-1809; Shelley, Yorkshire, 1809-10. In 1813 he was supplying Melbourne in Derbyshire. Miall records that his ministry at Skipton was marked by a decline in the congregation. Miall, p. 363. M. Pearson, *Northowram: Its History and Antiquities…* Halifax, King, 1898, p.192. Surman Index.

William Tapp, 1758–1819. Independent minister. Born at Hitchin, Hertfordshire. Educated at Heckmondwike Academy, 1779-82. Minister at Pontefract, 1782–1790. Minister at South Cave, East Riding of Yorkshire, 1791-1819. Died at South Cave, 1819. A.E. Trout, 'An Old Yorkshire Congregation, South Cave Congregational Church', *Transactions of the Congregational Historical Society,* September, 1931. Surman Index.

James Tetley, Independent minister. Educated at Heckmondwike Academy from 1762 and minister at Ravenstonedale, Westmorland, 1766-1775. He retired through ill-health but lived into the 1790s. Surman Index.

John Toothill, Independent minister. Born at Wilsden in 1760, the cousin of Jonathan Toothill of Hopton. Converted by hearing Joseph Cockin preach at a cottage meeting. He joined Cockin's congregation at Kipping and was sent by Cockin to the Academy at Heckmondwike. When the church at Booth, in the township of Midgley near Halifax, applied to Heckmondwike Academy for a preacher during a vacancy in 1782 Toothill was sent. He impressed the congregation who invited him to be their permanent minister. Toothill agreed but intended to continue his studies at the Academy. However James Scott died in January 1783 and John Toothill at once became minister at Booth. He remained only until August 1786 when he received a call from some of the Independent congregation at Rainford in Lancashire. This congregation was divided between the orthodox and many who favoured Arianism. Toothill accepted the call to Rainford after seeking the advice of the congregation at Square Chapel, Halifax. 'They were unanimously in favor (*sic*) of his accepting the invitation, on the ground that Booth would continue to enjoy the privileges of the gospel, and Rainford might be rescued from the evils of Arianism.' D. Jones, *Centenary Memorials of The Church and Congregation Assembling for Christian Worship in Booth Chapel near Halifax*. Halifax, Birtwhistle, 1861, pp.22-24. Miall, p.232.

Jonathan Toothill, Independent minister. He was converted by reading one of George Whitefield's sermons, hearing William Grimshaw and perhaps most importantly by a sermon in Kipping Chapel by Timothy Priestley the minister. Priestley encouraged him to enter the ministry and recommended him to James Scott of Heckmondwike. He was duly educated at the Academy. He was minister at Hopton, near Mirfield, 1768–1826 and was responsible for a great revival in the congregation at Hopton. He died there in 1826. G.G. Waddington, *Historical and Biographical Notices,* Dewsbury, Ward, 1886. pp.170-1, 175-196.

Samuel Walker, Independent minister. He was educated at Heckmondwike Academy, 1771-4, where he was reputed to be one of Scott's most able pupils. Minister of Heywood Chapel, Northowram, 1774-1793. On the death of John Scott in 1782 the Heckmondwike Academy was brought to Northowram to be taught by Walker. He resigned the pastorate at Northowram in 1793, due to a division in the congregation, but continued to conduct the Academy until 1795. In that year, perhaps because of doctrinal disagreements, he lost the support of the Northern Education Society that had financed both Heckmondwike and Northowram. Walker died in 1796. Miall, 1868, pp.164, 326. M. Pearson, *Northowram: its History and Antiquities,* Halifax, King, 1898, pp.148-149; 192-193.

John Walton, Baptist minister of Sutton in Craven from 1780 to 1807. Shipley recorded that 'his ministry was greatly blessed to the village, for he was a man of considerable ability and outstanding piety'. Shipley, p.183.

Abraham Webster, Baptist minister. He came to Pole Moor Chapel, Slaithwaite, from Liverpool in January 1808. Early in Webster's ministry at Pole Moor some of his congregation who followed William Gadsby's teachings broke away from the church and established a separate congregation. Webster augmented his income at Pole Moor by teaching a school and farming in a small way. Perhaps because of continued trouble from those inclining to Gadsby's high Calvinist views, Abraham Webster left Pole Moor for Hebden Bridge in 1818. Further schisms at Pole Moor resulted in Webster's recall and he remained minister there until his death in 1828. A. Crawshaw and M. Wilkinson, *Tabernacle on the Hill. A History of Pole Moor Baptist Chapel, Scammonden, 1787-1987*, privately printed, 1987, pp.15-22.

Glossary

The authorities for the definitions are indicated at the end of the entry.

The Oxford English Dictionary, Vols. I –XII, Oxford, The Clarendon Press, 1933, has been abbreviated to *O.E.D.*
J. Wright (ed.), *The English Dialect Dictionary*, Vols. I – VI, Oxford, The Clarendon Press, 1898–1905, has been abbreviated to *E.D.D.*

Baking stone. A flat stone for baking oatcakes on. *E.D.D.*

Balk or Baulk. The loft in the barn, often over the mistal, where the hay is stored. *O.E.D.*

Burden. A load of hay gathered up and tied with a rope so it could be carried on a person's back. W.B. Crump, *The Little Hill Farm*, London, Scrivener, 1951, pp.58-59.

Bushel. A measure of capacity equal to eight gallons.

Cess. A tax or rate. *O.E.D.*

Church Rate. A rate levied on all householders by the churchwardens for the purpose of maintaining the parish church. Until 1868 these rates were compulsory irrespective of whether or not the householder was a member of the Church of England. D. Hey, *The Oxford Companion to Local and Family History,* Oxford, Oxford University Press, 1986, p.90.

Clean. To bring forth the after-birth when a cow has calved. *E.D.D.*

Clout. A heavy blow. *O.E.D.*

Composition money. The payment of money in lieu of some other obligation. *O.E.D.* Ashworth recorded paying 'composition money' for the roads to the local surveyor of highways. He used the term because the surveyor was levying a highway rate instead of requiring householders to give free labour on the roads for six days per annum as they were obliged to do under the terms of the Statute Labour Act of 1555 as amended in

1563. D. Hey, *The Oxford Companion to Local and Family History*, Oxford, Oxford University Press, 1986, p.424.

Day's Work. One Day's Work in Halifax Measure equals 3136 square yards or two roods and twenty three perches. *Scale for Changing Statute Measure into Halifax Customary or Provincial Measure*, Halifax, Greenwood, 1847.

Double Russels. Russell is a ribbed or corded cloth made with a cotton warp and woollen weft. A double cloth is where two fabrics, each with its own warp and weft, are woven simultaneously on the same loom and held together by interweaving a certain number of the warp threads. The purpose of weaving doubles is to produce a heavy cloth with a fine face. *O.E.D.* and E. Ostick, *Textiles for Tailors,* London, The Tailor and Cutter, n.d.

Double Stuffs called two picks. Stuff is a worsted cloth and double stuffs are woven as a double cloth (see above).

Droughty. Dry. *O.E.D.* Joseph Rogerson of Leeds used the word in exactly this sense in his Diary of 1808. W.B. Crump, *The Leeds Woollen Industry,* Leeds, Thoresby Society Publications, Vol. XXXII, 1931, for example, p.87.

Easter Dues. In the parish of Halifax at least these appear to have been the small tithes commuted to a money payment. J. Watson, *The History and Antiquities of the Parish of Halifax*, London, Lowndes, 1775, pp.347-349.

Eddish. Grass that has grown after the field has been mowed. *O.E.D.*

Finely. Considerably. *E.D.D.*

Flitting. Moving house.

Fodering. Feeding. *O.E.D.*

Gogram. (Grogram). A coarse cloth made from a mixture of silk and wool. Usually worn by people of modest means. Admiral Vernon was unusual for a person of his rank in wearing a grogram cloak, which earned him the nick-name 'old grog'. The name 'grog' was then transferred to the mixture of rum and water that Vernon ordered to be served to men under his command in August 1740. *O.E.D.*

Graving. A method of preparing the land by hand for the sowing of seed. For further information see pp.50-52.

Hacking. Breaking up the soil with the use of a hack. See p.51.

Hattock. A stook or shock of corn consisting of several sheaves, often stacked with two sheaves laid across the top to keep the whole dry. *E.D.D.*

Hay Mow. A haystack. *O.E.D.*

Healding a warp. Drawing the warp through the healds and reed and winding it on to the cloth roller. See diagram on p.68.

Healds. The gear on a loom that lifts the warp threads, allowing the weft thread to be passed across and create the weave. See diagram on p.68.

House. To get under cover, to bring in. *E.D.D.*

Ketlock. A large umbelliferous plant such as cow parsnip, colewort or common charlock. *O.E.D.*

Knitting in. To tie the threads of a new warp to the ends of the old warp as a piece of cloth is finished. *E.D.D.*

Lead. To carry, cart or convey by cart. *E.D.D.*

Looming a warp. Putting the warp onto the loom.

Lathe. A barn. *E.D.D.*

Loss'd. Wet through. *E.D.D.*

Mainer. Manure. This spelling is frequently found in seventeenth-century inventories in the Halifax district.

Miding. Midden. *E.D.D.*

Mistal. The place in the barn where the cows were kept. *O.E.D*

Mooing. The process of placing hay or corn in a hay mow (haystack). Making a stack of corn or hay, inside or out. *O.E.D.*

Mooter. A toll paid at the mill. J. Collier, *The Miscellaneous Works of Tim Bobbin, Esq; Containing His View of The Lancashire Dialect*, Manchester, Haslingden, 1775.

Mossing. A method of rendering stone slate roofs waterproof by stuffing moss into the gaps under the slates. The moss required renewal at fairly frequent intervals. J. Walton, *Early Timbered Buildings of the Huddersfield District*, Huddersfield, Tolson Museum, 1955, p.50.

Necessary. A privy or any small ancillary building. *E.D.D.*

Pack of meal. This may be an indefinite quantity or a pack of 252 lbs, which was a recognised measure of meal. *O.E.D.*

Pocket of Hops. Hops were sold in 'pockets' or sacks that weighed from 1¼ to 1½ hundredweights.

Poor Cess. A rate levied by the overseers of the poor to cover the cost of poor relief within the township.

Rearing Feast. A celebratory feast given to the workmen when a roof has been put on a new building. *E.D.D.*

Rakings. The remnants of hay or corn left in the field after the crop has been gathered in. These are then raked up, hence the term. *E.D.D.*

Rope Shackles. A rope about sixteen feet long tied through a shaped wooden handle and used for carrying a burden of hay from the field to the barn or haystack. W.B. Crump, *The Little Hill Farm*, London, Scrivener, 1951, pp.58-59.

Rushbearing. An annual celebration that has its origin in the ancient practice of strewing rushes on the floors of churches. They would remain for a year until they were replaced with new rushes that were often brought to church in procession by elaborately loaded and decorated carts. The event was often the occasion of a general holiday. *E.D.D.*

Scouring. Washing wool to remove dirt and the natural grease by the use of water and a mild alkaline agent. In the eighteenth and nineteenth centuries in the West Riding this was usually a solution of stale urine. W.B. Crump and G. Ghorbal, *History of the Huddersfield Woollen Industry*, Huddersfield, Tolson Museum, 1935, p.36.

Share. To shear or cut. *O.E.D.* Wright records this as a West Riding usage, *E.D.D.* This word was wrongly transcribed as 'shave' by T.W.Hanson in 'The diary of a Grandfather; Cornelius Ashworth of Walt Royd', *Transactions of the Halifax Antiquarian Society*, 1916, p.235. This mistake was followed by F. Atkinson in the extracts from Ashworth's Journal which he published in F. Atkinson, *Some Aspects of the 18th Century Woollen Trade in Halifax*, Halifax, Halifax Museums, 1956, p.28. Unfortunately this misreading has often been quoted subsequently.

Sheave (Sheaf). A bundle of cut corn which has been bound up so it can be stacked. *O.E.D.*

Shelling. Husks or chaff produced by threshing. *O.E.D.*

Shilling. Grain, especially oats, which has been separated from the husk.

Sizing a warp. Treating a warp with a glutinous liquid made from animal bones to strengthen it. *O.E.D.* and K. Pointing (ed.), *Baines's Account of the Woollen Manufacture of England*, Newton Abbot, David and Charles, 1970, p.163.

Soft. With reference to the weather; mild. *E.D.D.*

Statedly. Regularly. *O.E.D.*

Strike of oats. A measure equal to two bushels in the West Riding, although it could vary from half a bushel to four bushels in other districts. *E.D.D.*

Swilling. The practice of spreading liquid manure from the mistal across the fields below it by using a system of shallow channels. W.B. Crump, *The Little Hill Farm*, London, Scrivener, 1951, p.51.

Tammy. A cloth with a worsted weft and cotton warp. K. Pointing (ed), *Baines's Account of the Woollen Manufacture of England*, Newton Abbot, David and Charles, 1970, p.164.

Thatching. Putting a roof on a building. In the area around Halifax this usually meant using 'thakstones' i.e. stone slates. *E.D.D.*

Tillage. Manure. *E.D.D.*

Turf. Peat.

Warp. The yarn placed lengthways on a loom, passing from the back or warp beam, through the healds and reed and on to the cloth roller at the front of the loom. See diagram on p.68.

Water-Furrowing. The practice of flooding a meadow in order to encourage an early and abundant growth of grass. See pp.45-48.

Weft. The yarn which runs from one side of the loom to the other. See p.68.

Winding on a warp. Putting the warp on to the warp beam of the loom. See diagram on p.68.

Window money. The window tax.

Winnowing. The process of separating the grain from the chaff after threshing. Often this process took place in the centre of a barn on the threshing floor with both front and back doors open to create a draught that would carry away the chaff. W.B. Crump, *The Little Hill Farm*, London, Scrivener, 1951, p.70.

INDEX TO THE INTRODUCTION

Footnotes and illustrations are not indexed

INDEX TO THE DIARIES 1782 – 1816
PLACES

1. References are to dates in the Diary.
2. Where possible, this index provides an indication of the location of place names but only when they are not marked on the extract of the map produced by J.F. Myers in 1834-35 reproduced at the end of this volume.
3. Variant spellings in the Diaries are in round brackets.
4. Modern spellings are provided, underlined and in square brackets, where the place name in the Diary is unclear.
5. Where the Diary spelling is significantly different from the modern name an additional entry is made under the modern name which is underlined.
6. Specific buildings and sites are indexed in the Subject Index, not in this index.
7. Halifax is not indexed as a place because of its ubiquity in the Diaries.

Gildersome *(28 Oct 1782) (11 June 1783)*

Glasgow *(2 April 1783)*

Gomersal *(28 Dec 1782) (4 Jan 1783) (26, 28, 30 May 1783) (2 June 1783) (30 March 1785) (23 April 1785) (5, 23 May 1785) (27 August 1785) (7 November 1785) (26 Dec 1785) (23 Jan 1809) (15 Aug 1809) (3, 12, 15, 19 April 1815) (14 June 1815) (10 July 1815) (12 Dec 1815)*

Grey Stones (Greystones), Wheatley *(11 April 1815) (22 July 1815)*

Haley (Haily; Hayley) Hill *(11 Nov 1783) (8 Feb 1809) (6 April 1809)*

Harwood (Highroad) Well *(1 June 1785) (24 October 1785) (29 Dec 1815)*

Hathershelf *(9 Jan 1809) (22, 27, 29 May 1809) (1 June 1809) (4 Aug 1809) (22 March 1815) (28 June 1815) (7, 10 July 1815) (16, 18 Nov 1815)*

Haworth (Howarth) *(1 March 1785) (2, 3 June 1809) (17 July 1809) (21 Nov 1815)*

Hebble Bridge (Brig), Salterhebble *(12-13, 25, 30-31 Jan 1786) (1 Feb 1786)*

Hepton [Hebden] Bridge *(10 Feb 1785)*

High Field, Ovenden *(21 August 1785)*

Hipperholme (Hipperholm) *(30 March 1809) (8 July 1809) (21, 28 Oct 1809) (17 Jan 1815) (9 June 1815) (25 Aug 1815) (23, 24 Oct 1815) (2 Nov 1815) (20, 23 Jan 1816)*

Holdsworth (Houldsworth; Houldworth) *(29 Nov 1782) (4 Sept 1783) (28 March 1785) (20 Jan 1786) (16 Jan 1809) (25, 27 Sept 1809) (6 Jan 1815) (28 July 1815)*

Holmfirth (Holmforth) *(14 May 1783) (3 Aug 1783) (12 June 1785)*

Hopton *(14 May 1783) (6 July 1783) (29 May 1785) 10 August 1785)*

Howarth (Haworth) *(2, 3 June 1809) (17 July 1809) (21 Nov 1815)*

Huddersfield *(9 April 1783) (27 June 1783) (27 Feb 1785) (8 May 1785) (31 July 1785) (1 Aug 1809)*

Hunsworth *(23 May 1785) (7 November 1785)*

Illingworth *(8 Oct 1782) (7 Jan 1783) (1, 21 Feb 1783) (21, 27 March 1783) (19 May 1783) (15, 26 June 1783) (10, 23, 30 Aug 1783) (8 Nov 1783) (17, 19 Jan 1785) (1, 15 Feb 1785) (6, 13, 28 March 1785) (11 May 1785) (1, 19, 24 June 1785) (7 July 1785) (27-28 October 1785) (29 Dec 1785) (4, 20 Jan 1786) (16 Jan 1809) (3 Feb 1809) (16, 28 March 1809) (2 July 1809) (20 Oct 1809) (2, 13 Jan 1815) (31 May 1815) (28 July 1815) (1, 7 Aug 1815) (4 Sept 1815) (9, 15 Jan 1816)*

Illingworth Moor *(16 Feb 1815)*

Italy *(15 April 1783)*

Jane Green, Causeway Foot *(6 Jan 1815)*

Jumples (Jumpls) Mill, Wheatley *(19-20, 22-23, 29 August 1785) (17 October 1785) (8 November 1785) (20-23 Dec 1785) (9-11, 14, 21, 23-24 Jan 1786) (3-4, 7-10, 13-14, 16-17 Feb 1786) (8 March 1786)*

Jumples, Wheatley *(14 Oct 1815)*

Keighley *(21 May 1783) (23 June 1783) (31 Aug 1815)*

King Cross *(25 June 1785) (8 Dec 1785) (16 Jan 1786) (16 Aug 1815)*

King Cross Lane, King Cross *(9 April 1809) (19 June 1809)*

Kiping *(13 July 1783)*

320

Kitten Clough, Mt Pellon *(8 Jan 1785)*

Lee Bank, Lee Mills *(26 May 1783)*

Lee Bridge, Lee Mills *(10 April 1783) (27 June 1785) (22 Jan 1816) (19 Nov 1815)*

Leebank Shroggs, Shroggs *(10-11 Mar 1786)*

Leeds *(20 Oct 1782) (21 Nov 1782) (4, 26 May 1783) (13 July 1783) (9 March 1785) (6, 19 April 1785) (19 June 1785) (4 May 1809) (22 June 1815) (13 Dec 1815) (28 Feb 1816)*

Little Brackenbed, Brackenbed *(11 Nov 1783)*

Liverpool *(6 Aug 1783) (8, 15 May 1785) (7, 11 Aug 1809) (11 Dec 1809)*

Lockwood *(16, 23 July 1809)*

London *(25 Sept 1782) (13 Dec 1782) (20 May 1783) (9 June 1783) (8 Aug 1783) (28 Oct 1783) (2 May 1785) (3, 17, 25 June 1785) (24 July 1785) (4 May 1809) (5, 7 June 1809) (31 Oct 1809) (1 Nov 1809) (11 Dec 1809) (4, 22 June 1815) (26, 31 July 1815) (26 Oct 1815) (10 Nov 1815) (13, 15 Dec 1815) (28 Feb 1816)*

Long House, Mixenden *(17Aug 1815)*

Lordship, Ovenden *(9 Jan 1785)*

Luddenden (Luddinden) *(2 Jan 1786) (2 May 1815) (16 Nov 1815)*

Luddenden Foot (Ludenden foot; Luddend Foot) *(2, 13 May 1815) (1 July 1815) (22 Aug 1815) (30 Sept 1815) (22, 25 Dec 1815)*

Manchester *(25, 27 June 1785) (2, 11 April 1809)*

Manningham *(23 June 1785)*

Messina *(15 April 1783)*

Midgley *(19 Jan 1786)*

Mile Cross *(16 March 1785)*

Mixenden *(8 Feb 1783) (28 April 1783) (18 May 1783) (11 Nov 1783) (5, 16 Jan 1785) (15 May 1785) (20 July 1785)*

Mixenden Ings *(8 Aug 1815)*

Mixenden Stones *(7 June 1815)*

Moorside (Moor Side). See Ovenden Moorside)

Morley *(22 June 1783)*

Mount Pellon *(16 March 1815) (23 Nov 1815)*

Naples *(15 April 1783)*

North Gate, Halifax *(27 Oct 1815)*

Northowram (Northouram) *(29 Nov 1782) (14 May 1783) (13 Aug 1783) (23 Jan 1785) (6, 13 March 1785) (11, 24 May 1785) (1, 9 June 1785) (20 November 1785) (19 Feb 1786) (30 March 1809) (21 Oct 1809) (19 May 1815)*

Ovenden *(15 Dec 1782) (6 Oct 1783) (9 Feb 1785) (1 March 1785) (1 June 1785) (31 July 1785) (18 October 1785) (10 November 1785) (17, 25 Dec 1785) (15, 16, 17 Jan 1815) (28 July 1815) (14 Oct 1815) (3, 17 Nov 1815) (4 Jan 1816)*

Ovenden Brook *(9 Jan 1875)*

Ovenden Wood (Ovendenwood) *(28 April 1783) (28 June 1783) (14 May 1785) (2, 6 Feb 1809)*

Ovenden Moorside *(28 Feb 1783) (1, 28 Oct 1783) (16 Jan 1809) (3 Feb 1809) (29 April 1809) (27 Sept 1809) (13 Jan 1815) (9 Feb 1815) (6, 29 April 1815) (28 July 1815) (15 Aug 1815) (4 Oct 1815) (3 Nov 1815)*

Paris *(18 March 1815)*

Pellon, Mount Pellon *(1 April 1783) (13 May 1815)*

Plymouth Dock (<u>Devonport</u>), (Devon) *(20 Jan 1809)*

Pole Moor, Scammonden *(14 May 1815)*

Pontefract *(13 Aug 1783)*

Roper Green, Illingworth *(2 March 1809)*

Rotheram *(9 Dec 1782)*

Sabden, (Whalley parish, Lancashire) *(20 April 1815) (13, 30 Sept 1815)*

Salter Hebble *(5 Dec 1809) (2, 7 Jan 1815) (17 June 1815) (16 Nov 1815) (12 Dec 1815)*

Savil Green, Savill Hall *(14 Jan 1786)*

Scotland *(2 April 1783)*

Shaw Hill, Halifax *(28 Jan 1809) (9 Feb 1815) (21 Oct 1815)*

Shaw Lane, Ovenden *(25, 27 Sept 1809) (6 Jan 1815) (13 Jan 1815) (28 July 1815)*

Sheffield *(5 June 1785)*

Shelf *(19 May 1815)*

Shorest *(12 Sept 1815)*

Sicily *(7, 15 April 1783)*

Skipton *(14 June 1809)*

Skircoat *(25 April 1783) (21 April 1809) (12 Jan 1815) (10 March 1815) (8 May 1815) (22 Aug 1815) (16 Nov 1815)*

Skircoat Green *(5, 9 May 1783)*

Slaithwaite *(14 May 1815)*

Slippy Lane *(24 May 1785)*

Sodhouse Green, Ovenden *(3 April 1783)*

Southowram (Southouram) *(5, 9, 28 May 1783) (23 June 1783) (21 June 1785) (19 May 1815) (9 June 1815) (23, 24 Oct 1815)*

Sowerby *(12 Jan 1815) (10 March 1815)*

Sowerby Bridge *(29 November 1785) (22 Feb 1809) (6 July 1809)*

Sowerby Street, Sowerby Bridge *(17 June 1815)*

Spain *(28 Jan 1783)*

Spring Hall, Halifax *(14 March 1815)*

Staincliff *(9 June 1785)*

Staincliffe (Staincliff) Hall *(26, 28 May 1783)*

Stannary (Stanry), Halifax *(30 Dec 1815) (3 Jan 1816)*

Soil (Swill) Hill *(8 Jan 1785) (25 Feb 1785) (6 April 1809) (23 Aug 1815)*

Soil (Swill) Hill End *(29 Nov 1782) (28 April 1783)*

Soil (Swill) Hill Top *(6, 13 March 1815) (8 Aug 1815) (5 Jan 1816)*

Triangle *(29 November 1785)*

Wakefield *(1 Aug 1809)*

Warley (Warely; Warely Town; Waretown) *(24, 28 Oct 1785) (21 April 1809) (6, 25 July 1809) (12 Jan 1815) (26 Feb 1815) (10 March 1815) (8, 29 April 1815) (2, 8 May 1815) (17 June 1815) (22 Aug 1815) (12 Sept 1815) (7 Oct 1815) (4, 16 Nov 1815) (22 Dec 1815) (12, 13 Feb 1816)*

Washer Lane, Halifax *(20 Aug 1815)*

Wheatley (Wheatly) *(21, 23, 25 Jan 1783) (14 March 1783) (8 April 1783) (2, 3 July 1783) (11 Nov 1783) (22, 27 Jan 1785) (23 Feb 1785) (6, 17, 28 March 1785) (20, 27 July 1785) (17, 24 October 1785) (29 Dec 1785) (23 April 1809) (4, 8 Feb 1815) (1, 6 May 1815) (8 June 1815) (28 July 1815) (17 Nov 1815)*

Wheatley Edge, Wheatley *(14-19, 21-26 November 1785) (5 Dec 1785)*

Whithill, Illingworth *(28 Feb 1783)*

York *(16 Aug 1783) (31 May 1815)*

INDEX TO THE DIARIES 1782 – 1816
PERSONS

1. References are to dates in the Diary.
2. This index makes no assumption that people of the same name at different dates are the same person. Only when there is clear evidence to the contrary are entries for different dates made under the same name.
3. Births are indexed under the parent only
4. Christian names are expanded where certain.
5. Individuals are defined by place where known.
6. Occupations and relationships where known are in brackets.
7. Variant spellings in the Diaries are in brackets.

(7 Oct 1815) (26-30 Dec 1815) (2-3 Jan 1816)

Ashworth, John; wife of (sister-in-law of Diarist) *(30 June 1783)*

Ashworth, John's daughter (niece of Diarist) *(7-8 Feb 1815)*

Ashworth, Mother (of Diarist) *(5 Aug 1783)*

Ashworth, Reverend (of Gildersome) *(11 June 1783)*

Ashworth, William (brother of Diarist) *(29 Dec 1785)*

Ashworth, William; wife of (sister-in-law of Diarist) *(30 June 1783)*

Aston, Reverend (of Lockwood near Huddersfield) *(16 July 1809)*

Ayston (of Holdsworth) *(28 March 1785)*

Bairston, Nacy *(25 Dec 1815)*

Bairstow, George *(9 May 1815)*

Bairstow, Nanny *(22 Nov 1815)*

Bairstow, William; wife of (of Ovenden) *(9 Feb 1785)*

Balmforth, William *(3 Aug 1815)*

Bancroft, James (of Roper Green) *(2 March 1809)*

Bancroft, Joseph *(7 Nov 1785)*

Banister, John *(3 Nov 1785)*

Banister, Reverend *(3 May 1809)*

Barraclogh, Samuel *(17 Sept 1815)*

Bates, Reverend John *(23 April 1815)*

Bates, Richard (of Skircoat) *(25 April 1783)*

Bently, Edward of Foor (Ford) in Northowram *(29 Nov 1782)*

Bever, Peter (of Wheatley) *(10 Jan 1786)*

Binns, Alice *(18 July 1785)*

Binns, Thomas (of Stanry (Stannary)) *(30 Dec 1815) (3 Jan 1816)*

Bins, Mrs (of Dean Clough) *(15 Jan 1786)*

Birdwhisler, Edward; son of *(2 Feb 1809)*

Blagborough, Joseph *(4-6 July 1815) (7 Aug 1815) (14-16, 20 Sept 1815)*

Blagborough, William *(5, 9 Nov 1785)*

Blagbrough (Blagboug), Benjamin *(22 Dec 1785) (10 Mar 1786)*

Blagbrough (Blagbroug), Sarah *(30 Oct 1785) (5 Jan 1786)*

Blagbrough, Barnaby *(19 Jan 1783)*

Blagbrough, Benjamin (of Illingworth) *(7 Jan 1783)*

Blagbrough, John *(18 Jan 1783) (19 June 1783)*

Blagbrough, Joseph *(10, 13 Nov 1809)*

Blagbrough, Thomas (of Illingworth) *(7 Jan 1783)*

Bonaparte *(18 March 1815)*

Booth, Reverend Thos (of Halifax) *(12 May 1785)*

Booth, Reverend Thos; wife of (of Halifax) *(17 April 1785)*

Boulton, James (of Ovenden) *(4 Jan 1816)*

Bowcock, William *(19, 23 Dec 1783)*

Brear, James *(27 Feb 1815)*

Brewer, Reverend (of Sheffield) *(5 June 1785)*

Brooksbank, Reverend Joseph (of London) *(24 July 1785)*

Bruce, Reverend (of Liverpool) *(6 Aug 1783)*

Burnet, Reverend *(5 March 1783)*

Butterfield, Mrs (of Halifax) *(10 Dec 1815)*

Butterworth, Mary *(17 Feb 1815)*

Butterworth, Mary (of Halifax) *(1 Oct 1809)*

Buttery, Betty *(28 Dec 1785)*

Bwilitt, Thomas *(7 April 1809)*

Carpmeal (of Halifax) *(17 April 1815)*

Casson, John *(9 Nov 1782)*

Chambers, Benjamin (of Halifax) *(6 Aug 1785)*

Chambers, Mary (of Halifax) *(28 May 1809)*

Chambers, Reverend John (of Warley) *(26 Feb 1815)*

Chapman, Dolly *(18 July 1785)*

Charnock, Harry *(4-6 July 1815) (14-16, 20 Sept 1815)*

Charnock, James *(30 Jan 1785) (24 March 1785) (18 Oct 1785) (23 Feb 1786)*

Charnock, Reverend James (of Haworth) *(17 July 1809)*

Charnock, Reverend James (of Haworth), wife of *(17 July 1809)*

Charnock, John (Jas) *(30 June 1783) (5 July 1783) (5, 12, 17 Sept 1783) (4 Nov 1783)*

Charnock, Joshua; child of *(7 July 1785)*

Charnock, Mary (daughter of James Charnock) *(24 March 1785)*

Charnock, Thomas (of Swill Hill Top) *(6, 13 March 1815)*

Charnock, William *(4 Dec 1809)*

Child, G.; sister of *(7 Feb 1815)*

Child, George *(22 Sept 1809)*

Clayton, Alice *(16 Feb 1815)*

Clayton, William *(8 Feb 1785)*

Clough, Joseph *(23 Nov 1782)*

Clough, Miss *(25 April 1783) (18, 23 June 1783)*

Cockin (Cocking, Cooking), Reverend Joseph (of Kipping (Kippin) Chapel, Thornton and later of Square Chapel, Halifax) *(12 March 1783) (15 June 1783) (13, 17, 24 July 1783) (19, 26 June 1785) (10 Aug 1785) (22 Feb 1809) (19 April 1809) (9 August 1809) (4 Oct 1809) (13 December 1809) (25 June 1815) (2, 9, 13, 16, 27 July 1815) (18 27 Aug 1815) (3, 10, 17 Sept 1815)*

Cockroft, Jonathan *(4 Oct 1783)*

Cockroft, Joshua; daughter of *(31 March 1783) (13 April 1783)*

Cockroft, Mark; child at *(9 Jan 1785)*

Cockroft, Samuel; child of (of Ovenden) *(10 Nov 1785)*

Cooper, Mary *(13 Dec 1782) (26 Jan 1785)*

Cordingly (Cordaly), Nancy *(23 Nov 1782)*

Cordingly (Cordingley), Joseph (cousin of Diarist's wife) *(23 Nov 1782) (14 Feb 1783) (21 March 1783) (12 July 1783)*

Cordingly, Aunt (of Diarist's wife) *(12, 16 July 1783)*

Crabtree (Crabter), Reverend (of Bradford) *(19 Feb 1786) (8 May 1785)*

Crabtree, David *(12 Feb 1783)*

Crabtree, widow *(8 July 1785)*

Crabtree, widow (of Wheatley) *(27 July 1785)*

Crapper, Benjamin *(20 March 1785)*

Craven, William *(9, 14 July 1785)*

Crossley, Hannah *(4 Jan 1815)*

Crossley, John *(15 Oct 1809)*

Crossley, John *(20 Jan 1785*

Crossley, Joseph *(3 Aug 1815)*

Crossley, Susee *(14, 16 July 1783)*

Crowther, C (Charles) *(19-20 Dec 1782) (10 Feb 1785) (21-24, 30 March 1785) (16, 19-21 May 1785) (13-15 June 1785) (18 July 1875) (12, 19, 22-23, 25-26 Aug 1785) (20 Oct 1785) (29 Nov 1785) (27-29 Dec 1785)*

Crowther, Doctor *(12 Jan 1809)*

Crowther, Hannah *(6 Nov 1783)*

Crowther, John *(2 April 1783) (27 Aug 1783) (1 Nov 1783) (11 Jan 1785) (24 May 1785) (25-26 Aug 1785) (29 Nov 1785) (1, 3, 9 Dec 1785)*

Crowther, John; wife of *(29 Nov 1785) (1 Dec 1785)*

Crowther, Joseph (of Northowram) *(1 June 1785)*

Crowther, Sarah *(24 Oct 1782) (2, 11 April 1809) (3 Sept 1809)*

Dawson, Reverend (of Cleckheaton) *(22 May 1785)*

Dean, John (of Bradshaw) *(11 May 1785)*

Dillott, Joseph (of Illingworth) *(31 May 1815)*

Dillott, Mary (of Ovenden) *(15 Jan 1815)*

Drake, Joseph (of Wheatley) *(8 Feb 1815)*

Drake, Sally (of Bradshaw) *(10 Mar 1786)*

Earnshaw, John (of Bradshaw) *(29 Nov 1782)*

Edwards, Reverend (of Leeds) *(6 April 1785)*

Elsworth, Mary (wife of Moses Elsworth) *(21 Feb 1786)*

Elsworth, Moses *(12 Oct 1783) (18 May 1785) (14-15 June 1785) (22, 25 Aug 1785)*

Etenfield, William (of Halifax) *(22 Jan 1785) (30 Jan 1785)*

Farnel (of Northowram) *(11 May 1785)*

Farrar, Elizabeth (wife of John Farrar) *(3, 16 Jan 1785)*

Farrar, John (of Mixenden) *(3, 16 Jan 1785)*

Farrar, Titus; wife of (of Denham Gate) *(15 Feb 1785)*

Farrar, widow (of alms house in Halifax) *(15 Feb 1785)*

Fawcett, Reverend (of Brearley Hall) *(11 June 1783)*

Fearly, John *(29 December 1809)*

Fearnely, Mary *(1 April 1816)*

Fearnly, Thos (of Ovenden) *(25 Dec 1785)*

Fetcher, Polly *(28 Dec 1785)*

Firth, Daniel (of Houldsworth) *(29 Nov 1782)*

Firth, Joseph *(15, 17 Aug 1783)*

Firth, Joseph *(22 April 1809)*

Firth, Susannah *(26 Oct 1809)*

Fletcher, Reverend Alexander *(27 July 1815)*

Foster, Henry *(31 July 1785)*

Fowler, Henry (of Edge End) *(29 Nov 1782)*

Foxhall, Mr *(28 July 1785)*

Gadsby, Reverend *(10 Oct 1809)*

Galland (Gallan or Gallen), Reverend (of Holmfirth) *(14 May 1783) (3 Aug 1783) (12 June 1785)*

Garforth, Elkanah (of Mixenden) *(27 July 1783) (11 Nov 1783)*

Garforth, John *(18 July 1785)*

Garforth, Richard *(26 May 1783)*

Garforth, Richard *(27, 31 Oct 1809)*

Garforth, Samuel; children of (of Mixenden) *(20 July 1785)*

Garlick, James (of Halifax) *(15 Sept 1815)*

Gath, William (of Halifax) *(13 Dec 1815)*

Gaukroger, Joseph (of Mount Pellon) *(16 March 1815)*

Gledhill, Sarah *(11 April 1815)*

Gledill, James *(4 Oct 1782)*

Green, Samuel *(4 Jan 1815)*

Green, Thomas; wife of (of Halifax) *(28 Jan 1785) (6 Feb 1785)*

Greenwood, John *(11 Nov 1783)*

Greenwood, Mr (of Wheatley) *(6 May 1815)*

Gregory, Ja^s Grarrson *(16 June 1785)*

Groves, Reverend (of Rotherham) *(9 Dec 1782)*

Hainsworth, James *(14 Nov 1785) (6 Dec 1785)*

Halliday, Ann (of Booth Town) *(18 Oct 1815)*

Hamilton, John (of Halifax) *(28 May 1783)*

Hargreaves, John *(3 Aug 1815)*

Hargreaves, Joseph *(3 Aug 1815)*

Hargreaves, Joseph (of Kitten Clough near Mount Pellon); wife of *(8 Jan 1785)*

Harper, Jas; wife of *(31 Dec 1815)*

Harrison, Reverend (of Berry) *(21-23 Aug 1809) (16 May 1815)*

Harrod, Jane (of Ovenden workhouse) *(15 Jan 1785)*

Hartley, Jane; child of *(28 Feb 1809) (6 April 1809)*

Hasleden, Job *(21 December 1809)*

Hebblethwait, G; wife of (of Mile Cross) *(16 March 1785)*

Hebblethwat, John (of Halifax) *(8 March 1815)*

Hebblethwat, Sarah (of Halifax) *(8 March 1815)*

Hemingway, Luke *(6 Nov 1783)*

Hepworth (of Illingworth) *(28 March 1785)*

Hepworth, Joshua (of Ovenden) *(1 March 1785)*

Hilbank, William *(14, 20 March 1785)*

Hiley, John *(8 Feb 1783)*

Hiley, Matthew *(14 Nov 1782) (1 Jan 1783) (8 Feb 1783)*

Hiley, Matthew (of Mixenden Stones) *(7 June 1815)*

Hill, Mr (of Halifax) *(20 Dec 1785)*

Hindle, Reverend John *(19 Jan 1783) (4 Sept 1783) (12 Oct 1783) (24 June 1785) (18, 25 Dec 1785) (12, 19 Feb 1786)*

Hindles, Joseph *(28 June 1783)*

Hindson, Richard (of Haily Hill) *(8 Feb 1809)*

Hirst, David; daughter of *(3 April 1783)*

Hirst, James *(19, 21 Sept 1809)*

Hirst, T/Thomas *(21 Feb 1815) (7 Aug 1815)*

Hirst, William (of Dean Clough) *(12 Feb 1785)*

Hodgson (of Halifax) *(20 March 1815)*

Hodgson, A. (of Halifax) *(4 Oct 1815)*

Holm, Mrs (of Lee Bridge) *(19 Nov 1815)*

Holroyd, Isaac: daughter of *(3 July 1785)*

Hooson, Henry *(18 March 1783)*

Horsfall, Jonathan *(21 Sept 1815)*

Horsfall, Mary (wife of Jonathan Horsfall) *(21 Sept 1815)*

Horsfield, Mrs (of Haworth) *(1 March 1785)*

Houdson, Charles *(11 Feb 1786)*

Hough (Hought), Reverend *(15 Dec 1782) (23 Feb 1783)*

Houlden, Mrs (of Halifax) *(6 Aug 1785)*

Houlden, Squire; wife of (of Ovenden Wood) *(6 Feb 1809)*

Houlden, Thomas; wife of (of Halifax) *(18 Dec 1785)*

Houlden, Thos; the younger of Illingworth *(26 June 1783)*

Houldsworth (Hauldsworth), John (overseer) *(31 May 1809) (24 Nov 1809)*

Houldsworth, Betty *(1-2 April 1783)*

Houldsworth, John *(22 May 1785)*

Houls, Mr *(24 Oct 1785)*

Houls, Nathaniel; wife of *(1 June 1785)*

Hoult, Joseph (of Halifax) *(8 Jan 1785)*

Howarth, James *(24-25 April 1809)*

Howarth, James (of Sabden) *(13 Sept 1815)*

Howarth, Nancy (of Sabden) *(13, 30 Sept 1815)*

Hoyland, Mr; painter (of Halifax) *(14 March 1785)*

Hoyle, James (of Bradshaw) *(5 Feb 1815)*

Hoyle, Thomas (of Halifax) *(13 Jan 1785)*

Hudson, Charles (of Shaw Hill) *(9 Feb 1815)*

Hudson, Charles; wife of *(28 Jan 1809)*

Ibbotson, George (of Halifax) *(25 June 1785)*

Iles, Dolly *(28 Jan or 4 Feb 1816)*

Illingworth, John *(14 Nov 1782) (17 Dec 1782) (23 Jan 1783) (8, 27 March 1783) (26, 28 April 1783) (26 May 1783) (28 June 1783) (12 July 1783) (21 Aug 1783) (22 Oct 1783) (22 Jan 1785) (19 May 1785) (10 June 1785) (6 July 1785)*

Illingworth, John (road surveyor) *(11 Jan 1809) (3 Oct 1809)*

Illingworth, Widow (of Moorside) *(9 Feb 1815)*

Illingworth, William *(18 Aug 1815)*

Ingham, Elizabeth (of Wheatley) *(14 March 1783)*

Ingham, Jermiah; wife of *(25 Nov 1785)*

Irvin, Mr *(2 April 1785) (18 May 1785) (13 June 1785)*

Irwin, John *(8 Jan 1783)*

Jones, Mrs (wife of Reverend Jones) (of Mixenden) *(15 May 1785)*

Jones, Reverend (of Mixenden Chapel) *(15 May 1785)*

Jowett, Jonas *(26 Oct 1815)*

Keighley, James *(19 Dec 1785)*

Kelly, Robert; son of (of Halifax) *(15 Jan 1785)*

Knight, Mr Joseph *(14 Sept 1783)*

Knight, Reverend Titus (Minister of Square Chapel, Halifax) *(27 Oct 1782) (3, 10, 17, 24 Nov 1782) (8, 19, 22, 25, 29 Dec 1782) (2, 5, 6, 12, 19, 26 Jan 1783) (2, 9, 16 Feb 1783) (9, 16, 20, 30 March 1783) (6, 13, 17, 20, 22, 24, 27 April 1783) (1, 11, 18, 22, 25 May 1783) (1, 8-9, June 1783) (8, 10, 14, 17, 21, 24, 28, 31 Aug 1783) (4, 7, 14, 21, 28 Sept 1783) (5, 12, 19, 26 Oct 1783) (2, 9, 16, 23 Nov 1783) (2,6,9,16,20,23,27,30 Jan 1785) (6, 13, 20, 27 Feb 1785) (6, 9, 13, 20, 27 March 1785) (3, 10, 17 April 1785) (1, 2, 8, 12, 15 May 1785) (10, 17, 24, 31 July 1785) (14, 21, 28 Aug 1785) (16, 20, 23, 30 Oct 1785) (3, 6, 13, 27 Nov 1785) (4, 11, 15, 18, 25 Dec 1785) (8, 15, 22, 29 Jan 1786) (5, 12 Feb 1786)*

Knight, Reverend Saml *(31 July 1785)*

Knight, Willam; wife of *(13 Feb 1785)*

Laistercliff, George *(25 Dec 1815)*

Langdon, Reverend (of Leeds) *(20 Oct 1782) (21 Nov 1782)*

Lees, John (of Halifax) *(3 Sept 1815)*

Lees, Mr *(25-26 July 1785)*

Lees, Mrs *(17 April 1785)*

Liley (a young woman) *(3 March 1809)*

Longbottom, Abraham *(30 June 1809) (1, 3 July 1809)*

Longbottom, Richard *(1 Nov 1785) (3, 11 Feb 1786)*

Longbottom, Thomas *(22 Jan 1785)*

Lonsdale, Michael *(21 December 1809)*

Lord of the Manor *(15 Jan 1816)*

Lord, Mr (pupil of Mr Walker of Northowram) *(20 Nov 1785)*

Lowell (Lowel), Reverend (of Halifax) *(15 May 1785) (2 June 1785)*

Marsden, Edmund (step-grandson of Diarist) *(9, 23 Jan 1809) (30 March 1809) (22, 30 May 1809) (1, 5 June 1809)*

Marsden, Edmund (stepson of Diarist) *(25 Sept 1782) (3, 9, 17, 21, 25, 27 June 1785) (27, 31 July 1809) (1, 4-5, 7, 11, 15 Aug 1809)*

Marsden, Hannah (step-granddaughter of Diarist) *(9, 23 Jan 1809) (17-18, 20-21 Feb 1809) (21, 23 May 1809)*

Marsden, John (step-grandson of Diarist) *(24 Jan 1815) (31 March 1815) (20 June 1815) (3, 26 July 1815)*

Marsden, Sarah (step-granddaughter of Diarist) *(6, 22 March 1815) (3, 19 April 1815) (7, 10, 17, 26 July 1815)*

Marsden, Susannah (stepdaughter-in-law of Diarist) *(13, 22 May 1809) (1-3, 5 June 1809) (22, 28 June 1815) (7,10,26 July 1815)*

Marsden, Sussanah (step-granddaughter of Diarist) *(9 Jan 1809) 22 May 1809) (1, 5, 7 June 1809)*

Marsden, Thomas (stepson of Diarist) *(18 Oct 1782) (24, 28 Dec 1782) (4, 7 Jan 1783) (23 June 1783) (25, 27 June 1785) (27 Aug 1785) (26 Dec 1785) (13, 22, 27, 29-30 May 1809) (1-3, 5, 7 June 1809) (22 June 1815) (10, 13, 16, 18, 21 Nov 1815) (12-15 Dec 1815)*

Marsden, William (step-grandson of Diarist) *(24 Jan 1815) (31 March 1815) (20 June 1815) (3, 10, 26 July 1815)*

Medley (Modley), Reverend (of Liverpool) *(8, 15 May 1785)*

Meldrum, Reverend (of Brighouse) *(20 July 1783)*

Meller, Reverend Thomas (of Lockwood near Huddersfield) *(23 July 1809)*

Midgley, Francis *(5 Sept 1815)*

Midgley, Francis; wife of *(5 Sept 1815)*

Midgley, James (stepson-in-law of Diarist) *(23 Jan 1809) (16-17, 21-24 March 1809) (4, 27 May 1809) (4, 7, 15 Aug 1809) (4 Sept 1809) (2-4 Oct 1809) (7, 9-10, 14 Feb 1815) (3-5. 20 April 1815) (14 June 1815) (3-5 July 1815) (14-16, 20, 18, 23, 25-29 Sept 1815) (11-13 Oct 1815) (26-30 Dec 1815) (2-3 Jan 1816)*

Midgley, John the younger (of Illingworth) *(19 Jan 1785)*

Midgley, Mariah *(9 April 1809)*

Midgley, Michael *(5 June 1809)*

Midgley, Sarah (stepdaughter of Diarist) *(4, 15 Aug 1809) (4 Sept 1809) (24 Feb 1815) (22 March 1815) (12, 15 April 1815)*

Mitchel, Jonathan (of Bradshaw) *(10 Jan 1786)*

Mitchell, Abraham (of Esps, Mount Pellon) *(23 Nov 1815)*

Mitchell, widow *(9 April 1809)*

Mitchell, widow (of Pellon) *(13 May 1815)*

Moor, James; wife of (of Long House, Mixenden) *(17 Aug 1815)*

Moorhouse, Reverend (of Huddersfield) *(12 March 1783) (27 July 1783) (8 May 1785)*

Muncaster (of Luddenden) *(2 May 1815)*

Norminton, Hannah *(4 Nov 1785)*

Norminton, Timothy *(4 Nov 1785)*

Norminton, William *(5 June 1809)*

Norminton, William; wife of *(5, 7 June 1809)*

Nuttall, Richard *(17 May 1815)*

Oddy, William *(8 Feb 1783)*

Oulton (Houlton), Reverend (of Northowram) *(23 Jan 1785) (6 March 1785)*

Page, Benjamin (of Mixenden) *(8 Feb 1783)*

Parker, Robert *(18 Oct 1785)*

Parsons (Parson), Reverend (of Leeds) *(6 April 1785) (19 June 1785)*

Patterson, Kenneth; wife of *(27 Oct 1815)*

Pearson, George wife of *(4 April 1815)*

Pickles (of Pellon) *(1 April 1783)*

Pollard, Mr *(15 October 1809)*

Pollard, William; wife of *(19 Jan 1783)*

Prescot, Mr (of Callico (Callco) Hall) *(20 February 1809)*

Presly, James *(18 Feb 1783)*

Prestly, George *(25 Feb 1783)*

Priestley (Priestly, Priesley), Thomas *(23 April 1809) (2 July 1809) (10 Aug 1809) (17 Oct 1809) (6, 9-11, 14, 21 Nov 1809) (24 December 1809)*

Priestley (Pristly), Nancy *(1, 6 Nov 1809) (9 Dec 1809)*

Priestley, Hariot *(23, 25, 27 Jan 1815) (31 March 1816)*

Priestley, James *(10 Nov 1815)*

Priestley, Jon.; daughter of *(5, 6 Jan 1785)*

Priestley, Jonathan (of Bradshaw); wife of *(11 April 1783)*

Priestley, Miss (of King Cross Lane) *(9 April 1809)*

Priestley, Sarah *(26 Oct 1815)*

Priestley, T. (in our yard) *(26 Oct 1815)*

Priestley, T.; wife of (in our yard) *(26 Oct 1815)*

Priestley, widow *(11 June 1809)*

Priestly, John (of Wheatley); son of Thomas *(8 April 1783)*

Priestly, Jonathan *(29 March 1785) (28 Nov 1785)*

Priestly, Thomas *(16 June 1815)*

Priestly, Thomas (of Wheatley) *(8 April 1783)*

Pye, Betty (of Halifax) *(22 Jan 1785)*

Ramsbottom, Mr *(7 Feb 1815)*

Ramsbottom, Rabort *(28 Sept 1815)*

Ramsden, John (of Highfield) *(21 Aug 1785)*

Ramsden, Robert (of Halifax) *(28 Oct 1815)*

Ramsden, Thomas *(10, 14 April 1809)*

Ransome, John (of Halifax) *(13 March 1785)*

Rawson, John *(29 Dec 1782)*

Rhodes, Charlotte (niece of Diarist) *(17, 25 June 1785)*

Rhodes, Jeremiah (nephew of Diarist) *(26 Feb 1815) (28 April 1815) (29 June 1815) (24 Sept 1815)*

Rhodes, Joseph (nephew of Diarist) *(26 June 1815)*

Rhodes, Misses (nieces of Diarist) *(24 Feb 1809) (19, 22, 27 May 1809)*

Rhodes, Mrs (Sister) (sister-in-law of Diarist) *(24 Oct 1782) (22, 26, 30 May 1783) (17, 25 June 1785) (9, 12 Nov 1785) (24 Feb 1809) (16, 19 May 1809) (15 Aug 1809) (19 June 1815)*

Rhodes, Rhoda (niece of Diarist) *(27 May 1809)*

Rhodes, Rhoda (niece of Diarist) *(24 Oct 1782) (22 May 1783) (8-9, 11 March 1815)*

Rhodes, Sally (niece of Diarist) *(24 Oct 1782) (8 Nov 1782) (17, 22 June 1785)*

Rhodes, Shechaniah (nephew of Diarist) *(19 June 1815)*

Rhodes, Shechaniah (Brother; Uncle; Sheepaniah; Shecpaniah; Sheckainah) (of Gomersal) (brother-in-law of Diarist) *(28 Dec 1782) (4 Jan 1783) (22, 28, 30 May 1783) (4 Aug 1783) (2, 5 March 1785) (2, 23 April 1785) (22, 25 June 1785) (26 Feb 1815) (3 April 1815) (10, 17-18 July 1815) (3 or 10 Feb 1816)*

Rhodes, Sheaniah junior (nephew of Diarist) *(27-28 May 1809)*

Rhodes, Theodora (Theo) (niece of Diarist) *(27 May 1809) (28 April 1815) (12 May 1815)*

Rigley, Benj (of Hayley Hill) *(11 Nov 1783)*

Riley, James *(26 Oct 1782) (22-23 Nov 1782) (11, 24 March 1783) (23 June 1783)*

Riley, Widow (of Sodhouse Green); son of *(3 April 1783)*

Robertshaw, Ann *(10 March 1783)*

Robertshaw, Jonas *(18 July 1785)*

Rothera, John; wife of *(15 Jan 1809)*

Savil, John (of Wheatley) *(4 Feb 1815)*

Savil, John; child of (of Wheatley) *(23 Feb 1785)*

Scott, Thomas (of Illingworth) *(31 May 1815)*

Sharp, Isaac *(28-30 Nov 1785) (1-2 Dec 1785)*

Sharp, Reverend John *(17 December 1809) (23 July 1815)*

Shaw, John (of Ovenden) *(15 Jan 1815)*

Shaw, Jonathan (of Grey Stones) *(11 April 1815)*

Shaw, Joseph (of Keighley) *(31 Aug 1815)*

Shaw, Luke (of Halifax) *(18 Dec 1815)*

Sheard, John *(28-29 Nov 1785)*

Sheard, Matthew *(14, 30 Nov 1782)*

Sheard, Samuel *(4, 8 Oct 1782)*

Smith, James (of Illingworth) *(17 Jan 1785)*

Smith, James (of Shaw Hill) *(21 Oct 1815)*

Smith, John *(14 Nov 1785) (6 Dec 1785)*

Smith, Joseph (of Washer Lane) *(20 Aug 1815)*

Smith, Mary (of Ovenden) *(1 June 1785)*

Smith, Mary (of Wheatley) *(22 Jan 1785)*

Smith, Mary (widow of James Smith) (of Illingworth) *(17 Jan 1785)*

Smith, Timothy (of Cleckheaton) *(20 May 1785)*

Smith, Timothy (of Hunsworth) *(23 May 1785)*

Smith, William; child of (of Wheatley) *(20 July 1785)*

Snowden, Robert *(18 Jan 1815)*

Snowden, Thomas *(18 Jan 1785)*

Soltanstall, Mark *(16 Aug 1783)*

Spencer (Spencr), Jonas (of Greystones) *(22 July 1815 [2 Sept 1832])*

Spencer, George *(22 July 1815 [2 Sept 1832])*

Spencer, Hannah (daughter-in-law of Jonas Spencer) *(22 July 1815 [2 Sept 1832])*

Spencer, Harriet *(22 July 1815 [2 Sept 1832])*

Spencer, Hiram *(1, 3 April 1809)*

Spencer, Malty (of Swillhill) *(8 Jan 1785)*

Spencer, Thomas *(16 Aug 1783)*

Stancliff, Joshua *(4 Sept 1815)*

Stancliff, Joshua; wife of *(6 Nov 1815)*

Stanicliff, Zachara *(13 March 1785)*

Steadman, Reverend *(3 May 1809)*

Steel, Mr (of Ovenden) *(31 July 1785)*

Street, Reverend (of London) *(4 June 1815)*

Sugden, Reverend (of Skipton) *(14 June 1809)*

Sunderland, Doctor *(23 Feb 1809)*

Sunderland, Rufus: child of (of Ovenden Workhouse) *(11 May 1785)*

Sutcliff, Aron (of Wheatley) *(8 June 1815)*

Sutcliff, James (of Halifax) *(19 Sept 1809) (12 Nov 1809)*

Sutcliff, John (of Jumples in Ovenden) *(14 Oct 1815)*

Sutcliff, John; son of James *(19 Sept 1809)*

Sutcliff, Mr (preacher at St Anns Chapel in the Briars) *(17 April 1785)*

Sutcliff, Samuel (of Ovenden) *(15 Jan 1815)*

Sutcliff, William *(31 May 1815)*

Sutcliffe, Aron; child of (of Wheatley) *(28 March 1785)*

Sutcliffe, Aron; wife of (of Wheatley) *(27 Jan 1785)*

Swaine (Swain), Henry *(22 Sept 1809) (8, 11 December 1809)*

Swaine, Joseph *(3 or 10 Feb 1816)*

Swaine, Mr John (brother-in-law of Diarist) *(20-26, 29-30 May 1783)*

Swaine, Mrs Sarah (sister-in-law of Diarist) *(20, 26, 30 May 1783)*

Swaine, William (Brother) (brother-in-law of Diarist) *(28 Oct 1782) (17, 21, 23, 25, 27 June 1785)*

Swift, Henry *(27 July 1783)*

Swift, Jonathan; wife of *(2 Nov 1783)*

Tap, Reverend (of Pontefract) *(29 June 1783) (13 Aug 1783)*

Tattersall, Mrs; daughter of (of Wheatley) *(17 March 1785)*

Taylor, Charles *(9, 16 Feb 1783)*

Taylor, Noah (of Swill Hill end) *(29 Nov 1782)*

Taylor, Reverend *(6 March 1785)*

Taylor, Richard (of Midgley) *(19 Jan 1786)*

Tetley, Abraham (of Northowram) *(11 May 1785)*

Tetley, John *(29 Dec 1785)*

Tetley, Reverend *(23 March 1783)*

Thomas (of Halifax) *(7 March 1815)*

Thomas, John (of Mixenden) *(18 May 1783)*

Thomas, William (of Illingworth) *(16 March 1809)*

Thompson, James (of Staincliffe Hall near Dewsbury) *(28 May 1783)*

Thompson, Joseph (of Southowram) *(28 May 1783)*

Thompson, Mr *(2 March 1785)*

Thompson, Mr (of Southowram) *(21 June 1785)*

Toabman, Reverend (of Gainsborough, Lincs) *(31 Aug 1783)*

Toothill, Reverend John (of Booth Chapel) *(15 June 1783) (9 March 1785) (10 Aug 1785)*

Toothill, Reverend Jonathan (John) (of Hopton) *(14, 18 May 1783) (6 July 1783) (10 Aug1783) (29 May 1785) (10 Aug 1785)*

Towler, H *(5 Jan 1785)*

Town, George *(17-19, 21-22 Oct 1782) (22-23 Nov 1782) (28-31 Jan 1783) (22, 24-26 March 1783) (12, 14 April 1783) (9, 11, 18-20 Aug 1783) (16-20, 22 Sept 1783) (17-19, 21-24 March 1785) (20-21 May 1785) (14, 18 July 1785)*

Town, Hannah *(10, 13 Oct 1782)*

Town, Jacob *(25 Oct 1783)*

Town, John *(9 Aug 1783) (29 March 1785) (28 Dec 1785) (3 Feb 1786, 10 Mar 1786)*

Turner (Turer), Marsden *(25-26 Aug 1785) (3 Dec 1785)*

Turner, Ann *(20 Feb 1815)*

Turner, Ann *(31 March 1785)*

Turner, Jacob *(9 July 1785)*

Turner, Marsden *(22 Aug 1783)*

Turner, Reverend (of Leeds) *(4 May 1783) (13 July 1783)*

Varely (Varley), John *(19-20 May 1785)*

Varely, David *(30 Dec 1785)*

Varely, John (of Brockholes) *(9 April 1809)*

Varley, Jonas (of Birks Lane near Lee Bridge) *(10 April 1783)*

Vickerman, Charles *(4 Jan 1815)*

Vickers, Abram *(22 Sept 1809)*

Wade, Matthew *(5 April 1783)*

Wade, Thomas (of Spring Hall) *(14 March 1815)*

Wadsworth, James *(9 Aug 1809)*

Wadsworth, Timothy (of Northowram) *(13 March 1785)*

Wadsworth, William (of Haily Hill) *(6 April 1809)*

Wainhouse (of King Cross) *(19 Jun 1809)*

Wainhouse, Mrs (of North Gate Halifax) *(27 Oct 1815)*

Walker, Reverend (of Northowram) *(13 Aug 1783) (23 Jan 1785) (6 March 1785) (26 May 1785) (9 June 1785) (20 Nov 1785) (19 Jan 1786) (19 February 1786)*

Walsh, William (of Wheatley) *(1 May 1815)*

Walter, David (of Illingworth) *(7 Aug 1815)*

Walton, John (of Highroad Well) *(29 Dec 1815)*

Walton, Mary (of Luddenden Foot) *(13 May 1815)*

Walton, Reverend John (of Sutton) *(24 December 1809)*

Walton; wife of (of Norland) *(16 Aug 1815)*

Wash, Timothy *(3 Feb 1786)*

Webster, Reverend Abraham (of Slaithwait, Pole Moor) *(14 May 1815)*

Webster, Thos (of Wheatley) *(6 March 1785)*

Webster, Thos (of Wheatley); wife of *(6 March 1785)*

Wesley, Reverend John *(7 Sept 1783)*

Wharf, Mr (of Sowerby Bridge) *(22 Feb 1809)*

Whitehead, John (of Warley Town) *19 April 1815)*

Whitely, William (of Halifax) *(2 Feb 1785)*

Whitworth, James (of Ovenden) *(18 Oct 1785)*

Widdop, C. *(14-16, 20 Sept 1815)*

Widdop, Charles *(17 Oct 1809)*

Wigglesworth, Ely; wife of *(9 Dec 1785)*

Wigglesworth, John *(18 July 1785)*

Wiglesworth, John *(7 Aug 1783)*

Wilkinson, John (of Halifax) *(15 Aug 1815)*

Wilson, John (of Lee Bridge) *(27 June 1785*

Wilson, John; child of *(7 July 1785)*

Wood, Judith *(23 Feb 1783) (2 March 1783)*

Woodhead, William *(5 April 1785)*

Wormald, James *(of Luddenden) (16 Nov 1815)*

Wormald, John *(9 July 1785)*

Wormald; child of (of Ovenden Wood) *(14 May 1785)*

Worstenholm, Mrs *(6 Nov 1815)*

INDEX TO THE DIARIES 1782 – 1816
SUBJECTS

1. References are to dates in the Diary.
2. This index is to the Diary entries only, not the footnotes.

Box, sent to London *(28 Oct 1783)*
(31 Oct 1809) (26 Oct 1815)
Bread
    pot ashes in *(23 Sept 1783)*
    wheat loaf *(23 Sept 1783)*
Breaking up
    Grey Stones Croft *(14 June 1785)*
    inclosed ground *(13 June 1785)*
Briar Close, digging *(4 April 1785)*
Briars (Briers)
    cutting up *(17 May 1815)*
    pulling *(24 June 1785)*
        Gatefield *(28 June 1785)*
        Little Field *(27 June 1785)*
        Sun Door Field *(21 June 1785)*
Broad Tree, Ovenden *(22 Nov 1815)*
Brook below house *(19 Aug 1783)*
Burdens (bursdens) of hay rakeings
(28 July 1783) (5 July 1785)
Burials. **See also** Deaths, Graves. *(24
  Feb 1785)*
    110 children *(29 Dec 1782)*
    Appleyard, Samuel *(12 Jan 1809)*
    Bairstow, wife of William
      Bairstow of Ovenden *(9 Feb
      1785)*
    Banister, John *(3 Nov 1785)*
    Binns, Thomas of Stanry *(3 Jan
      1815)*
    Blagborough, William *(9 Nov
      1785)*
    Blagbrugh, Thomas *(7 Jan 1783)*
    Butterfield, Mrs of Halifax *(10
      Dec 1815)*
    Butterworth, Mary *(1 Oct 1809)*
    Bwilitt, Thomas *(7 April 1809)*
    Casson, John *(9 Nov 1782)*
    Charnock, daughter of Joshua
      Charnock *(7 July 1785)*
    Charnock, wife of James
      Charnock of Haworth *(17 July
      1809)*

Child, sister of G. *(7 Feb 1815)*
Clayton, Alice of Illingworth
  Moor *(16 Feb 1815)*
Cockroft, child of Samuel
  Crockcroft of Ovenden *(10 Nov
  1785)*
Cooper, Mary *(26 Jan 1785)*
Crabtree, Charles; daughters *(12
  Feb 1783)*
Crabtree, Widow *(8 July 1785)*
Crabtree, Widow of Wheatley *(27
  July 1785)*
Crapper, Uncle Benjamin *(20
  March 1785)*
Crossley, Susan *(16 July 1783)*
Crowther, Joseph *(1 June 1785)*
Crowther, wife of John Crowther
  (1 Dec 1785)
Dean, John of Bradshaw *(11 May
  1785)*
Dillot, Mary of Ovenden *(15 Jan
  1815)*
Farnel of Northowram *(11 May
  1785)*
Farrar, wife of Titus Farrar of
  Denham Gate *(15 Feb 1785)*
Farrer, Widow of Halifax alms
  houses *(15 Feb 1785)*
Garforth, children of Samuel
  Garforth of Mixenden *(20 July
  1785)*
Green, wife of Thomas Green of
  Halifax *(28 Jan 1785)*
Halliday, Ann of Booth Town *(18
  Oct 1815)*
Hargreaves, wife of Joseph
  Hargreaves of Kitten Clough,
  Mt Pellon *(8 Jan 1785)*
Harper, wife of James *(31 Dec
  1815)*
Harrod, Jane of Ovenden
  workhouse *(15 Jan 1785)*

Burials (continued)

Hebblethwaite, wife of G. of Milecross *(16 March 1785)*

Hebblethwat, Sarah of Halifax *(8 March 1815)*

Hiley, Matthew of Mixenden Stones *(7 June 1815)*

Hirst, James *(21 Sept 1809)*

Holm, Mrs of Lee Bridge *(19 Nov 1815)*

Holroyd, daughter of Isaac Holroyd *(3 July 1785)*

Horsfield, Mrs of Haworth *(1 March 1785)*

Houls, wife of Nathaniel Houls of Northowram *(1 June 1785)*

Hoyle, James of Bradshaw *(5 Feb 1815)*

Hoyle, Thomas of Halifax *(13 Jan 1785)*

Ibbotson, George of Halifax *(25 June 1785)*

Iles, Dolly *(28 Jan or 4 Feb 1816)*

Irwin, John *(8 Jan 1783)*

Jowett, Jonas *(26 Sept 1815)*

Kelly, son of Robert Kelly of Halifax *(15 Jan 1785)*

Knight, wife of William Knight *(13 Feb 1785)*

Liley *(3 March 1809)*,

Longbottom, child of Richard Longbottom *(1 Nov 1785)*

Marsden, Hannah *(20-21 Feb 1809)*

Midgley, daughter of James *(5 April 1815)*

Mitchell, Abraham of Esps near Mount Pellon *(23 Nov 1815)*

Paterson, wife of Kennith *(27 Oct 1815)*

Pollard, William; wife *(19 Jan 1783)*

Prescot, Mr of Callico (Callco) Hall *(20 Feb 1809)*

Presly, James *(18 Feb 1783)*

Priestley, Widow *(11 June 1809)*

Ramsden, John of High Field *(21 Aug 1785)*

Ramsden, Robert of Halifax *(28 Oct 1815)*

Rawson, John *(29 Dec 1782)*

Savil, child of John Savil of Wheatley *(23 Feb 1785)*

Shaw, John of Ovenden *(15 Jan 1815)*

Sheard, Samuel *(8 Oct 1782)*

Smith, child of William Smith of Wheatley *(20 July 1785)*

Smith, Mary of Ovenden *(1 June 1785)*

Smith, Timothy of Hunsworth *(23 May 1785)*

Snowden, Robert *(18 Jan 1815)*

Spencer, Malty of Swillhill *(8 Jan 1785)*

Sunderland, child of Rufus Sunderland in Ovenden workhouse *(11 May 1785)*

Sutcliff, Aron of Wheatley *(8 June 1815)*

Sutcliff, John of Jumples in Ovenden *(14 Oct 1815)*

Sutcliffe, child of Aron Sutcliffe of Wheatley *(28 March 1785)*

Sutcliffe, Samuel of Ovenden *(15 Jan 1815)*

Sutcliffe, wife of Aron Sutcliffe of Wheatley *(27 Jan 1785)*

Swift, Henry *(27 July 1783)*

Swifts, Jonathan *(2 Nov 1783)*

Taylor, Charles *(9 Feb 1783)*

Tetley, Abraham of Northowram *(11 May 1785)*

Town, Hannah *(13 Oct 1782)*

Burials (continued)

Varely, John of Brockholes *(9 April 1809)*

Varley, Jonas; child *(10 April 1783)*

Wade, Matthew *(5 April 1783)*

Wadsworth, Timothy of Northowram *(13 March 1785)*

Wadsworth, William of Haily Hill *(7 April 1809)*

Walton, John of High Road Well *(29 Dec 1815)*

Wharf, Mr of Sowerby Bridge *(22 Feb 1809)*

Whitely, William of Halifax *(2 Feb 1785)*

Wigglesworth, wife of Ely Wigglesworth *(9 Dec 1785)*

Wilkinson, John of Halifax *(15 August 1815)*

Wilson, child of John Wilson *(7 July 1785)*

Wilson, John of Lee Bridge *(27 June 1785)*

Wood, Judith *(23 Feb 1783)*

Bursting lumps *(5 April 1783)*

Callico (Callco) Hall *(20 Feb 1809)*

Calverley Mill *(17 Dec 1809)*

Calves. **See** Cows

Carrying pieces. **See** Pieces

Cart and horse *(22 Nov 1782) (24 March 1785) (18 July 1785) (28 Feb 1815) (1 March 1815) (19 July 1815)*

Casual workers (unnamed) *(27 Feb 1815)*

ashes

leading *(9 March 1809) (1 March 1815)*

spreading *(27, 29 March 1815)*

breaking clods *(9 April 1785)*

bursting lumps *(5 April 1783)*

carpenters *(9 May 1785)*

dung

leading *(19 July 1815)*

spreading *(20-21 July 1815)*

field work *(28 Feb 1815)*

furrowing *(31 March 1815)*

gardening *(1 April 1815)*

graving *(28 Feb 1815) (1-3 March 1815)*

hacking *(31 March 1783) (1-2 April 1783) (5-6 April 1785) (23-25, 27 March 1815)*

harrowing *(3-4 April 1783) (29-31 March 1815)*

hattocks

housing *(16, 18 Oct 1782)*

sharing *(10-11 Oct 1782) (12, 13, 15 Sept 1783)*

hay

cutting *(28 Feb 1815)*

hay mow dressing *(18 July 1815)*

making *(14-15, 19, 22-26, 28 July 1783) (11-16, 19, 21-23 July 1785) (13-15, 17-22 July 1809) (4-8, 10-12 July 1815)*

leading

ashes *(9 March 1809) (1 March 1815)*

dung *(19 July 1815)*

rubbish *(19 July 1815)*

mowing *(8-9, 11-12 July 1785) (3, 7-8 July 1815)*

opening sheaves *(29 Sept 1809)*

reaping *(8-9, 11 Sept 1809)*

removing earth *(12 Sept 1783)*

rubbish, leading *(19 July 1815)*

shearers *(26-27, 29 Aug 1785)*

thrashing *(26 Sept 1815)*

water-furrowing *(4-5 April 1783) (9 April 1785)*

water regulation in holms *(7 April 1815)*

Casual workers (unnamed)
(continued)
  weeding summer pastures *(18 July 1815)*
Chairs, mending *(8-9 May 1809)*
Chambers, great and little *(6 Jan 1786)*
Chapels
  Baptist Chapel (Halifax) *(20, 21 Feb 1809)*
  Booth *(10 Aug 1785)*
  Methodist in Halifax *(9 Jan 1786)*
  Mixenden *(15 May 1785; (16 May 1815)*
  of Mr Barraclogh [in Stainland] *(17 Sept 1815)*
  of Mr Crabtree in Bradford *(8 May 1785)*
  of Mr Edwards in Leeds *(6 April 1785)*
  Zion Independent Chapel in Halifax *(17 Sept 1815)*
  Square Chapel repairs *(25 June 1815)*
  soliciting money for debt repayment *(31 Aug 1815)*
  St Anns in Briars (Southowram) *(17 Apr 1785)*
Cherries, picking *(21 July 1783)*
Chest, mending *(18 Oct 1785)*
Children
  burial *(29 Dec 1782) (19 Jan 1783)*
  deaths
    from fever *(3, 8, 13 April 1783)*
    from small pox *(29 Dec 1782) (3 April 1783)*
Christmas holiday of Thomas Marsden *(24 Dec 1782) (7 Jan 1783)*
Church, Halifax *(14 Sept 1783) (21 Oct 1815)*
Church meetings *(20 April 1809) (15 June 1809) (27 July 1809) (24 Aug 1809) (21 Sept 1809) (23 Nov 1809) (25 Dec 1809) (19 Jan 1815) (20 April 1815) (18 May 1815) (15 June 1815) (11 August 1815) (12 Oct 1815) (9 Nov 1815) (11 Jan 1816) (15 Feb 1816)*
Church rates *(4 Oct 1815)*
Churchyard, Halifax *(29 Dec 1782) (19, 26 Jan 1783)*
Churning *(24 Oct 1782) (1, 8, 16, 30 Nov 1782) (8, 19 Feb 1783) (1 March 1783) (14, 19, 26 June 1783) (1, 8 July 1783) (4, 16, 23, 30 Aug 1783) (29 Oct 1783) (8 Nov 1783)*
Clockmaker *(7 Nov 1785)*
Clod breaking *(9 April 1785) (31 March 1809) (1, 3-4 April 1809)*
Coal
  box making *(14 Dec 1782)*
  clouting *(23 Oct 1782)*
  laying a heap *(24 Dec 1782)*
  sacks of *(19, 23 Dec 1782)*
Coal house (necessary)
  building *(17 Sept 1783) (4 Nov 1783) (6-9, 21 Nov 1809)*
  removing earth for *(12 Sept 1783)*
  stone gathering for *(5 Sept 1783)*
  thatching *(7 Aug 1815)*
Composition money, payments *(11 Jan 1809) (3 Oct 1809) (28 Sept 1815)*
Constable rates *(4 Oct 1815)*
Consumption, death from *(27 July 1783)*
Corn. **See also** Oats
  drying *(10 Oct 1809)*
  housing *(16, 18 Oct 1782) (18 Sept 1783) (10 Oct 1809)*
    hattocks *(16 Aug 1783)*
  laying up *(30 Sept 1809) (10 Oct 1809)*
  light corn *(5 Oct 1809)*

red polled cow *(8 Apr 1785)*

Crime

    breaking in *(31 May 1815)*

    hanging of rioters *(16 Aug 1783)*

    Prosecution Society meetings *(2 Jan 1815) (1 Aug 1815)*

    theft at counting house *(6 May 1815)*

    transport of prisoners to York *(31 May 1815)*

Dams

    Jumples mill *(19, 25-26 Aug 1785) (3, 17-18 Feb 1786)*

    swilling *(11 June 1785)*

Deaths. **See also** Burials, Graves

    accidents

        coal pit *(23 Aug 1815)*

        drowning *(9 Jan 1785) (21 Oct 1815)*

        workplace *(4 Oct 1782)*

    from

        burning *(11 Nov 1783)*

        illness *(15 Sept 1815)*

          consumption *(27 July 1783)*

          fever *(10, 14, 31 March 1783) (1, 3, 8, 11, 13 April 1783) (27 Jan 1785) (12 Feb 1785) (13, 16-17, 28 March 1785)*

          smallpox *(29 Dec 1782) (12, 25 Feb 1783) (3 Apr 1783) (14 May 1785) (20 July 1785)*

          throwing up blood *(15 Sept 1815)*

    killed *(16 Aug 1815)*

    suicide *(25 April 1783) (7 Nov 1785) (19 June 1809)*

Deaths of named persons

    Ashworth, daughter of John (brother of Diarist) *(8 Feb 1815)*

    Bates, Richard *(25 April 1783)*

    Bever, Peter of Wheatley *(10 Jan 1786)*

Binns, Thomas of Stanry *(30 Dec 1815)*

Bins, Mrs of Dean Clough *(15 Jan 1786)*

Birdwhisler, son of Edward of Ovenden Wood *(2 Feb 1809)*

Blagborough, William *(5 Nov 1785)*

Blagbrough, Sarah *(5 Jan 1786)*

Booth, wife of Thomas of Halifax *(17 April 1785)*

Boulton, James of Ovenden *(4 Jan 1815)*

Carpmeal of Halifax *(17 April 1815)*

Chambers, Mary of Halifax *(28 May 1809)*

Cockroft, Joshua; daughter *(13 April 1783) (31 March 1783)*

Crossley, John *(15 Oct 1809)*

Crossley, Susee *(14 July 1783)*

Crowther, wife of John *(29 Nov 1785)*

Drake, Joseph of Wheatley *(8 Feb 1815)*

Elsworth, Mary *(21 Feb 1786)*

Etenfield, William of Halifax *(22 Jan 1785)*

Farrer, Elizabeth *(3 Jan 1785)*

Foster, Henry of Huddersfield *(31 July 1785)*

Foxhall, Mr *(28 July 1785)*

Garforth, Elkanah *(11 Nov 1783)*

Garlick, James of Halifax *(15 Sept 1815)*

Gath, William of Halifax *(13 Dec 1815)*

Gaukroger, Joseph of Mount Pellon *(16 March 1815)*

Gregory, Jas Grarrson *(16 June 1785)*

Deaths of named persons
(continued)

Hartley, child of Jane *(7 April 1809)*

Hebblethwat, Sarah of Halifax *(8 March 1815)*

Hill, Mr of Halifax *(20 Dec 1785)*

Hindson, Richard of Haily Hill *(8 Feb 1809)*

Hirst, David; daughter *(3 April 1783)*

Hirst, James *(19 Sept 1809)*

Hirst, William of Dean Clough *(12 Feb 1785)*

Hodgson of Halifax *(20 March 1815)*

Houlden, wife of Squire Houlden of Ovenden Wood *(6 Feb 1809)*

Houldsworth, Betty *(2 April 1783)*

Houldsworth, John *(22 May 1785)*

Hoult, Joseph of Halifax *(8 Jan 1785)*

Hoyland, Mr of Halifax *(13 March 1785)*

Hudson, Charles of Shaw Hill *(9 Feb 1815)*

Hudson, wife of Charles of Shaw Hill *(28 Jan 1809)*

Illingworth, Widow of Moorside *(9 Feb 1815)*

Ingham, Elizabeth *(14 March 1783)*

Ingham, wife of Jermiah *(25 Nov 1785)*

Jones, Mrs of Mixenden *(15 May 1785)*

Lees, John of Halifax *(3 Sept 1815)*

Lees, Mrs *(17 April 1785)*

Lonsdale, Michael *(21 Dec 1809)*

Marsden, Hannah *(17-18 Feb 1809)*

Midgley, Maria *(9 April 1809)*

Mitchel, Jonathan of Bradshaw *(10 Jan 1786)*

Mitchell, Widow *(9 April 1809)*

Mitchell, Widow of Pellon *(13 May 1815)*

Moor, wife of James of Mixenden *(17 August 1815)*

Norminton, wife of Timothy *(4 Nov 1785)*

Pearson, wife of George *(4 April 1815)*

Prestly, George *(25 Feb 1783)*

Priesley, T *(24 Dec 1809)*

Priestley, Jonathan; wife *(11 April 1783)*

Priestley, Miss of King Cross lane *(9 April 1809)*

Priestley, Sarah of Walt Royd yard *(26 Oct 1815)*

Priestly, John *(8 April 1783)*

Pye, Betty of Halifax *(22 Jan 1785)*

Ramsden, Thomas *(10 April 1809)*

Ransome, John of Halifax *(13 March 1785)*

Riley, Widdow; son *(3 April 1783)*

Robertshaw, Ann *(10 March 1783)*

Rothera, wife of John *(15 Jan 1809)*

Savil, John of Wheatley *(4 Feb 1815)*

Shaw, Luke of Halifax *(18 Dec 1815)*

Sheard, Samuel; in a quarry *(4 Oct 1782)*

Smith, James of Shaw Hill *(21 Oct 1815)*

Smith, Joseph of Washer Lane *(20 August 1815)*

Deaths of named persons
(continued)
Smith, Mary of Illingworth *(17 Jan 1785)*
Smith, Mary of Wheatley *(22 Jan 1785)*
Smith, Timothy (near Cleck Heaton) *(20 May 1785)*
Stanicliff, Zacharia *(13 March 1785)*
Steel, Mr of Ovenden *(31 July 1785)*
Sutcliff, James *(19 Sept 1809)*
Sutcliff, John *(19 Sept 1809)*
Sutcliff, wife of Avon of Wheatley *(27 Jan 1785)*
Swift, Henry *(27 July 1783)*
Taylor, C. *(17 Jan 1783)*
Thomas of Halifax *(7 March 1815)*
Thomas, William of Illingworth *(16 March 1809)*
Town, Hannah *(10 Oct 1782)*
Vickers, Abram *(22 Sept 1809)*
Wade, Thomas of Spring Hall *(14 March 1815)*
Wainhouse, Mrs of North Gate, Halifax *(27 Oct 1815)*
Walsh, William *(1 May 1815)*
Walton, Mary of Luddenden Foot *(13 May 1815)*
Walton, wife of Norland *(16 August 1815)*
Whitehead, John of Warley Town *(29 April 1815)*
Wood, Judith *(2 Feb 1783)*
Wormald, child of; of Ovenden Wood *(14 May 1785)*
Wormald, James of Luddenden *(16 Nov 1815)*
Debts of Baptist Chapel in Keighley *(31 Aug 1815)*

Digging *(6 Sept 1815)*
in Briar Close *(4 April 1785)*
in garden *(1 Sept 1809)*
Ditches
filling up in holms *(24, 26 May 1809)*
opening
in holms *(8-10 March 1809) (3-5 April 1815)*
in Pomfret (Pontefract) *(27, 31 Oct 1809) (2 Nov 1809) (14 Feb 1815)*
holms (holmes) *(23 Nov 1782) (22, 25 March 1783) (23 March 1785) (8-10 March 1809) (3-5 April 1815)*
road *(4 Nov 1785)*
Doctor *(10 Feb 1785)*
for Brother John *(11 Oct 1809)*
for physic *(12 Jan 1809)*
Double Russels, weaving *(27 Aug 1783)*
Double Stuff, weaving *(4, 6 Oct 1783)*
Drains
covering *(2 April 1785)*
in yard *(2-3 Aug 1785)*
making *(26 March 1783)*
stones for *(24 March 1783)*
Drowning *(21 Oct 1815)*
child *(9 Jan 1785)*
Dung (dull). **See also** Manure
gathering *(16 May 1815)*
laying up *(14 Jan 1785) (13 Jan 1809) (27 March 1809) (15 Nov 1809) (20 March 1815) (7 Nov 1815) (21 Dec 1815) (17,24 Jan 1816)*
leading *(9, 12 Aug 1809) (12, 19 July 1815) (24 March 1785)*
spreading *(19 July 1783) (21 March 1785) (8 June 1785)*

Funeral sermons for (continued)

 Thomas Webster and wife *(6 March 1785)*

 Thos Green's wife *(6 Feb 1785)*

 Thos Houlden's wife *(18 Dec 1785)*

 William Etenfield *(30 Jan 1785)*

 William Hillbank *(20 March 1785)*

Funerals

 James and John Sutcliffe *(19 Sept 1809)*

 Thomas Ramsden *(14 April 1809)*

Furniture, sale of *(2 May 1815)*

Furrowing *(31 March 1815)*

Garden work *(12, 14 April 1783) (6, 7, 9 June 1783) (12, 20 Aug 1783) (9, 17 June 1785) (11, 13, 17 Aug 1785) (14, 29 March 1809) (8 June 1809) (1 April 1815) (8 June 1815) (7 Sept 1815)*

 digging *(1 Sept 1809) (6 Sept 1815)*

 weeding *(19 June 1783) (2, 21 July 1783) (1 June 1785) (1 Sept 1809) (10 Aug 1815) (6 Sept 1815)*

Gate Field

 gathering stones *(30 May 1785) (2-3, 7 June 1785)*

 inclosed ground in *(8 June 1785)*

 pulling briers *(28 June 1785)*

 walling *(19, 21 Oct 1785) (19 June 1809)*

 weeding *(19 June 1809)*

 worked in *(6 June 1785) (5 July 1785) (20-21 June 1809)*

Gates, painting *(17 May 1783)*

Goods, packing of *(26 Oct 1815)*

Grass

 mowing *(13 July 1809)*

 weeding *(22 July 1783)*

Grave stone for Hannah Marsden *(23 May 1809)*

Graves

 digging in Illingworth *(19 May 1783)*

 open in Halifax churchyard *(29 Dec 1782) (19, 26 Jan 1783)*

Graving *(22 March 1783) (15-18, 20-21, 25 March 1809) (28 Feb 1815) (1-3 March 1815)*

 wheatfield *(29 March 1785)*

Grey (Gray) Stones Croft

 breaking up *(14 June 1785)*

 worked in *(15-16 June 1785) (4, 6, 12 Aug 1785)*

Grograms, weaving *(1 Nov 1783)*

Hacking *(31 March 1783) (1-2 April 1783) (5-6 April 1785) (16-18, 21-22, 25 March 1809) (23-25, 27 March 1815)*

Hanging

 of rioters *(16 Aug 1783)*

 suicide *(25 April 1783) (7 Nov 1785) (19 June 1809)*

Harrowing *(3-4 April 1783) (23-24, 25 March 1809) (29-31 March 1815)*

Hashers *(5-6 April 1785)*

Hat purchase *(11 June 1785)*

Hattocks. **See also** Sheaves. *(19 March 1785) (29 Dec 1785) (7 Jan 1786).*

 housing *(16, 18 Oct 1782) (16 Aug 1783)*

 milling *(26 Oct 1782) (25 Aug 1783) (22 Sept 1783) (3 Oct 1783) (5 Oct 1809)*

 number of strikes from *(31 Jan 1783)*

 removing hoods *(28 Sept 1809)*

House jobs (continued) *(13 Aug 1785)*
(26-29 Oct 1785) (10, 12 Nov 1785)
(15, 24, 26 Dec 1785) (3, 6, 17-20 Jan
1786) (17 April 1809) (30 Dec 1809)

House, new
    building in yard *(13 June 1783)*
    taking possession *(30 June 1783)*

Housing
    corn *(18 Sept 1783)*
    hattocks *(16 Oct 1782) (16 Aug 1783)*
    hay *(16 July 1783) (13, 15, 21 July 1785)*
    oats *(6 Oct 1809) (23, 25-26, 29 Sept 1815)*
    sheaves *(29 Sept 1809)*
    turfs *(8 July 1783)*

Husbandry jobs *(1, 8, 10, 17-18, 22, 26 Jan 1785) (2 Feb 1785) (17, 25, 31 Oct 1785) (1, 5 Nov 1785) (7-10, 15, 17, 26 Dec 1785) (9 Jan 1786) (8 Aug 1809) (11 Sept 1809) (15 Nov 1809) (14, 28 Feb 1815) (20 March 1815) (25, 27 April 1815) (17-18 Aug 1815) (22 Sept 1815) (3 Nov 1815)*

Illness. **See** Sickness

Inclosed ground
    breaking up *(13 June 1785)*
    in Gate field *(8 June 1785)*

Inclosure *(1 or 8 Feb 1816)*
    Commissioners Meeting *(13 Nov 1815)*
    meetings *(16 Jan 1815) (13 Nov 1815)*
    sale of lots *(17 Jan 1815)*

Injury to finger *(5 June 1783)*

Jobbing. **See also** House jobs, Lathe jobs, Loom jobs, Garden work; Field work; Husbandry; Property maintenance; Yard jobs
    general *(29 Oct 1782) (21 Dec 1782) (1, 4, 17 Jan 1783) (24 Feb*

1783) (12 April 1783) (17 May 1783) (14, 17, 20 ,23-24 June 1783) (1-3, 8-9 July 1783) (9, 25, 30 Aug 1783) (6, 10, 22 Sept 1783) (20, 25, 27 Oct 1783) (2 Dec 1785)
    at Jumples Mill *(18, 20, 22-23, 29 Aug 1785) (8 Nov 1785) (20-23 Dec 1785) (9-11, 14, 21, 23-24 Jan 1786) (3, 4, 6-11, 13-16, 20-25 Feb 1786) (8 March 1786)*
        measuring stone *(17 Oct 1785)*
        mill dam (day) *(19, 25-26 Aug 1785) (3, 17-18 Feb 1786)*
    at Wheatley Edge *(14-19, 21-26 Nov 1785) (5 Dec 1785)*
    mistal *(27 Jan 1783)*
    near Hebble Bridge *(12-13, 25-28, 30-31 Jan 1786) (1-2 Feb 1786)*
    outside work *(23 Oct 1782) (4 Jan 1783)*

Joiners, helping *(6 May 1783) (4 Nov 1783)*

Journeys of Diarist. **See also** Chapel attendance in Halifax; Lectures; Meetings
    Bingley *(6 Dec 1785)*
    Birstal *(2 June 1783)*
    Bradford *(29 May 1783) (8, 15 May 1785)*
    Bradshaw *(28 April 1783) (19 May 1783) (15 Aug 1785) (6 April 1809)*
    Cattering Slack *(28 Feb 1783)*
    Causeway Foot *(8 August 1815) (5 Jan 1816)*
      Jane Green *(6 Jan 1815)*
    Cleckheaton *(30 May 1783)*
    Coley (Coly) *(30 March 1809) (21 Oct 1809) (17 Jan 1815) (19 May 1815) (25 August 1815)*
    Elland *(12 Jan 1809)*

Journeys of Diarist (continued)

Manningham, Fair Wather Green *(23 June 1785)*

Midgley *(19 Jan 1786)*

Mixenden *(8 Feb 1783) (28 April 1783) (5 Jan 1785)*

Mixenden Ings *(8 August 1815)*

Northowram *(24 May 1785) (30 March 1809) (21 Oct 1809) (19 May 1815)*

Ovenden *(15 Nov 1782) (1, 6, 28 Oct 1783) (18 Oct 1785) (17 Dec 1785) (17, 22 Nov 1815)*

> Broad Tree *(22 Nov 1815)*
>
> Jumples *(14 Sept 1815)*

Ovenden Moorside *(28 Feb 1783) (1, 28 Oct 1783) (16 Jan 1809) (3 Feb 1809) (29 April 1809) (27 Sept 1809) (13 Jan 1815) (6, 29 April 1815) (28 July 1815) (15 Aug 1815) (4 Oct 1815) (3 Nov 1815)*

Ovenden Wood *(28 April 1783) (28 June 1783)*

Ovenden Workhouse *(20 Jan 1786) (1 Dec 1809)*

Salter Hebble wharf *(8, 13, 19 Dec 1785) (15 Dec 1809)*

Salter Hebble *(5 Dec 1809) (7 Jan 1815) (17 June 1815) (16 Nov 1815) (12 Dec 1815)*

Shaw Lane, near Ovenden Cross *(25, 27 Sept 1809)*

Shelf *(19 May 1815)*

Shorest *(12 Sept 1815)*

Skircoat *(21 April 1809) (12 Jan 1815) (10 March 1815) (8 May 1815) (22 August 1815) (16 Nov 1815)*

Skircoatgreen *(5, 9 May 1783)*

Southowram *(5, 9 May 1783) (19 May 1815) (9 June 1815) (23-24 Oct 1815)*

Sowerby *(12 Jan 1815) (10 March 1815)*

Sowerby Bridge *(6 July 1809)*

Sowerby Street *(17 June 1815)*

Soil (Swill) Hill *(6 April 1809)*

Soil (Swill) Hill End *(28 April 1783)*

Soil (Swill) Hill Top *(6, 13 March 1815) (8 August 1815) (5 Jan 1816)*

Triangle *(29Nov 1785)*

Warley (Warely; Warely Town; Waretown) *(24, 28 Oct 1785) (21 April 1809) (6, 25 July 1809) (12 Jan 1815) (10 March 1815) (8 April 1815) (2, 8 May 1815) (17 June 1815) (22 August 1815) (12 Sept 1815) (7 Oct 1815) (4, 16 Nov 1815) (22 Dec 1815) (12-13 Feb 1816)*

Wheatley *(23, 25 Jan 1783) (2-3 July 1783) (11 Nov 1783) (17 Oct 1785) (29 Dec 1785) (28 July 1815) (17 Nov 1815)*

Whithill *(28 Feb 1783)*

Journeys of others

Gomersal *(23 Jan 1809) (15 Aug 1809)*

Hathershelf *(22, 27, 29 May 1809)*

Huddersfield *(1 Aug 1809)*

Leeds for London *(4 May 1809)*

Liverpool *(7, 11 Aug 1809) (11 Dec 1809)*

London *(5 June 1809) (11 Dec 1809)*

Wakefield *(1 Aug 1809)*

Justice meeting *(6 Dec 1785)*

Kitchen

building work *(21 June 1783)*

sweeping roof and walls *(24 Dec 1782)*

Letter from relatives *(31 July 1815)*
Letter writing *(25 Jan 1783) (29 Oct 1783)*
Lime
    buying *(8 July 1809)*
    laying up *(14 March 1809)*
    spreading *(22 March 1809)*
Linen, hanging to dry *(21 August 1815)*
Little Field
    drain *(24, 26 March 1783)*
    leading stones *(24 March 1783)*
    pulling up briers, thistles and ketlock *(27 June 1785)*
    worked in *(27 March 1783) (21 June 1809)*
Long Field
    corn weeding *(22 July 1783)*
    leading earth *(24 March 1783)*
    leading manure (maner) *(27 March 1783)*
    stone gathering *(7 April 1783) (30 June 1785)*
    weeding *(30 June 1785) (4 July 1785) (16 Sept 1815)*
    worked in *(27 March 1783) (6-8 July 1785) (20-21 June 1809)*
Loom
    fitting for weaving double stuff *(4 Oct 1783)*
    of John C. *(5 Sept 1783)*
    time at *(22, 29 Aug 1783)*
    weaving at Charles Crowthers' *(20 Oct 1785)*
Loom jobs *(7 Dec 1782) (18 Oct 1783)*
Loomed a warp. **See** Warp
Lumps, bursting *(5 April 1783)*
Lunatic, suicide *(25 April 1783)*
Manure (mainer). **See also** Dung
    gathering *(30-31 Oct 1815)*

leading *(22-23 Nov 1782) (24 March 1783) (7 Aug 1783) (18 July 1785)*
spreading *(20 Dec 1782) (19 July 1783) (8-9 Aug 1783) (18, 21 July 1785)*
Marriages
    Acroyd, Jonathan *(1 Jan 1783)*
    Blagbrough, Benjamin and Drake, Sally *(10 March 1786)*
    Chambers, Benjamin and Houlden, Mrs *(6 Aug 1785)*
    Clayton, William *(8 Feb 1785)*
    Crowther, H. and Hemingway, L. *(6 Nov 1783)*
    Garforth, Elkanah *(27 July 1783)*
    Garforth, John and Chapman, Dolly *(18 July 1785)*
    Hepworth and Ayston *(28 March 1785)*
    Hepworth, Joshua *(1 March 1785)*
    Laistercliff, George and Bairston, Nacy *(25 Dec 1815)*
    Robertshaw, John and Binns, Alice *(18 July 1785)*
    Shaw, Jonathan and Gledhill, Sarah *(11 April 1815)*
Mason, helping *(12, 21 June 1783) (4 Nov 1783)*
Master of Thomas Marsden *(7 Jan 1783)*
Meadows
    dung ['dull' in text] gathering *(16 May 1815)*
    dung spreading *(1 Jan 1816) (29 Jan or 5 Feb 1816) (16 Feb 1816)*
    husbandry *(3 Nov 1815)*
    mole hill spreading *(29 Jan or 5 Feb 1816) (14, 16 Feb 1816)*
    swilling *(1, 17 Jan 1816)*
    weeding *(26 May 1809)*

Meal (meall)
  grinding *(2 Oct 1815) (8 Jan 1816)*
  packs *(26 Oct 1782) (2 Oct 1815)*
  stones of *(25 Aug 1783) (3 Oct 1783) (26 March 1785)*
  strikes of *(7 Jan 1786)*
Measures
  burdens (bursdens) of rakeings *(28 July 1783) (5 July 1785)*
  bushels of seed oats *(21 March 1815)*
  dozens of lime *(8 July 1809)*
  loads of
    shilling *(10 Oct 1809)*
    wheat *(10 June 1785)*
  packets (pockets) of hops *(13 Dec 1785) (2, 4 Jan 1815) (7 Oct 1815)*
  packs of meal *(26 Oct 1782) (2 Oct 1815)*
  quarters of
    oats *(10 Oct 1809) (2 Oct 1815)*
    oats/corn *(19, 22 Oct 1782)*
  stones of
    flour *(10 June 1785)*
    meal *(25 Aug 1783) (3 Oct 1783) (26 March 1785)*
  strikes of
    light corn *(5 Oct 1809)*
    meal *(7 Jan 1786)*
    oats *(26 Oct 1782) (31 Jan1783) (5 Feb 1783) (25 Aug 1783) (22 Sept 1783) (3 Oct 1783) (19, 26 March 1785) (29 Dec 1785) (5, 10 Oct 1809)*
    shilling (shelling) *(26 Oct 1782) (5 Feb 1783) (25 Aug 1783) (3 Oct 1783) (26 March 1785) (7 Jan 1786)*
Medicine *(10 Feb 1785)*
  cow *(22-23 Jan 1783)*
  oil *(23 Sept 1783)*

Meetings. **See also** Church meetings
  Baptist Ministers at Bradford *(1 March 1809)*
  cow club *(7 Aug 1815)*
  inclosure of waste lands in Ovenden *(16 Jan 1815) (13 Nov 1815)*
    Commissioners Meeting *(13 Nov 1815)*
  Justice *(6 Dec 1785)*
  prayer meeting *(25 Oct 1809)*
  Prosecution Society *(2 Jan 1815) (1 Aug 1815)*
Mending equipment
  chest *(18 Oct 1785)*
  rake *(11 July 1783)*
  shuttle *(1 Jan 1783)*
Midden (miding), laying up *(14 Nov 1782) (24 Dec 1782) (1 Feb 1783) (26 April 1783) (25 Oct 1783)*
Militia, balloting for *(31 March 1785)*
Mill
  making at *(26 Oct 1782) (5 Feb 1783) (25 Aug 1783) (22 Sept 1783) (3 Oct 1783) (26 March 1785) (7 Jan 1786) (10 Oct 1809) (16 Feb 1815)*
  oats to *(5 Oct 1809)*
  filling new dam *(5 July 1785)*
  Jumples Mill *(18, 20, 22-23, 29 Aug 1785) (8 Nov 1785) (20-23 Dec 1785) (9-11, 14, 21, 23-24 Jan 1786) (3, 4, 6-11, 13-16, 20-25 Feb 1786) (8 March 1786)*
    measuring stone *(17 Oct 1785)*
    mill dam (day) *(19, 25-26 Aug 1785) (3, 17-18 Feb 1786)*
    rearing *(14 Jan 1786)*
  meal grinding *(2 Oct 1815) (8 Jan 1816)*
  Mr Lees' *(25-27 July 1785)*
  viewing new site *(29 Nov 1785)*

working at *(18 Aug 1785)*

Mistal, jobs in *(27 Jan 1783)*

Mob at Halifax *(7 June 1783) (16 Aug 1783)*

Mole hills, spreading *(21-22 March 1785) (28 March 1809) (29 Jan or 5 Feb 1816) (14, 16 Feb 1816)*

Moles, catcher paid for *(15 April 1809)*

Mooing corn *(18 Oct 1782) (18 Sept 1783*

Mooter (Moolter) *(3 Oct 1783) (5 Feb 1783) (7 Jan 1786)*

Mossing, William Charnock's house *(4 Dec 1809)*

Moving house (flitting) *(23 June 1783) (5 July 1783) (24 May 1785) (3 Dec 1785)*

Mowing. **See also** Haymaking. *(14, 24 July 1783) (8-9, 11-12, 14-15 July 1785) (3, 7-8 July 1815)*
   grass *(13 July 1809)*

Necessaries
   cleaning *(29 July 1785)*
   thatching of coal necessary *(7 Aug 1815)*

New house. **See** House

Newspapers *(28 Jan 1783) (15 April 1783)*

Nursing *(24 Oct 1782)*

Oats. **See also** Corn
   drying *(10 Oct 1809)*
   Friesland *(19 March 1785)*
   grinding *(2 Sept 1815) (8 Jan 1816)*
   harrowing for *(31 March 1815)*
   housing *(6 Oct 1809) (23, 25-26, 29 Sept 1815)*
   laying *(10 Oct 1809)*
   quarters of *(10 Oct 1809)*
   reaping *(8-9, 11 Sept 1809) (14-16, 20 Sept 1815)*
   rolling *(12 May 1809)*

seed *(20 March 1809) (21 March 1815)*

sowing *(30 March 1815)*

strikes of *(26 Oct 1782) (31 Jan1783) (5 Feb 1783) (25 Aug 1783) (22 Sept 1783) (3 Oct 1783) (19, 26 March 1785) (29 Dec 1785) (5, 10 Oct 1809)*

thrashing *(2-6 Oct 1809) (25-29 Sept 1815) (26-30 Dec 1815)*

weeding *(7 July 1809)*

winnowing *(19, 22 Oct 1782) (5-6 Oct 1809) (29 Sept 1815)*

Occupations
   carpenters *(9 May 1785)*
   painter *(13 March 1785)*

Oil as medication *(23 Sept 1783)*

Oratorio (oratoria) at Halifax Old Church *(21 Oct 1815)*

Ordination of ministers
   John Toothill *(10 Aug 1785)*
   Mr Parsons *(6 April 1785)*

Oven, setting *(21 Dec 1809)*

Ovenden Workhouse *(1 Dec 1809)*

Overseer of the Poor
   paying of poor allowance *(1 Dec 1809)*
   receipts of Poor cess *(31 May 1809) (24 Nov 1809)*

Painting *(14 May 1785)*
   gates *(17 May 1783)*

Pan, setting of *(1 Dec 1785)*

Pastures
   weeding *(5, 7 July 1809) (23-24 August 1815) (16, 18-19 Sept 1815)*
     Summer Pastures *(18-19 July 1783) (1 Aug 1785) (26 May 1809) (10 July 1809) (18 July 1815)*

Payments
   church rates *(4 Oct 1815)*

353

354

Services at (continued)

Illingworth Chapel *(19, 24 June 1785)*

Holdsworth *(4 Sept 1783)*

Mixenden *(16 May 1815)*

Square Chapel *(27 Oct 1782) (3, 10, 17, 24 Nov 1782) (8-9, 15, 19, 22, 25, 29 Dec 1782) (2, 5, 12, 19, 26 Jan 1783) (2, 9, 16 Feb 1783) (5, 9, 12, 16, 20, 23, 30 March 1783) (6, 13, 17, 20, 22, 24, 27 April 1783) (1, 11, 18, 22, 25 May 1783) (1, 8, 22, 29 June 1783) (6, 13, 17, 20, 24, 27 July 1783) (3, 6, 10, 14, 17, 21, 24, 28, 31 Aug 1783) (7, 14, 21, 28 Sept 1783) (5, 12, 19, 26 Oct 1783) (2, 9, 16, 23 Nov 1783) (2, 6, 9, 16, 20, 23, 27, 30 Jan 1785) (6, 13, 20, 27 Feb 1785) (6, 9, 13, 20, 27 March 1785) (3, 10, 17 April 1785) (1, 12, 22, 26, 29 May 1785) (2, 5, 9, 12, 19, 26 June 1785) (10, 17, 24, 31 July 1785) (14, 21, 28 Aug 1785) (16, 20, 23, 30 Oct 1785) (6, 13, 20, 27 Nov 1785) (4, 11, 15, 18, 25 Dec 1785) (8, 15, 22, 29 Jan 1786) (5, 12, 19 Feb 1786)*

Pellon Lane Chapel *(19 Feb 1786) (1, 8, 15, 22, 29 Jan 1809) (5, 19, 26 Feb 1809) (5, 12, 19, 26 March 1809) (2, 9, 16, 23, 30 April 1809) (3, 7, 14, 21, 28 May 1809) (4, 11, 18, 25 June 1809) (2, 9, 16, 23, 30 July 1809) (6, 13, 20, 27 Aug 1809) (3, 10, 17, 24 Sept 1809) (1, 8, 22, 25, 29 Oct 1809) (5, 12, 19, 26 Nov 1809) (3, 10, 17, 24, 25, 31 Dec 1809) (1, 8, 15, 22 Jan 1815) (5, 12, 19, 26 March 1815) (2, 9, 16, 23, 30 April 1815) (7, 14, 21, 28 May 1815) (4, 11, 18, 25 June 1815) (2, 9, 13, 16, 23, 27, 30 July 1815) (6, 13, 20, 27 August 1815) (3, 10, 17, 24 Sept 1815) (1, 8, 15, 22, 29 Oct 1815) (5, 12, 19, 26 Nov 1815) (17, 24, 31 Dec 1815) (7, 14 Jan 1816) (11, 26 Feb 1816)*

Unspecified *(1 Dec 1782) (23 Feb 1783) (2 March 1783) (4 May 1783) (3 July 1785) (1 Jan 1786) (26 Feb 1815)*

Services, visiting preachers

at Pellon Lane Chapel *(20 Oct 1782) (21 Nov 1782) (11 June 1783)*

at Mr Crabtree's chapel, Bradford *(8 May 1785)*

at Square Chapel *(23 Jan 1785) (27 Feb 1785) (6, 9 March 1785) (15, 22, 26, 29 May 1785) (2, 5, 9, 12, 19, 26, June 1785) (3, 24 July 1785) (20 Nov 1785) (19 Feb 1786)*

Sewing *(24, 25 Sept 1783)*

Sexton at Illingworth *(19 May 1783)*

Sharing (shearing)

corn *(27, 28 Aug 1783)*

hattocks *(8-11 Oct 1782) (9, 11-12 Aug 1783) (3, 12-13, 15-16 Sept 1783) (26-27, 29 Aug 1785)*

Sheaves. **See also** Hattocks

housing *(29 Sept 1809)*

opening and spreading *(29 Sept 1809)*

Shilling (shelling)

loads *(10 Oct 1809)*

strikes of *(26 Oct 1782) (5 Feb 1783) (25 Aug 1783) (3 Oct 1783) (26 March 1785) (7 Jan 1786)*

Shreading *(22 Feb 1783)*

Shuttle, mending *(1 Jan 1783)*

Sickness

Blagborough, Sarah *(30 Oct 1785)*

Sickness (continued)

bowels *(4-6, 13, 20, 27 Feb 1785)*
(6, 13 March 1785)

coughing blood *(15 Sept 1815)*

Diarist *(29 Mar 1783) (23 Sept
1783) (6-8, 10, 12 Feb 1809) (12-
14 Oct 1809) (26, 29-30 Jan 1815)
(5-6, 12 Feb 1815)*

fever *(27 Jan 1785) (12 Feb 1785)
(13, 16-17, 28 March 1785)*

Houlden, Thomas *(26 June 1783)*

smallpox *(14 May 1785) (20 July
1785)*

Stanicliff, Zachara *(13 March
1785)*

toothache *(14 Jan 1785)*

Turner, E. Marsden *(22 Aug 1783)*

wife of Diarist, leeches *(17 April
1815)*

Sising a warp. **See** Warp, sising

Smallpox deaths *(29 Dec 1782) (12, 25
Feb 1783) (3 Apr 1783) (14 May
1785) (16 June 1785) (20 July 1785)*

Snow shovelling *(13 Jan 1809) (21
Dec 1815)*

Soliciting money *(31 Aug 1815)*

Sowing *(23 March 1809)*

hay seed *(12 May 1809)*

oats *(30 March 1815)*

Spreading

ashes *(22, 25 March 1809) (27, 29-
30 March 1815) (8 June 1875)*

dung *(19 July 1783) (21 March
1785) (8 June 1785) (5 Aug 1785)
(28 March 1809) (9-12 Aug 1809)
(12, 20-21 July 1815) (18 Sept
1815) (1, 3 Jan 1816) (29 Jan or 5
Feb 1816) (16 Feb 1816)*

grass *(3 July 1815)*

water *(25 May 1785)*

Stable, cleaning *(18 Feb 1815)*

Stage coach, from London to Leeds
(22 June 1815)

Stall for a calf *(18 Jan 1783)*

Stone

for building *(14-19, 21-26 Nov
1785)*

for coal house *(5 Sept 1783)*

for drain *(24 March 1783)*

for walling *(21 May 1785)*

gathering *(7, 8 April 1783)*

in fields *(30 May 1785) (2-3, 7,
30 June 1785)*

getting *(10 March 1786)*

leading of *(7 Nov 1809)*

measure of meal *(25 Aug 1783) (3
Oct 1783)*

measuring *(17 Oct 1785)*

Straw, shaking of *(17-18 March 1785)
(28 Dec 1785) (3-4 Oct 1809) (27-29
Sept 1815) (26-30 Dec 1815)*

Strikes

measure of oats *(26 Oct 1782) (31
Jan 1783) (5 Feb 1783) (25 Aug
1783) (22 Sept 1783) (3 Oct 1783)*

measure of shelling (shilling) *(26
Oct 1782) (5 Feb 1783) (25 Aug
1783) (3 Oct 1783)*

Suicide by hanging *(25 April 1783) (7
Nov 1785) (19 June 1809)*

Summer pasture

dung spreading *(19 July 1783)*

weeding *(18, 19 July 1783)*

Sun Door Field

briers in *(21 June 1785)*

clod breaking *(4 April 1809)*

mending gap *(1 Nov 1815)*

working in *(9 Aug 1785) (13
March 1809) (5, 10 April 1809)*

Surveyor of Roads, John Illingworth
(11 Jan 1809)

Sweeping, roof and wall of kitchen
(24 Dec 1782)

Swilling *(22 Feb 1783) (2 Feb 1785) (7 Feb 1815) (1, 3, 17, 24 Jan 1816)*
    dam *(11 June 1785)*
    in Lathe Croft *(28-29 Nov 1809)*
Tammy (Tamy), weaving *(20 Oct 1785)*
Thatching
    ashes house *(16 May 1785)*
    payment *(7 August 1815)*
Thistles
    pulling of *(26 May 1809)*
    cutting up *(17 May 1815)*
    pruning *(21 August 1815)*
Threshing (thrashing) *(16-18, 21-22 Oct 1782) (29-31 Jan 1783) (18-19 Aug 1783) (16-17, 19-20 Sept 1783) (17-18 March 1785) (27-28 Dec 1785) (30 Sept 1809) (2-6 Oct 1809) (2 Jan 1816) (8-11. 13-14 Feb 1815)*
    hand staff for *(2 Oct 1809)*
    oats *(25-29 Sept 1815) (26-30 Dec 1815)*
Tillage. **See** Manure
Trees, cut down and sold *(18 Jan 1783)*
Turfs, fetching and housing *(8 July 1783)*
Turnips, weeding *(13 June 1815) (16-17 August 1815)*
Vent, fitting *(28 Nov 1785)*
Visits. **See also** Journeys
Visits from
    Acroyd, Alice *(28 Dec 1785)*
    Armitage, Polly *(28 Dec 1785)*
    Ashworth, John (brother of Diarist) *(20 Jan 1809)*
    Buttery, Betty *(28 Dec 1785)*
    Crowther, Sarah (from Manchester) *(2-11 April 1809) (3 Sept 1809)*
    Firth, Joseph *(22 April 1809)*
    Fletcher, Polly *(28 Dec 1785)*

Harrison, Reverend (of Berry) *(21-23 Aug 1809)*
Horsfall, Mary and children *(21 Sept 1815)*
Howarth, James *(24-25 April 1809)*
Howarth, Nancy of Sabden *(13 Sept 1815)*
Marsden, Edmund (step-grandson of Diarist) *(9 Jan 1809) (30 March 1809)*
Marsden, Edmund (stepson of Diarist) *(3, 17 June 1785) (27 July 1809)*
Marsden, Hannah (granddaughter of Diarist) *(9 Jan 1809)*
Marsden, John (step-grandson of Diarist) *(20 June 1815)*
Marsden, Sarah (step-granddaughter of Diarist) *(24 Feb 1815) (17 July 1815)*
Marsden, Susannah (stepdaughter-in-law of Diarist) *(9 Jan 1809) (13 May 1809) (1-5 June 1809) (22 June 1815)*
Marsden, Susannah (step-granddaughter) *(1-5 June 1809)*
Marsden, Thomas (stepson of Diarist) *(13 May 1809) (1-5 June 1809) (10 Nov 1815)*
Marsden, William (step-grandson of Diarist) *(20 Jume 1815)*
Midgley, Francis and wife *(5 Sept 1815)*
Midgley, Sarah (stepdaughter of Diarist) *(24 Feb 1815)*
Priestley, Nancy *(1 Nov 1809)*
Rhodes, Charlotte (niece of Diarist) *(17-25 June 1785)*

Visits from (continued)

Rhodes, Jeremiah (nephew of Diarist) *(26 Feb 1815) (28 April 1815) (29 June 1815) (24 Sept 1815)*

Rhodes, Joseph and son (nephew and great nephew of Diarist) *(26 June 1815)*

Rhodes, Rhoda (niece of Diarist) *(19, 22 May 1809) (8-11 March 1815) (12 May 1815)*

Rhodes, Sally (niece of Diarist) *(17-22 June 1785)*

Rhodes, Shechaniah (nephew of Diarist) *(27 May 1809) (26 Feb 1815) (3 April 1815) (19 June 1815) (10, 17-18 July 1815) (2 or 9 Feb 1816)*

Rhodes, Shechaniah (Shepaniah) (brother-in-law of Diarist) *(2, 5 March 1785) (2 April 1785) (22 June 1785)*

Rhodes, Susannah/Sister/Mrs (sister-in-law of Diarist) *(17-25 June 1785) (9-12 Nov 1785) (16-19 May 1809) (19 June 1815)*

Rhodes, Theodora (niece of Diarist) *(19-28 May 1809) (28 April 1815-12 May 1815)*

Shaw, Joseph of Keighley *(31 Aug 1815)*

Stancliff, Joshua's children *(4 Sept 1815)*

Stancliff, Joshua's wife *(6 Nov 1815)*

Swain, Mr H *(8 Dec 1809)*

Swaine, Joseph *(2 or 9 Feb 1816)*

Swaine, William (brother-in-law of Diarist) *(17 June 1785)*

Thompson, Mr *(2 March 1785)*

three nephews (of Diarist) *(26 Dec 1785)*

Turner, Ann *(31 March 1785) (20 Feb 1815)*

Worstenholm, Mrs *(6 Nov 1815)*

Visits of Diarist to

Bentlys, Edward *(29 Nov 1782)*

Blagbrough, John *(19 June 1783)*

Charnock, Thomas *(6, 13 March 1815)*

Crossley, Hannah *(4 Jan 1815)*

Doctor Crowther *(12 Jan 1809)*

Doctor Sunderland *(23 Feb 1809)*

Earnshaw, John *(29 Nov 1782)*

Father (of Diarist) *(27 June 1783) (11 Nov 1783)*

Firth, Daniel *(29 Nov 1782)*

Fowler, Henry *(29 Nov 1782)*

Garforth, Richard *(26 May 1783)*

Green, Samuel *(4 Jan 1815)*

Greenwood, John

Hiley, John *(8 Feb 1783)*

Hiley, Matthew *(1 Jan 1783) (8 Feb 1783)*

Hilup, Matt *(14 Nov 1782)*

Hindle, Joseph *(28 June 1893)*

Hooson, Henry *(18 March 1783)*

Houlden, Thomas *(26 June 1783)*

Illingworth, John *(14 Nov 1782) (17 Dec 1782) (23 Jan 1783) (8, 27 March 1783) (26, 28 April 1783) (26 May 1783) (28 June 1783) (12 July 1783) (21 Aug 1783) (22 Oct 1783) (19 May 1785) (10 June 1785) (6 July 1785)*

Oddy, William *(8 Feb 1783)*

Page, Benj *(8 Feb 1783)*

Parker, Robert *(18 Oct 1785)*

Potter's house *(24 May 1785)*

Rigley, Benj *(11 Nov 1783)*

Sales

H. Towler *(5 Jan 1785)*

James Keighley *(19 Dec 1785)*

Mr Houls *(24-25 Oct 1785)*

Weeding (continued)
    garden *(19 June 1783) (2, 21 July 1783) (1 June 1785) (1 Sept 1809) (2 June 1815) (10 August 1815)(6 Sept 1815)*
    grass and hay *(22 July 1783)*
    Lathe Croft *(30 May 1785)*
    Long Field *(30 June 1785) (4 July 1785)*
    meadow *(26 May 1809)*
    oats *(7 July 1809)*
    pastures *(5, 7 July 1809) (23-24 August 1815) (16, 18-19 Sept 1815)*
        Summer Pasture *(18-19 July 1783) (1 Aug 1785) (26 May 1809) (10 July 1809) (18 July 1815)*
    peas *(16-17 August 1815)*
    potatoes *(16 June 1815)*
    turnips *(13 June 1815) (16-17 August 1815)*
    Wheat field *(29 June 1785)*
Weft, scouring *(14, 24 Jan 1785) (1 Feb 1785)*
Well, covering drain to *(2 April 1785)*
Whacking (whecking; whicking) clods *(31 March 1809) (4 April 1809)*
Wheat, purchase *(10 June 1785)*
Wheat Field
    graving *(29 March 1785)*
    weeding *(28 June 1785)*
    working in *(4 April 1785)*
Wheatley Edge, working at *(14-19, 21-26 Nov 1785) (5 Dec 1785)*

Wheelbarrow, purchase *(11 June 1785)*
Wheeling, dung and earth *(5 Aug 1785)*
White sand *(19 Dec 1782) (31 May 1783)*
Whitsun Tide *(15 May 1815)*
Wig, wearing *(25 March 1785)*
Window money, payment *(20 March 1809) (22 Sept 1809) (21 Feb 1815) (7 August 1815)*
Window shutters *(6 Jan 1786)*
Winnowing. **See also** Straw, shaking. *(19, 22 Oct 1782) (31 Jan 1783) (20 Aug 1783) (20, 22 Sept 1783) (19 March 1785) (29 Dec 1785) (24 March 1809) (5-6 Oct 1809) (29 Sept 1815) (2 Jan 1816)*
Wood Field
    cutting up briers and thorns *(17 May 1815)*
    housing hay *(15 July 1785)*
    mowing grass *(12 July 1785)*
    worked in *(27 March 1783) (25 Jan 1785)*
Wood, loading *(29 Mar 1783)*
Workhouse (Ovenden) *(15 Jan 1785) (11 May 1785) (20 Jan 1786)*
Working. **See** Jobbing
Yard
    cleaning *(18 Feb 1815)*
    jobs *(25 Jan 1783) (27 March 1809)*
    new house in *(13 June 1783)*
    repairing of *(12, 15 Sept 1809)*
York Assizes *(16 Aug 1783)*

List of Subscribers

The following people have kindly supported this book by subscribing to it:

Name	Location
Adams, Sarah	Uppermill
Armitage, Mavis	Soyland
Ashworth, John Gareth	Cheltenham
Atack, Barbara & John	Hebden Bridge
Atkinson, Anthea	Cullingworth
Bailey, Ernie & Angela	Sheffield
Bailie, Ruth, J.P.	Moorfields, Northern Ireland
Baldwin, John & Lesley	"Big Six"
Bardsley, Roy	Saddleworth
Barraclough, Tony	Northowram
Barrow, Neil	Diggle, Saddleworth
Bates, Chris	Stroud
Baxter, W. & D.	Northowram
Begley, Christian R.	Hipperholme
Benson, Oliver	Uppermill
Botten, Brenda & Jim	Hebden Bridge
Bowers, George	Halifax
Bowman, Christine	Saddleworth
Brayshaw, Les	Northowram
Brember, Ivy	Bingley
Brian, Maureen	Hebden Bridge
Brill, Douglas, F.G.A.	Northowram
Brooke, John	Lightcliffe
Brown, Chris	Elland
Bryant, John	Halifax
Buckless, Anthony	Mixenden
Buckley, Anne	Northowram
Buckley, Mike	Dobcross, Saddleworth
Burton, Peter A.	Holmfirth

Name	Location
Button, Ian & Yelena	Stonehurst, Halifax
Cant, Jennifer	Mytholmroyd
Carter, Phil	Savile Park
Chambers, J.N.	Orwell
Cheetham, Ernest	Saddleworth
Chell, Sue	Leeds
Chetham's Library	Manchester
Clark, Jennifer	Delph
Collinge, Rodney & Margaret	Luddenden
Connolly, Eileen	Northowram
Cooke, Georgina	Bingley
Coomber, Richard	Shipley
Craven, David	Ovenden
Croft, Linda	Todmorden
Davies, Alison	Aberystwyth
Davies, Andrew G.	Leeds
de Verteuil, Sue	Thornton
Dewhirst, Tim	Harrogate
Dobson, Alison	Halifax
Doyle, J. Barry	Northowram
Eades, Gemma	Aberford
Farmer, Peter	Bramhope
Farrar, R.M.	Brighouse
Fawthrop, Pearl	Brighouse
Fellows, Hilary & Adrian	Hebden Bridge
Fisher, E.M.	Luddendenfoot
Ford, Pauline	Shipley
Freeman, Jo	Northowram
Gee, Stephen	Halifax
Giles, Colum	York
Glover, David C.	Pellon, Halifax
Graham, Sheila	Hebden Bridge
Grayshon, Ivy	Bucknell

Name	Location
Greenwood, Alan	Cragg Vale
Greenwood, Howard	Skircoat Green
Greenwood, Robin	Martyr Worthy, Hants
Gregory, Peter	Mytholmroyd
Gregory, Ray	Bingley
Haigh, Donald	Liversedge
Haigh, Peter	Wetherby
Halifax Antiquarian Society	Halifax
Halliday, Peter	Sowerby Bridge
Halliwell, Brian	Halifax
Hamilton, J.B.	Nottingham
Hammond, Ross	Halifax
Hargreaves, Dr John A.	Halifax
Harrison, Barry	Guisborough
Harrison, Brett & Felicity	Thornbury
Harrison, Kathryn	Mirfield
Heywood, Malcolm & Freda	Todmorden
Higgins, Peter	Diggle
Hill, Susan E.	Mixenden
Hobbs, Jeff	Whitley Bay, Northumberland
Holroyd, Brian	Halifax
Holt, Gillian	Midgley
Horne, Bob	Lightcliffe
Horrocks-Taylor, Patricia	Shibden, Halifax
Horsfall, Stephen	Hebden Bridge
Howcroft, Brian	Sowerby Bridge
Hugill, Ian	High Hoyland
Ineson, Philip & Jennifer	Warley
Jackson, Paul	Skircoat Green
Jacquest, Sylvia	Ormskirk
Jorissen, V.S.	Warley
Kelsall, Freda	Hebden Bridge
Khadem, Victor	Uppermill, Saddleworth

Name	Location
Kilbey, Ann	Cragg Vale
Kirker, Anne	Rishworth
Knight, David	Halifax
Knowles, Lynn	Hipperholme
Leach, John	Rastrick, Brighouse
Lee, Sybil & David	Wheatley, Halifax
Leonard, Steven	Wakefield
Leslie, Michael	Bingley
Lister, John	Halifax
Lister, Molly	Hipperholme
Lloyd, Clive R.	Luddenden
Longbottom, Paul	Sutton-in-Craven
Malay, Jessica	Mirfield
Marland, Brian	St Leonards-on-Sea
Martin, Dave	Wheatley
Martin, David	Midgehole
McCallam, David	Warley
McDonald, Corinne & Neil	Halifax
Mitchell, Graham	Lightcliffe
Monahan, Diana	Hebden Bridge
Moore, Brian	London
Morgan, Leslie	Heysham
Morton, Nancy I.	Handforth, Wilmslow
Mulhall, Irene	Illingworth
Murphy, Peter	West Wellow
Nash, David M.	Skircoat
Norris, Terry	West Slaithwaite
Nortcliffe, David & Margaret	Hipperholme
Northowram Historical Society	Northowram
Ogden, J.	Helensburgh
Oldham, David	Stamford
Page, John D.	Slack Top, Heptonstall
Paget, Elizabeth	Leeds

Name	Location
Patchett, John	Halifax
Patterson, Martin	Canton of Graubünden
Pearce, Cyril	Golcar, Huddersfield
Percy, N.	Riddlesden
Priestley, D.M.	Shelf
Quarmby, J.	Guisborough
Ray, Christine	Halifax
Reardon, Barbara	Hartshead
Robertshaw, Leslie	Darlington, Co. Durham
Robinson, Gertrude	Halifax
Robinson, Peter W.	Halifax
Rodgers, Mary	Delph, Saddleworth
Roe, Joanne	Ripponden
Royle, Edward	York
Saddleworth Historical Society	Saddleworth
Sarjeant, Chris	Holme
Scargill, Peter	Mixenden
Schofield, Alan	Stalybridge
Scott, Joyce	Lightcliffe
Scott, Michael	Hipperholme
Sell, Alan P.F.	Milton Keynes
Semper, John	Wigtown
Shepherd, David	Heptonstall
Shore, David	Fixby
Smalley, David	Rodmer Clough
Smith, Andrew	Ripponden
Smith, Barry & Eileen	Clifton
Smith, Jean	Warley
Smithies, Dr Oliver	North Carolina, USA
Speechley, Lisa	Heptonstall
Staples, Martin	Ripponden
Stell, Christopher	Hertfordshire
Stout, Jane	Norland

Name	Location
Stratford, Jessica	Rishworth
Swallow, Angela	Huddersfield
Sweeting, Audrey	Keighley
Thompson, Barry	Rishworth
Thornton, Jan	Kirkburton
Tiller, Kate	Oxford
Toole, Chris	Halifax
Travis, John S.	Ripponden
Travis, Susan I.	Denshaw, Saddleworth
Turner, Mike & Pauline	Northowram
Uttley, David & Jean	Eastwood, Todmorden
Uttley, Margaret	Cobham, Surrey
Uttley, Max & Jane	Wheatley
Uttley, Roz & Peter	Devon
Waite, Iain	Skircoat
Ward, D.	Shibden, Halifax
Watkins, Liz	Hebden Bridge
Watson, Ian	Shipley
Wellings, Martin	Oxford
Wilcock, Elisabeth	Leeds
Wild Rose Heritage and Arts	Hebden Bridge
Wilkinson, Jeff	Calderside
Williams, Ngaire	Rishworth
Williams, Veronica Eileen	Eccleston, St Helens
Wilson, Douglas & Heather	Todmorden
Woolrych, Frank	Pennine Horizons, Hebden Bridge